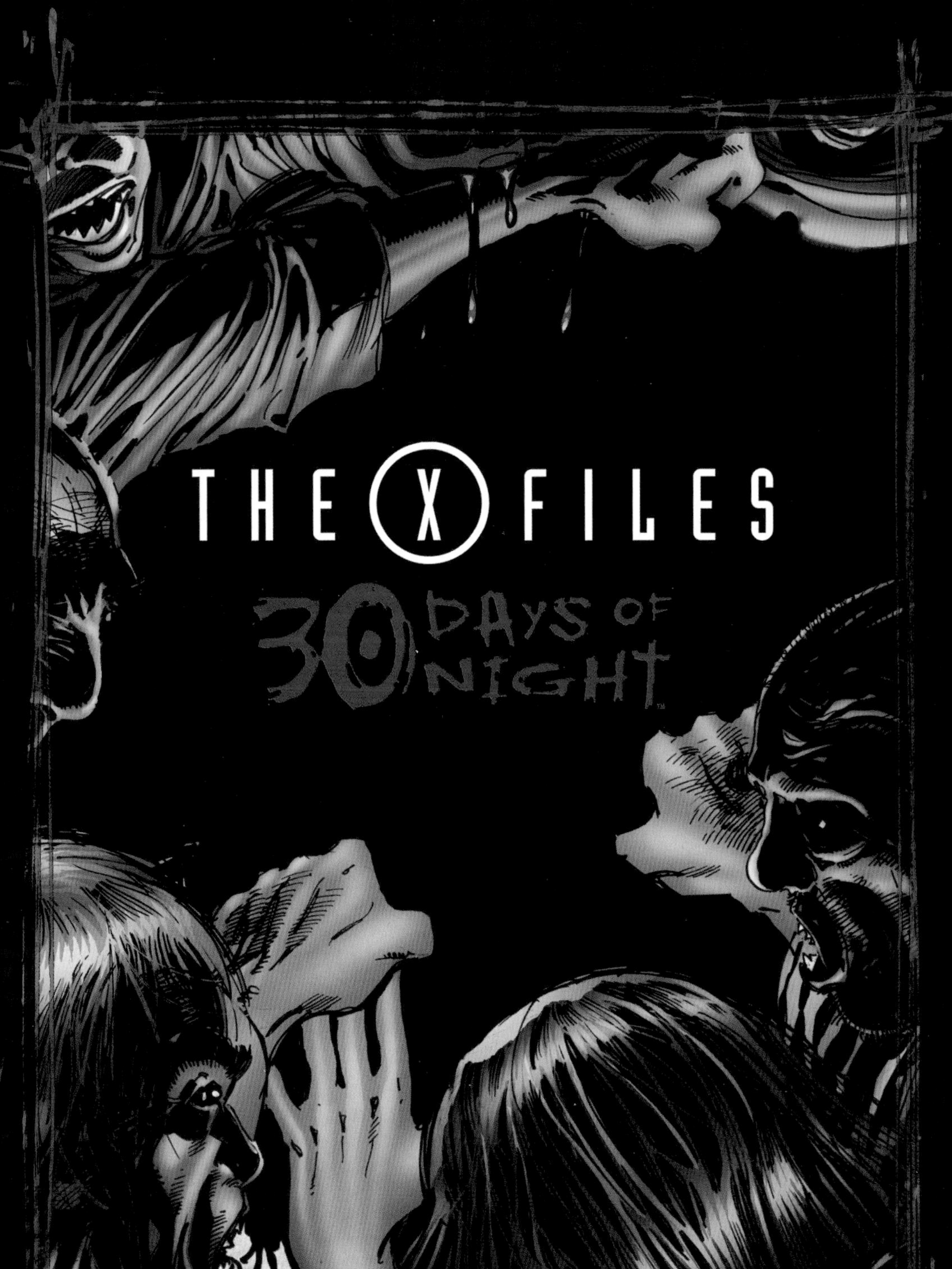
THE X FILES
30 DAYS OF NIGHT

THE ⊗ FILES

Written by
Steve Niles and Adam Jones

Art by
Tom Mandrake

Colors by
Darlene Royer with Gabe Eltaeb (Parts 4 and 6)
and Jorge Gonzalez (Part 6)

Letters by
Ed Dukeshire

Series Edits by
Shannon Denton, Ben Abernathy, and Kristy Quinn

Special thanks to Joshua Izzo and Nicole Spiegel at Twentieth Century Fox and Gabe Rotter at Ten Thirteen Productions.

Ted Adams, CEO & Publisher
Greg Goldstein, President & COO
Robbie Robbins, EVP/Sr. Graphic Artist
Chris Ryall, Chief Creative Officer/Editor-in-Chief
Matthew Ruzicka, CPA, Chief Financial Officer
Alan Payne, VP of Sales
Dirk Wood, VP of Marketing
Lorelei Bunjes, VP of Digital Services
Jeff Webber, VP of Digital Publishing & Business Development

www.IDWPUBLISHING.com
IDW founded by Ted Adams, Alex Garner, Kris Oprisko, and Robbie Robbins

Facebook: **facebook.com/idwpublishing**
Twitter: **@idwpublishing**
YouTube: **youtube.com/idwpublishing**
Tumblr: **tumblr.idwpublishing.com**
Instagram: **instagram.com/idwpublishing**

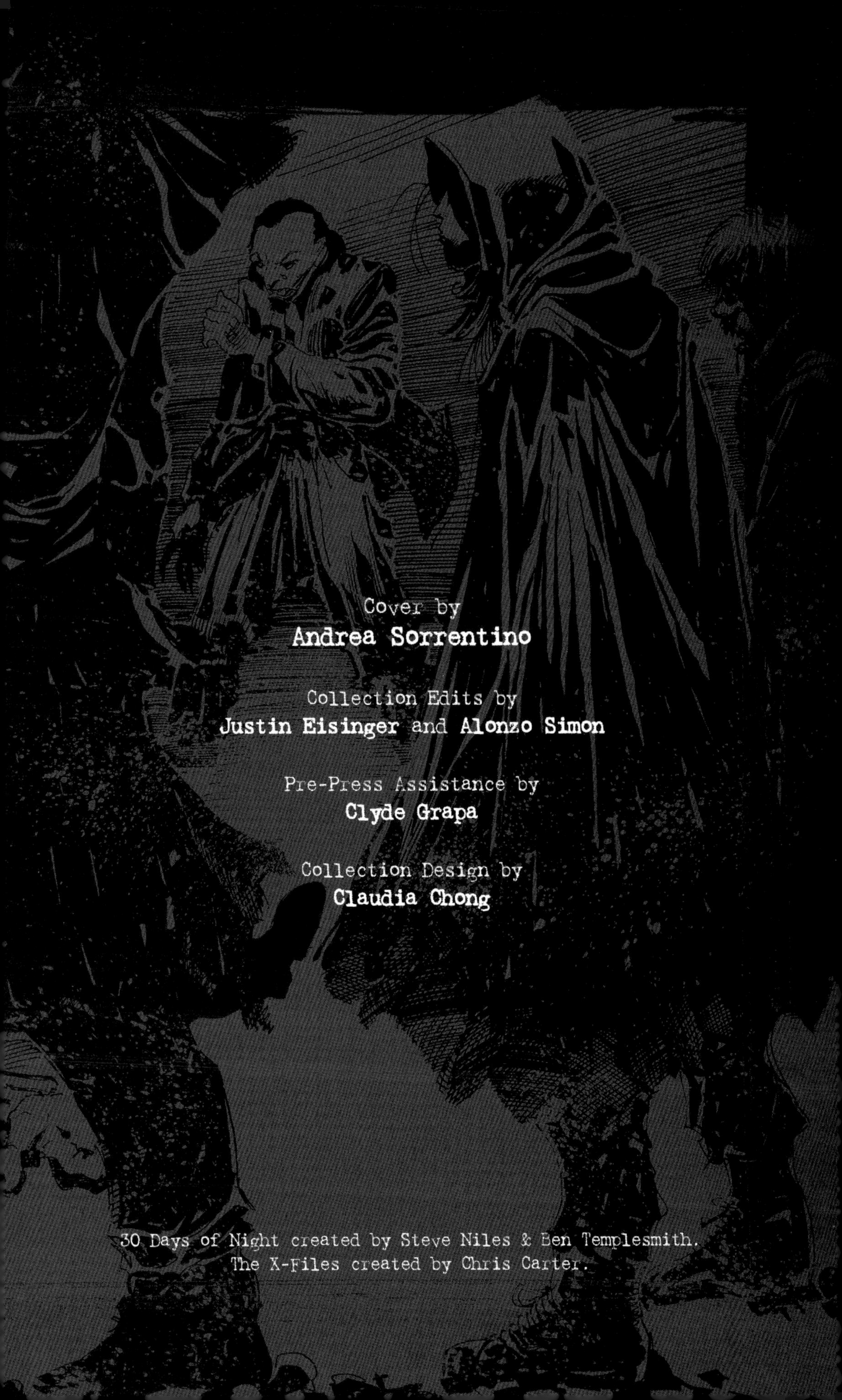

Cover by
Andrea Sorrentino

Collection Edits by
Justin Eisinger and **Alonzo Simon**

Pre-Press Assistance by
Clyde Grapa

Collection Design by
Claudia Chong

30 Days of Night created by Steve Niles & Ben Templesmith.
The X-Files created by Chris Carter.

art by: Andrea Sorrentino

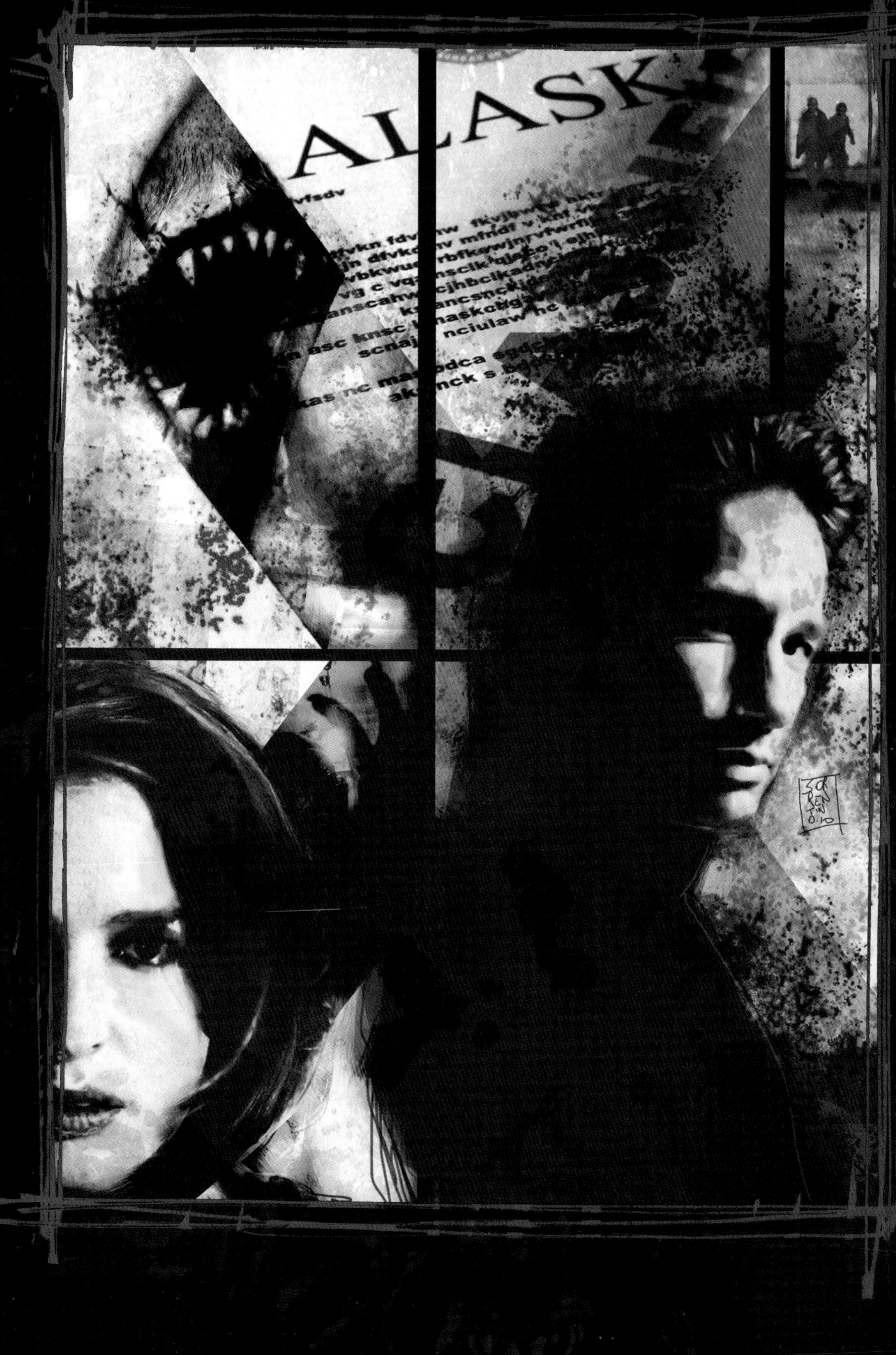
ALASK

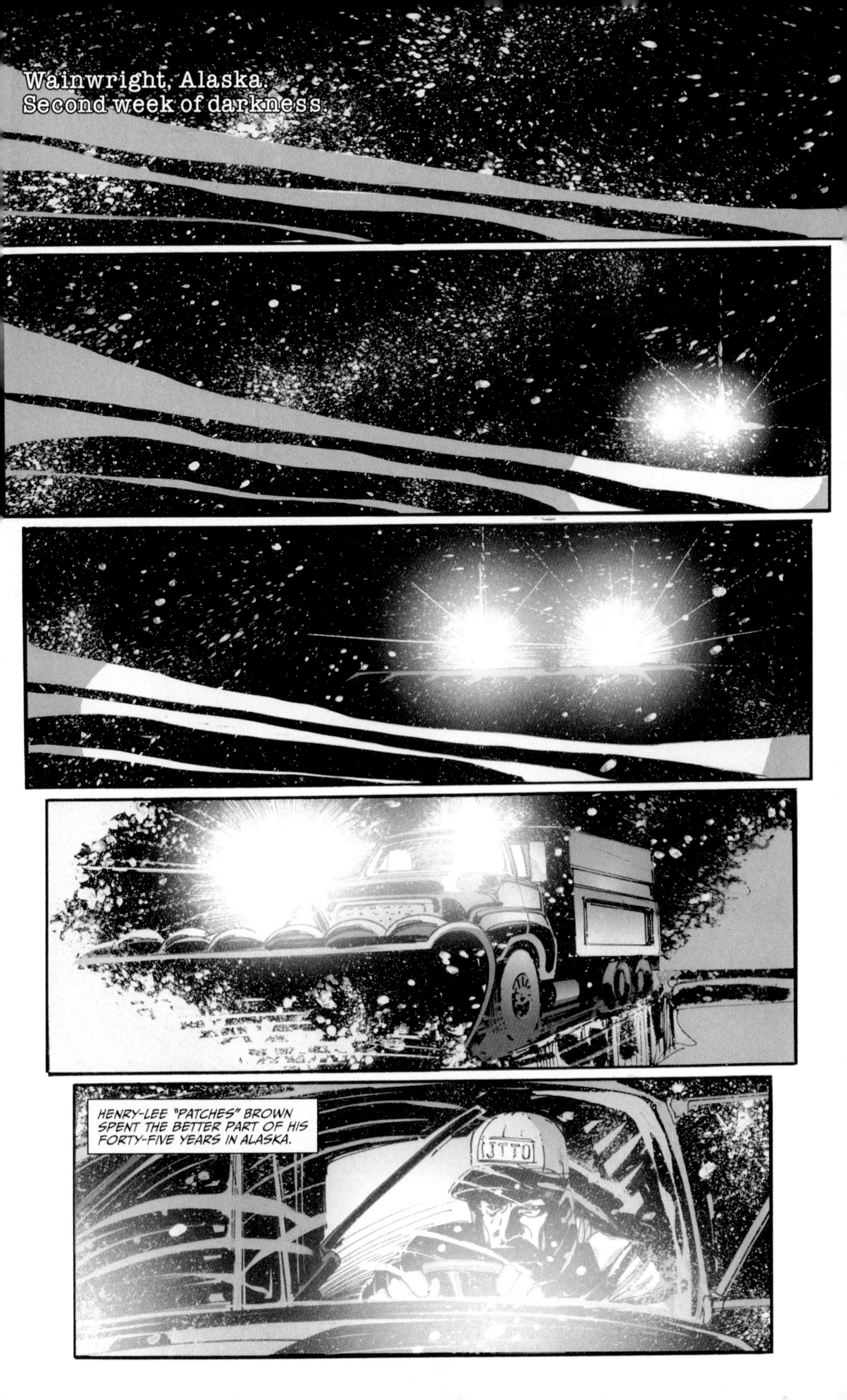
Wainwright, Alaska.
Second week of darkness.
HENRY-LEE "PATCHES" BROWN SPENT THE BETTER PART OF HIS FORTY-FIVE YEARS IN ALASKA.
JTTO

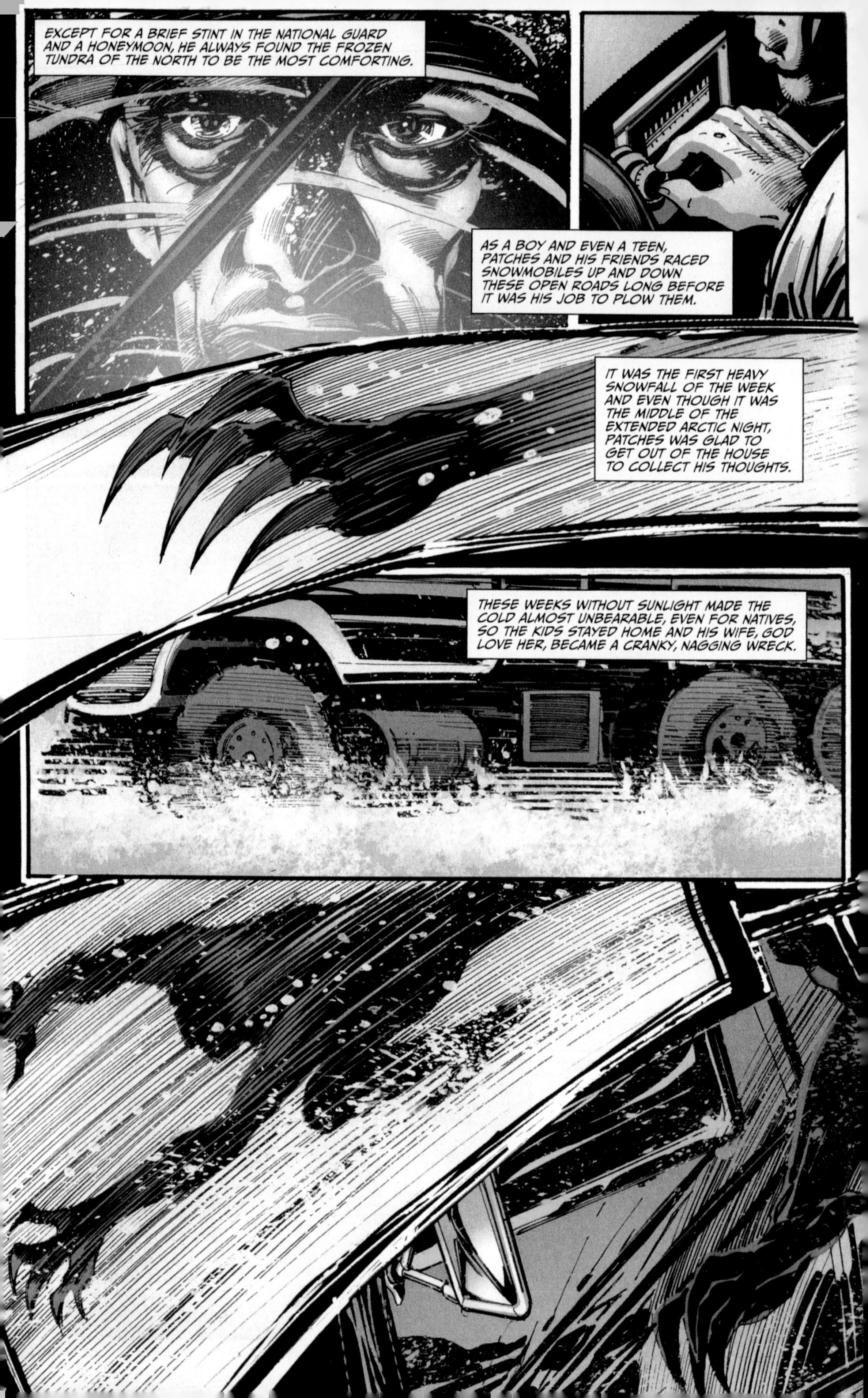
EXCEPT FOR A BRIEF STINT IN THE NATIONAL GUARD AND A HONEYMOON, HE ALWAYS FOUND THE FROZEN TUNDRA OF THE NORTH TO BE THE MOST COMFORTING.
AS A BOY AND EVEN A TEEN, PATCHES AND HIS FRIENDS RACED SNOWMOBILES UP AND DOWN THESE OPEN ROADS LONG BEFORE IT WAS HIS JOB TO PLOW THEM.
IT WAS THE FIRST HEAVY SNOWFALL OF THE WEEK AND EVEN THOUGH IT WAS THE MIDDLE OF THE EXTENDED ARCTIC NIGHT, PATCHES WAS GLAD TO GET OUT OF THE HOUSE TO COLLECT HIS THOUGHTS.
THESE WEEKS WITHOUT SUNLIGHT MADE THE COLD ALMOST UNBEARABLE, EVEN FOR NATIVES, SO THE KIDS STAYED HOME AND HIS WIFE, GOD LOVE HER, BECAME A CRANKY, NAGGING WRECK.

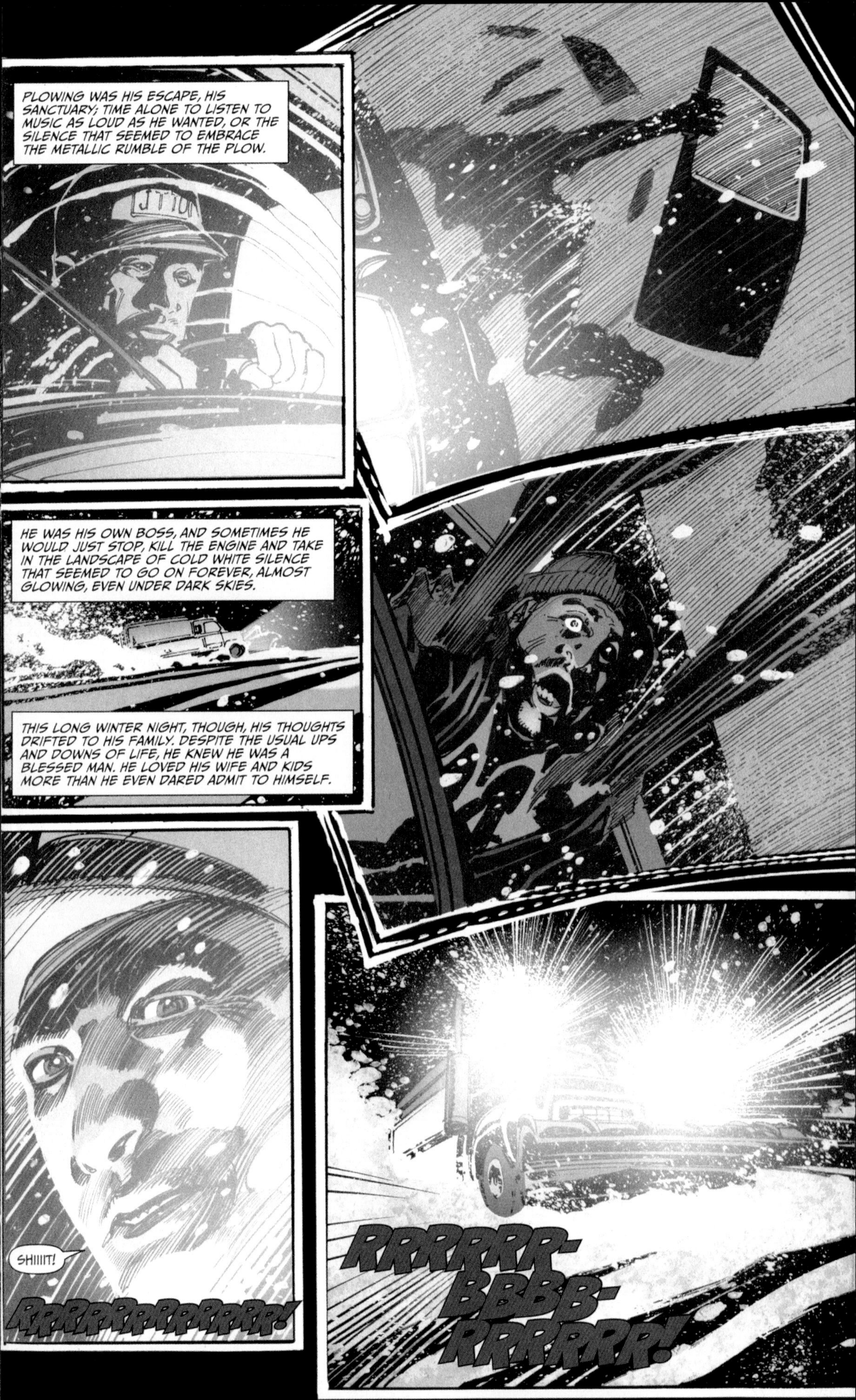
PLOWING WAS HIS ESCAPE, HIS SANCTUARY; TIME ALONE TO LISTEN TO MUSIC AS LOUD AS HE WANTED, OR THE SILENCE THAT SEEMED TO EMBRACE THE METALLIC RUMBLE OF THE PLOW.
HE WAS HIS OWN BOSS, AND SOMETIMES HE WOULD JUST STOP, KILL THE ENGINE AND TAKE IN THE LANDSCAPE OF COLD WHITE SILENCE THAT SEEMED TO GO ON FOREVER, ALMOST GLOWING, EVEN UNDER DARK SKIES.
THIS LONG WINTER NIGHT, THOUGH, HIS THOUGHTS DRIFTED TO HIS FAMILY. DESPITE THE USUAL UPS AND DOWNS OF LIFE, HE KNEW HE WAS A BLESSED MAN. HE LOVED HIS WIFE AND KIDS MORE THAN HE EVEN DARED ADMIT TO HIMSELF.
SHIIIIT!
RRRRRRRRRRRRRR!
RRRRRR-BBBB-RRRRRRR!

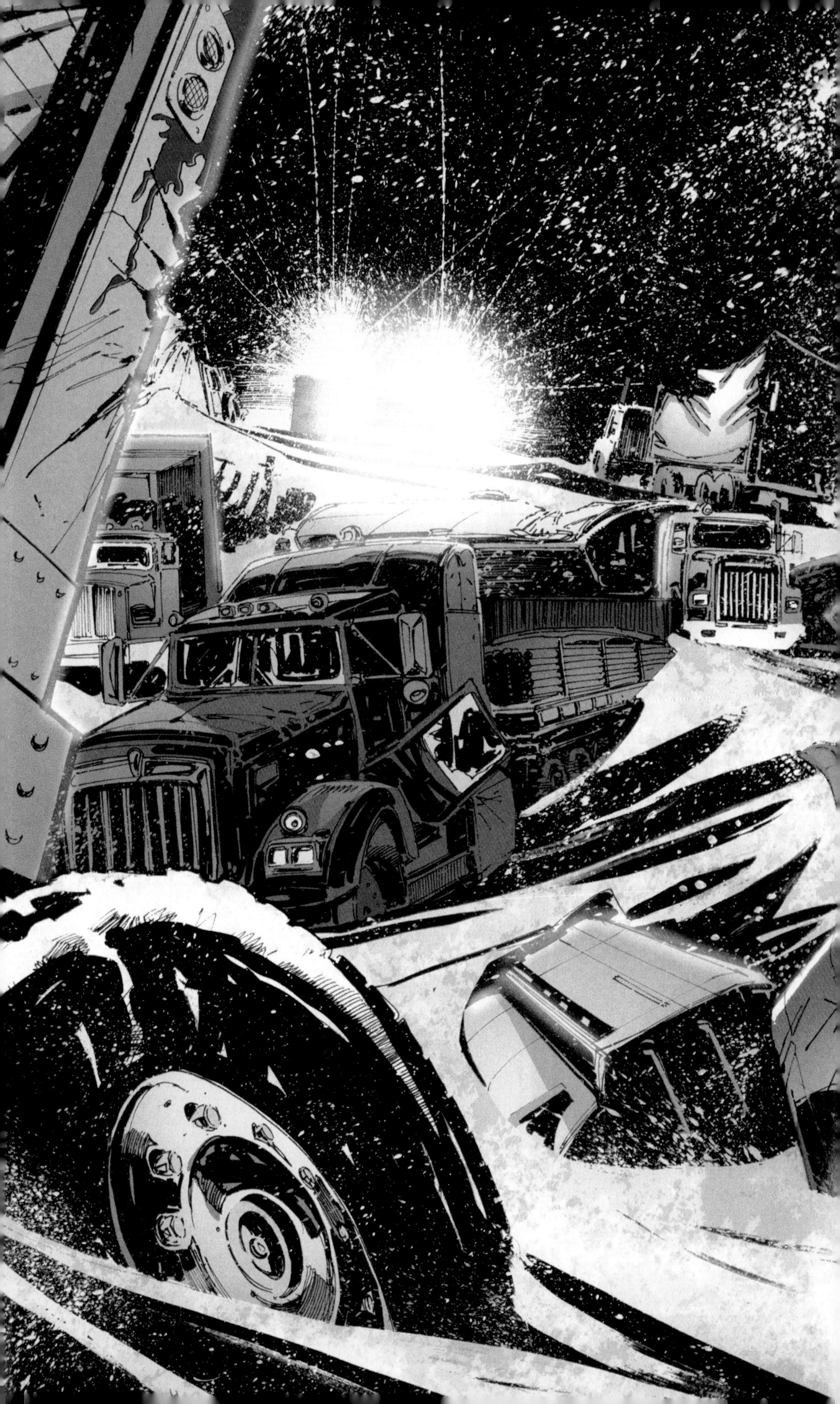

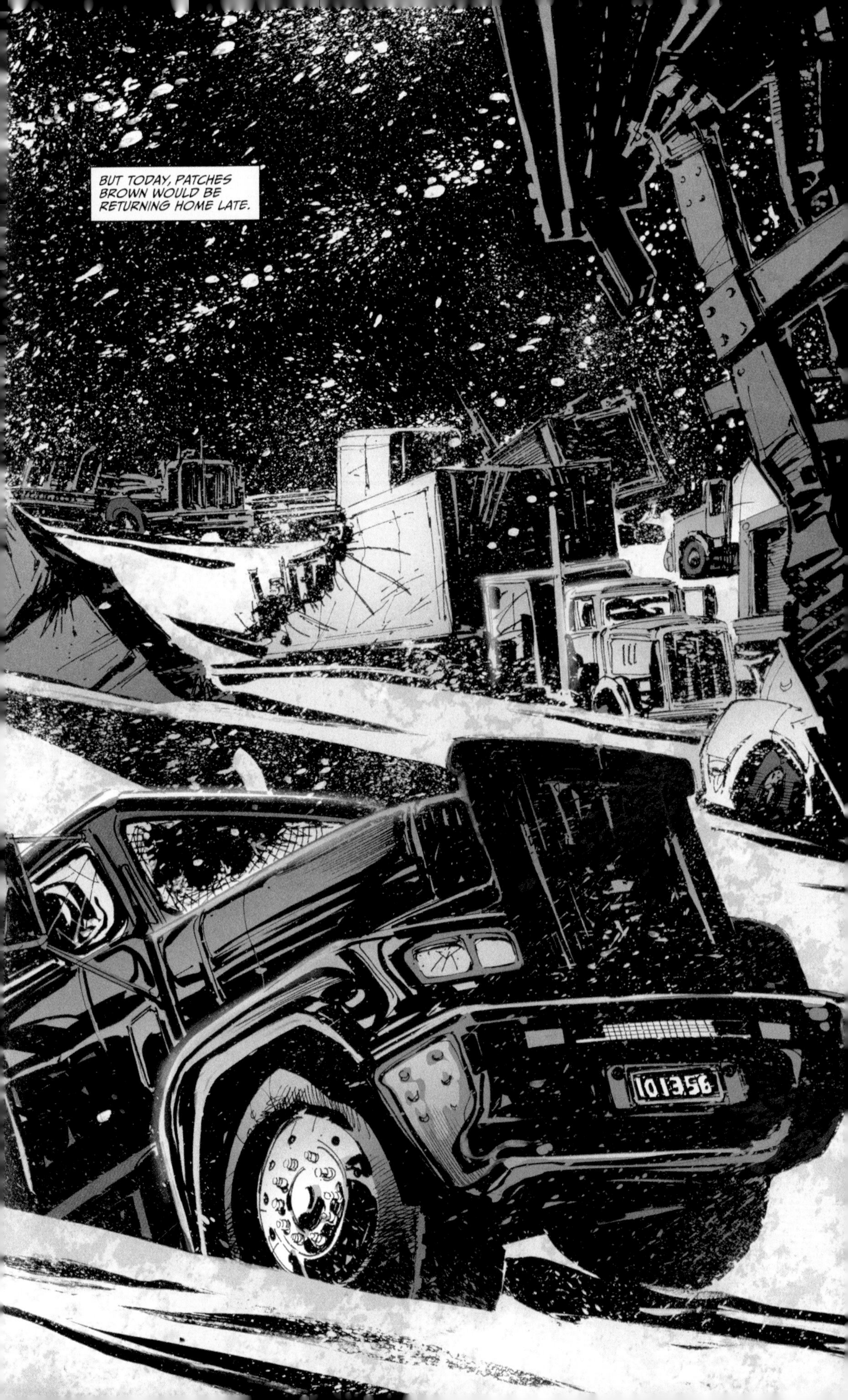
BUT TODAY, PATCHES BROWN WOULD BE RETURNING HOME LATE.
101356

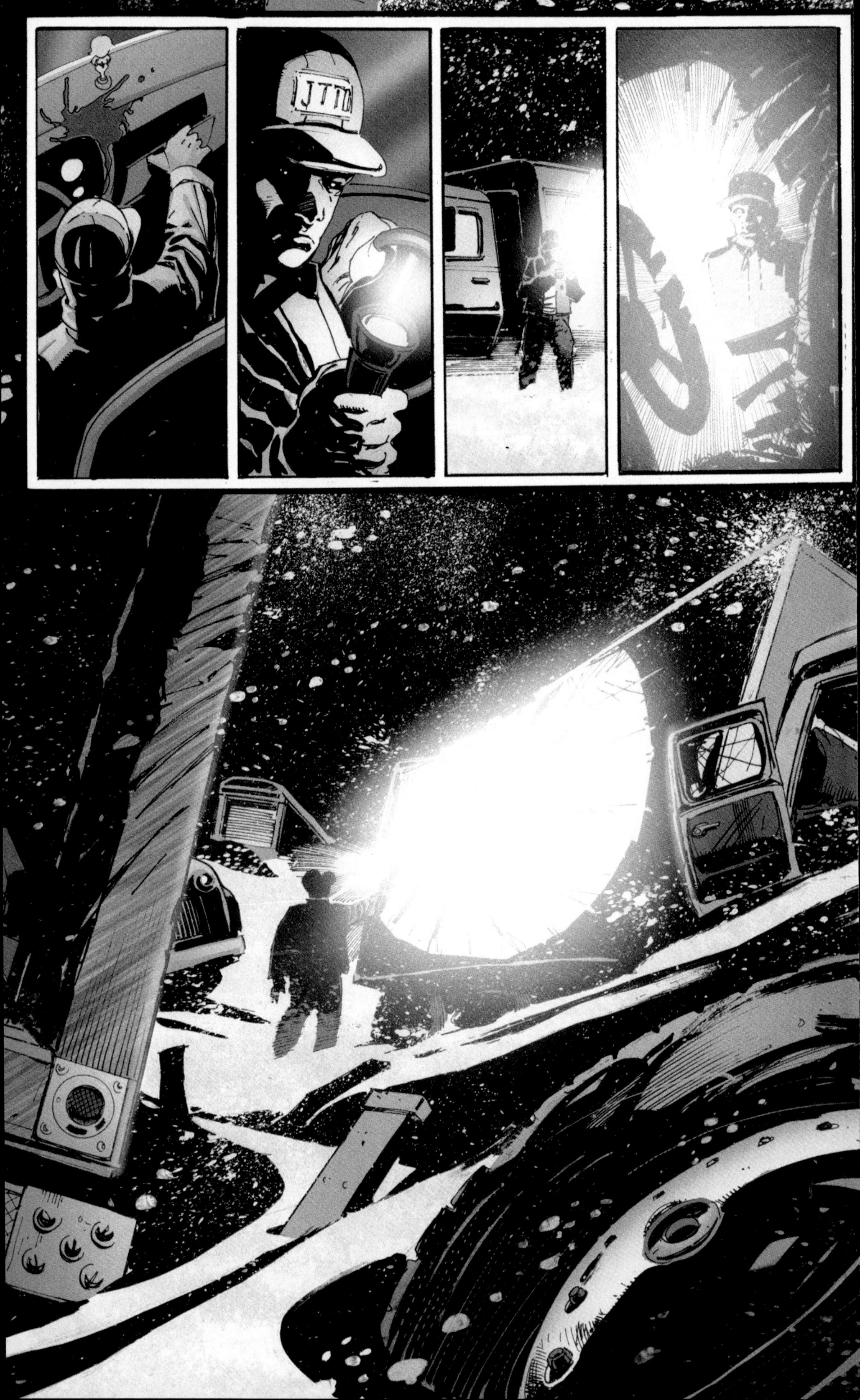

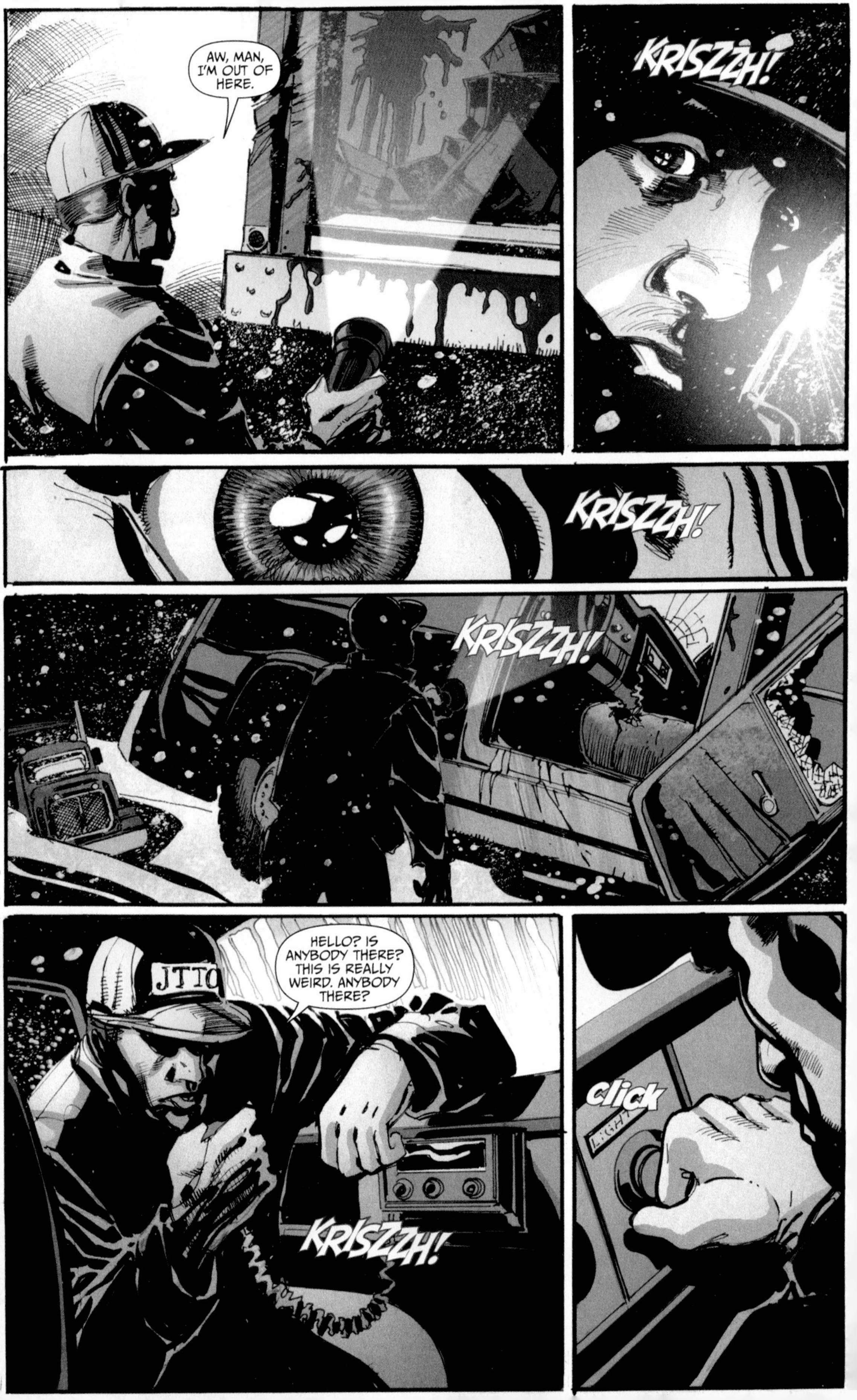
AW, MAN, I'M OUT OF HERE.
KRISZZH!
KRISZZH!
KRISZZH!
HELLO? IS ANYBODY THERE? THIS IS REALLY WEIRD. ANYBODY THERE?
JTTC
KRISZZH!
click
LIGHT

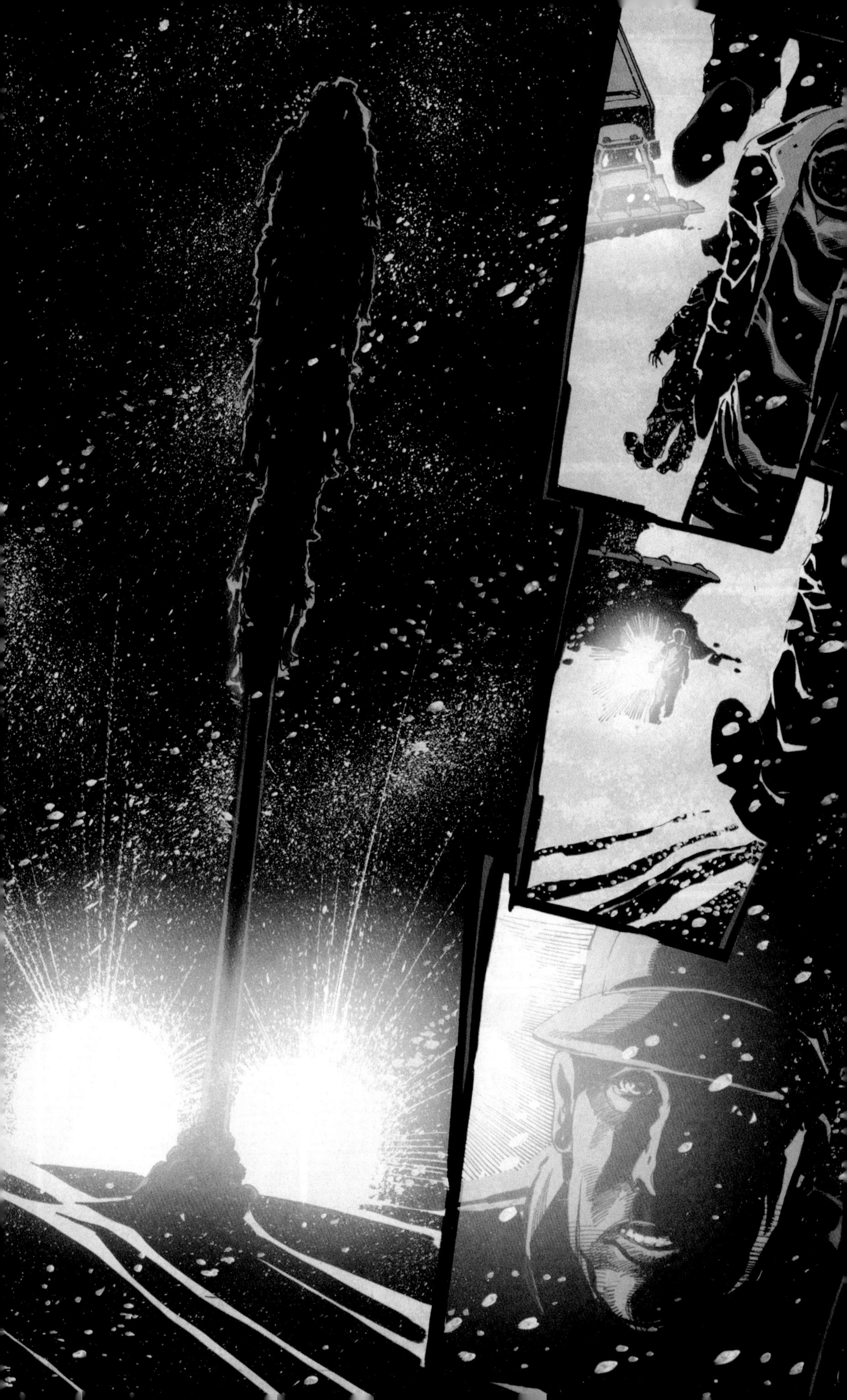

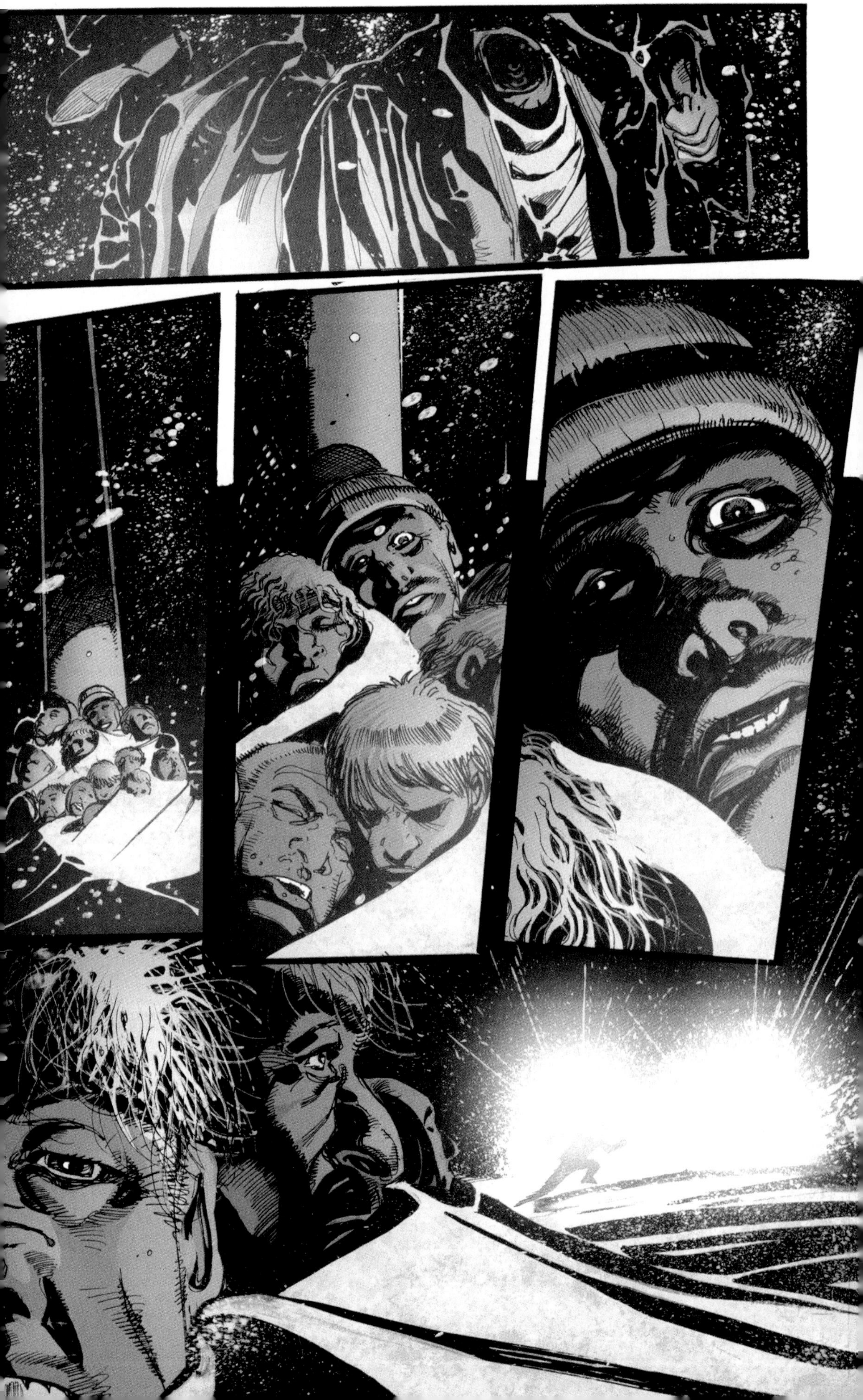

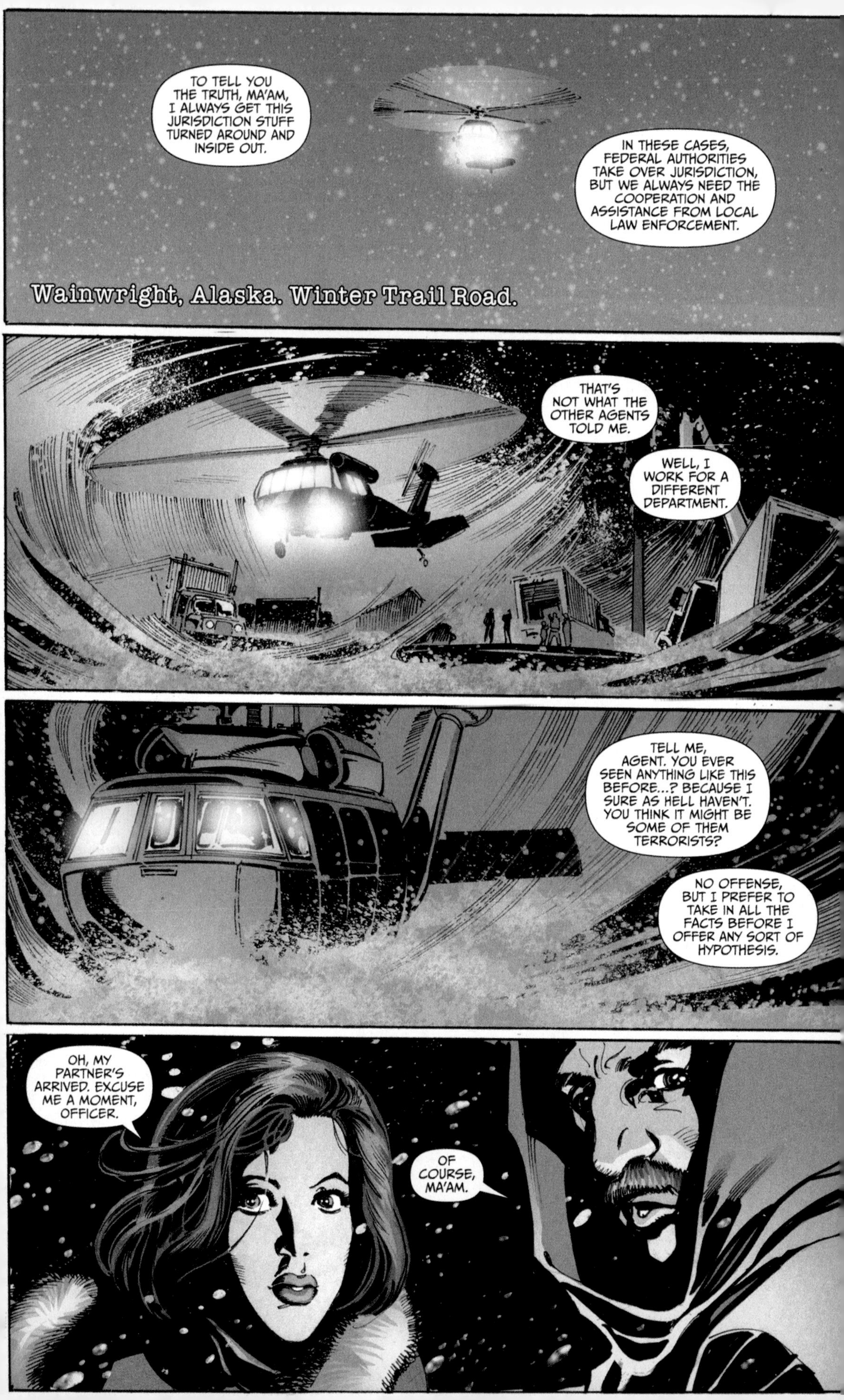
Wainwright, Alaska. Winter Trail Road.
TO TELL YOU THE TRUTH, MA'AM, I ALWAYS GET THIS JURISDICTION STUFF TURNED AROUND AND INSIDE OUT.
IN THESE CASES, FEDERAL AUTHORITIES TAKE OVER JURISDICTION, BUT WE ALWAYS NEED THE COOPERATION AND ASSISTANCE FROM LOCAL LAW ENFORCEMENT.
THAT'S NOT WHAT THE OTHER AGENTS TOLD ME.
WELL, I WORK FOR A DIFFERENT DEPARTMENT.
TELL ME, AGENT. YOU EVER SEEN ANYTHING LIKE THIS BEFORE...? BECAUSE I SURE AS HELL HAVEN'T. YOU THINK IT MIGHT BE SOME OF THEM TERRORISTS?
NO OFFENSE, BUT I PREFER TO TAKE IN ALL THE FACTS BEFORE I OFFER ANY SORT OF HYPOTHESIS.
OH, MY PARTNER'S ARRIVED. EXCUSE ME A MOMENT, OFFICER.
OF COURSE, MA'AM.

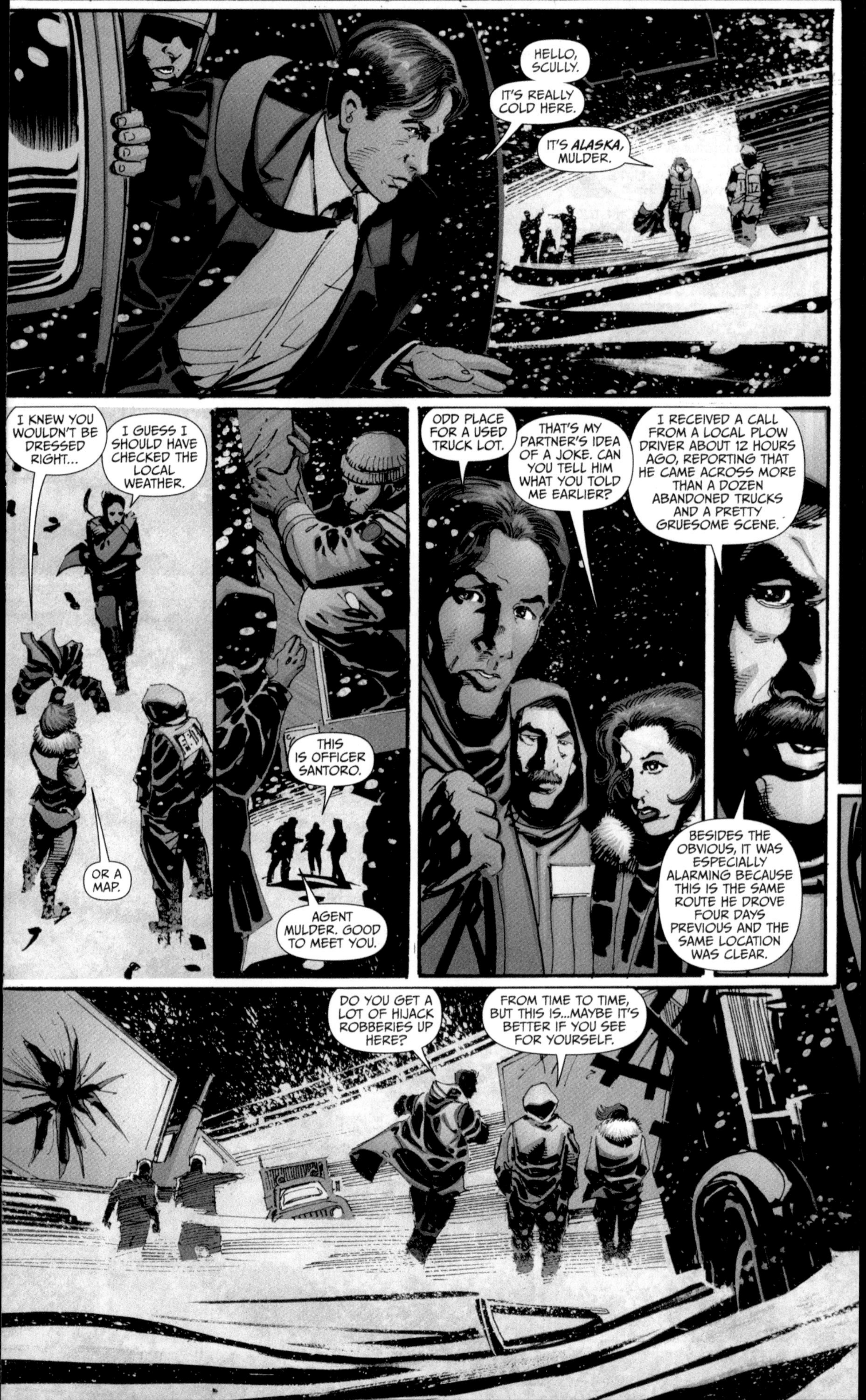
HELLO, SCULLY.
IT'S REALLY COLD HERE.
IT'S *ALASKA,* MULDER.
I KNEW YOU WOULDN'T BE DRESSED RIGHT...
I GUESS I SHOULD HAVE CHECKED THE LOCAL WEATHER.
OR A MAP.
THIS IS OFFICER SANTORO.
AGENT MULDER. GOOD TO MEET YOU.
ODD PLACE FOR A USED TRUCK LOT.
THAT'S MY PARTNER'S IDEA OF A JOKE. CAN YOU TELL HIM WHAT YOU TOLD ME EARLIER?
I RECEIVED A CALL FROM A LOCAL PLOW DRIVER ABOUT 12 HOURS AGO, REPORTING THAT HE CAME ACROSS MORE THAN A DOZEN ABANDONED TRUCKS AND A PRETTY GRUESOME SCENE.
BESIDES THE OBVIOUS, IT WAS ESPECIALLY ALARMING BECAUSE THIS IS THE SAME ROUTE HE DROVE FOUR DAYS PREVIOUS AND THE SAME LOCATION WAS CLEAR.
DO YOU GET A LOT OF HIJACK ROBBERIES UP HERE?
FROM TIME TO TIME, BUT THIS IS...MAYBE IT'S BETTER IF YOU SEE FOR YOURSELF.

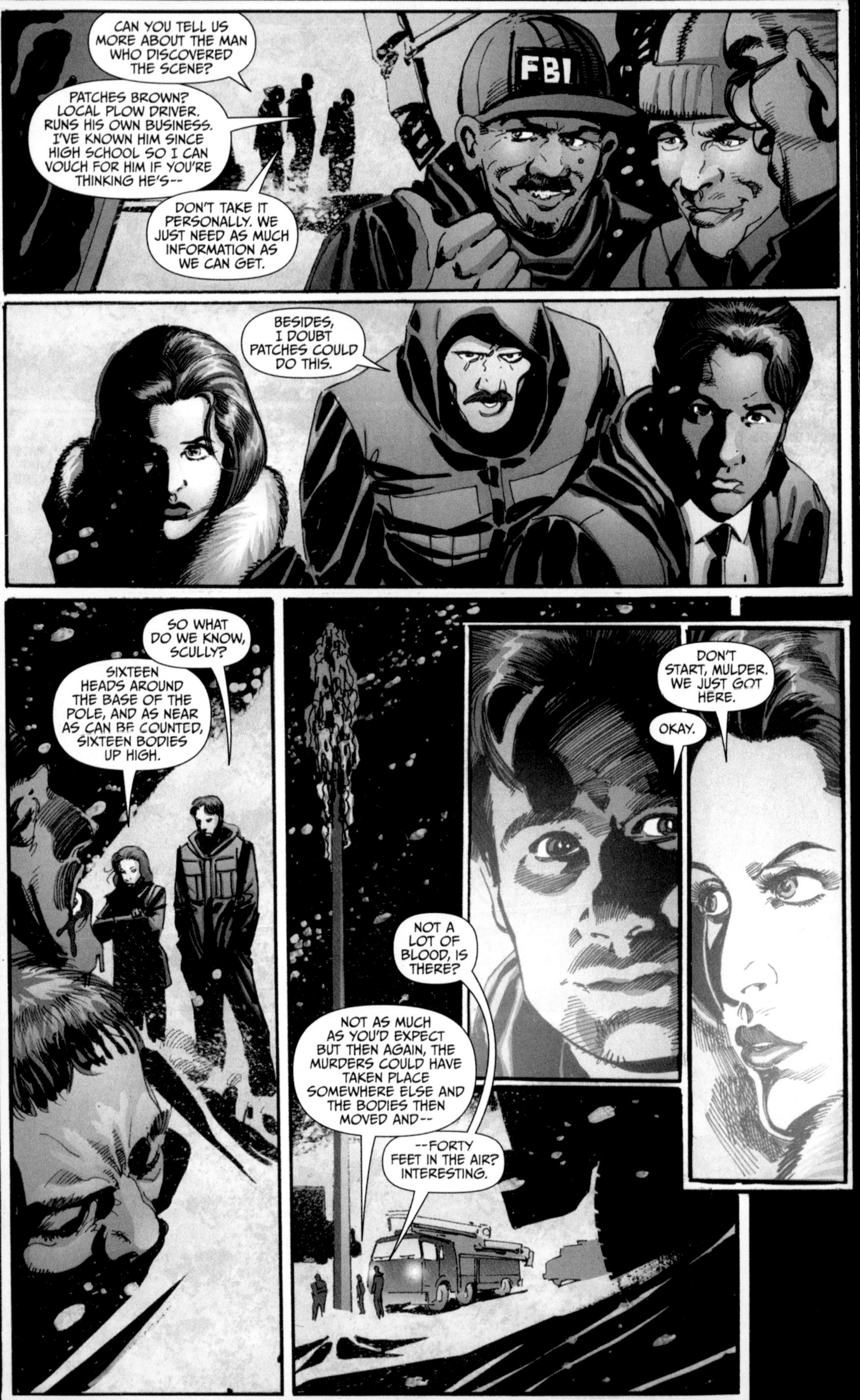
CAN YOU TELL US MORE ABOUT THE MAN WHO DISCOVERED THE SCENE?
PATCHES BROWN? LOCAL PLOW DRIVER. RUNS HIS OWN BUSINESS. I'VE KNOWN HIM SINCE HIGH SCHOOL SO I CAN VOUCH FOR HIM IF YOU'RE THINKING HE'S--
FBI
DON'T TAKE IT PERSONALLY. WE JUST NEED AS MUCH INFORMATION AS WE CAN GET.
BESIDES, I DOUBT PATCHES COULD DO THIS.
SO WHAT DO WE KNOW, SCULLY?
SIXTEEN HEADS AROUND THE BASE OF THE POLE, AND AS NEAR AS CAN BE COUNTED, SIXTEEN BODIES UP HIGH.
NOT A LOT OF BLOOD, IS THERE?
NOT AS MUCH AS YOU'D EXPECT BUT THEN AGAIN, THE MURDERS COULD HAVE TAKEN PLACE SOMEWHERE ELSE AND THE BODIES THEN MOVED AND--
--FORTY FEET IN THE AIR? INTERESTING.
DON'T START, MULDER. WE JUST GOT HERE.
OKAY.

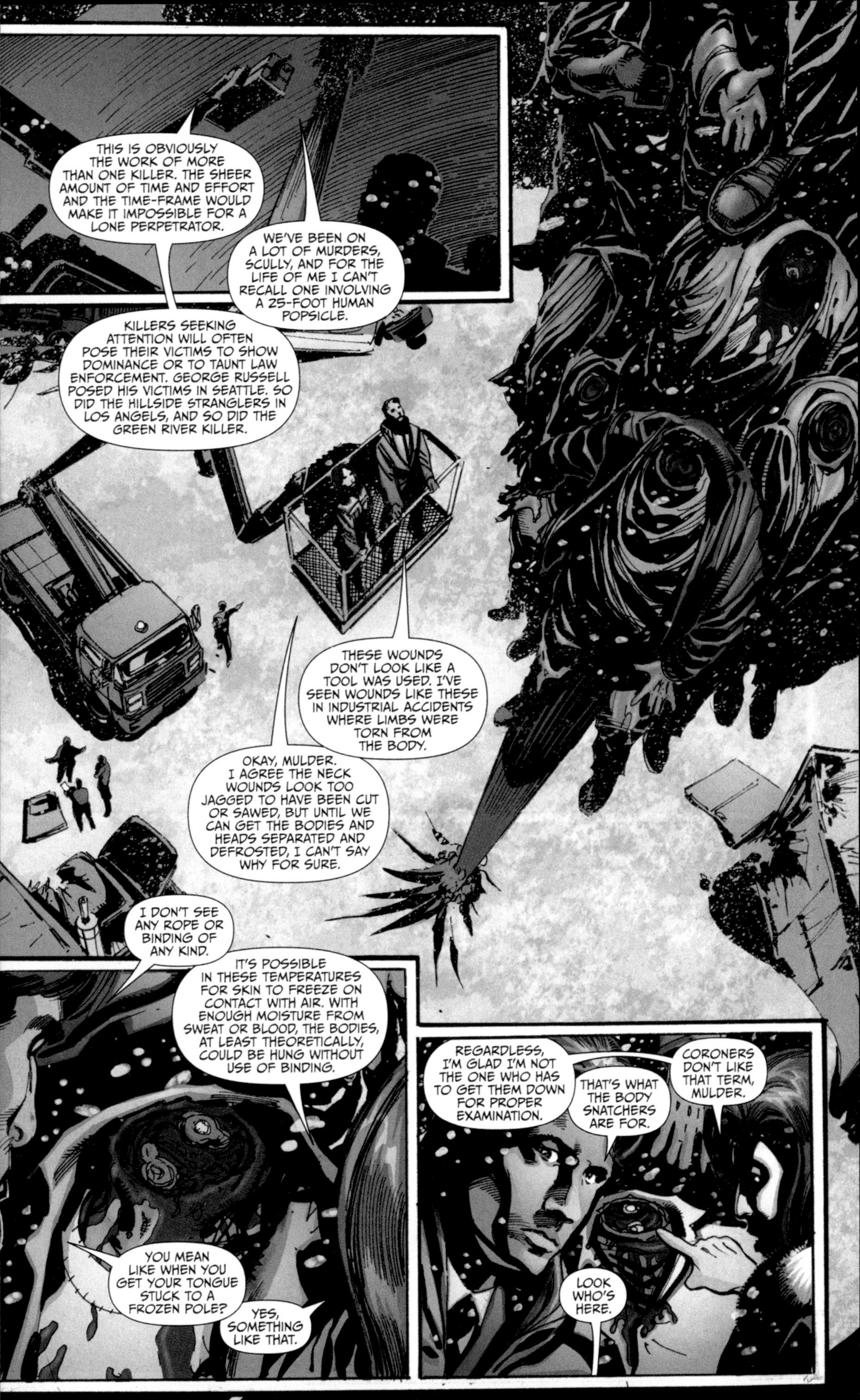
THIS IS OBVIOUSLY THE WORK OF MORE THAN ONE KILLER. THE SHEER AMOUNT OF TIME AND EFFORT AND THE TIME-FRAME WOULD MAKE IT IMPOSSIBLE FOR A LONE PERPETRATOR.
WE'VE BEEN ON A LOT OF MURDERS, SCULLY, AND FOR THE LIFE OF ME I CAN'T RECALL ONE INVOLVING A 25-FOOT HUMAN POPSICLE.
KILLERS SEEKING ATTENTION WILL OFTEN POSE THEIR VICTIMS TO SHOW DOMINANCE OR TO TAUNT LAW ENFORCEMENT. GEORGE RUSSELL POSED HIS VICTIMS IN SEATTLE. SO DID THE HILLSIDE STRANGLERS IN LOS ANGELS, AND SO DID THE GREEN RIVER KILLER.
THESE WOUNDS DON'T LOOK LIKE A TOOL WAS USED. I'VE SEEN WOUNDS LIKE THESE IN INDUSTRIAL ACCIDENTS WHERE LIMBS WERE TORN FROM THE BODY.
OKAY, MULDER. I AGREE THE NECK WOUNDS LOOK TOO JAGGED TO HAVE BEEN CUT OR SAWED, BUT UNTIL WE CAN GET THE BODIES AND HEADS SEPARATED AND DEFROSTED, I CAN'T SAY WHY FOR SURE.
I DON'T SEE ANY ROPE OR BINDING OF ANY KIND.
IT'S POSSIBLE IN THESE TEMPERATURES FOR SKIN TO FREEZE ON CONTACT WITH AIR. WITH ENOUGH MOISTURE FROM SWEAT OR BLOOD, THE BODIES, AT LEAST THEORETICALLY, COULD BE HUNG WITHOUT USE OF BINDING.
YOU MEAN LIKE WHEN YOU GET YOUR TONGUE STUCK TO A FROZEN POLE?
YES, SOMETHING LIKE THAT.
REGARDLESS, I'M GLAD I'M NOT THE ONE WHO HAS TO GET THEM DOWN FOR PROPER EXAMINATION.
THAT'S WHAT THE BODY SNATCHERS ARE FOR.
CORONERS DON'T LIKE THAT TERM, MULDER.
LOOK WHO'S HERE.

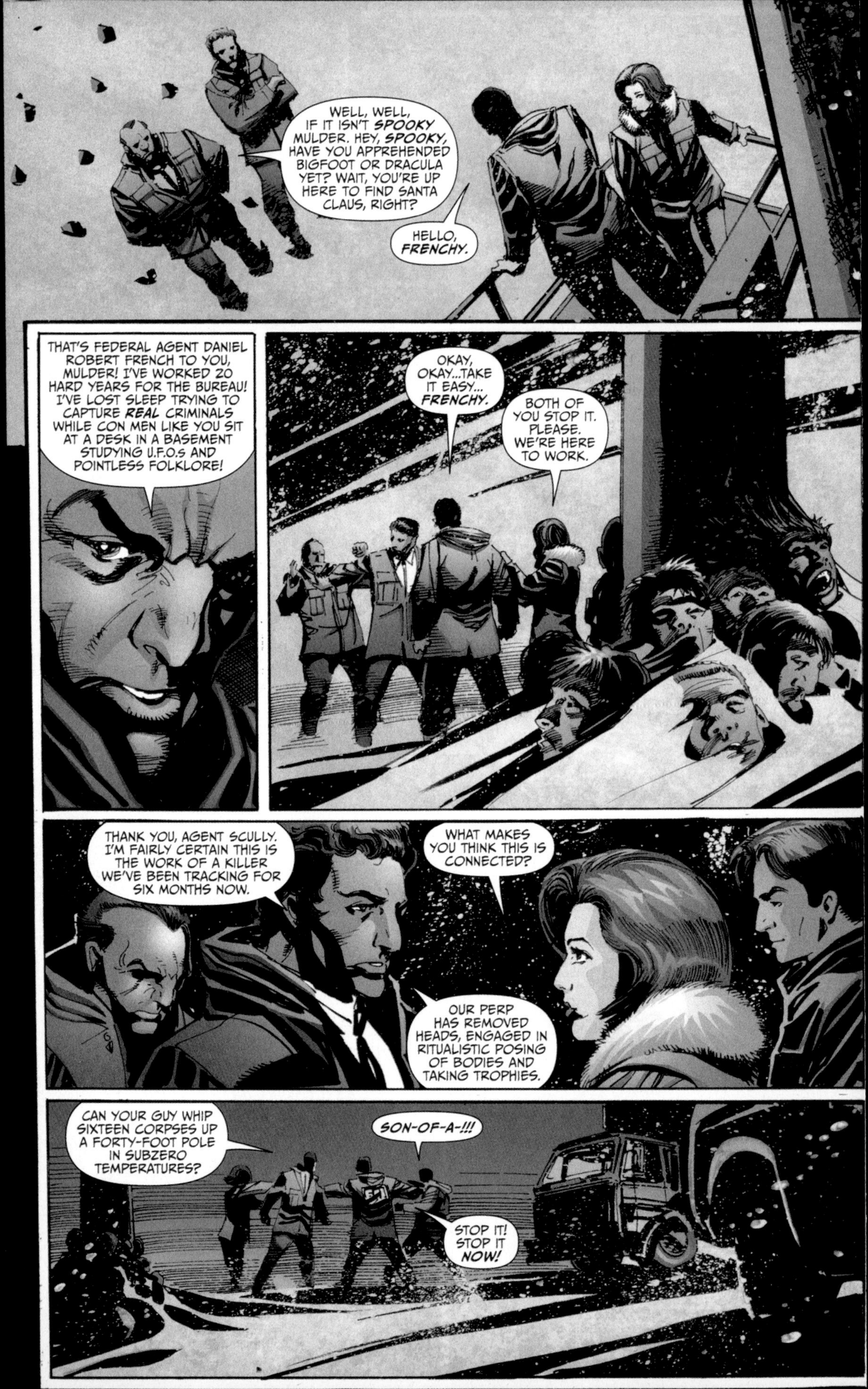
WELL, WELL, IF IT ISN'T SPOOKY MULDER. HEY, SPOOKY, HAVE YOU APPREHENDED BIGFOOT OR DRACULA YET? WAIT, YOU'RE UP HERE TO FIND SANTA CLAUS, RIGHT?
HELLO, FRENCHY.
THAT'S FEDERAL AGENT DANIEL ROBERT FRENCH TO YOU, MULDER! I'VE WORKED 20 HARD YEARS FOR THE BUREAU! I'VE LOST SLEEP TRYING TO CAPTURE REAL CRIMINALS WHILE CON MEN LIKE YOU SIT AT A DESK IN A BASEMENT STUDYING U.F.O.S AND POINTLESS FOLKLORE!
OKAY, OKAY...TAKE IT EASY... FRENCHY.
BOTH OF YOU STOP IT. PLEASE. WE'RE HERE TO WORK.
THANK YOU, AGENT SCULLY. I'M FAIRLY CERTAIN THIS IS THE WORK OF A KILLER WE'VE BEEN TRACKING FOR SIX MONTHS NOW.
WHAT MAKES YOU THINK THIS IS CONNECTED?
OUR PERP HAS REMOVED HEADS, ENGAGED IN RITUALISTIC POSING OF BODIES AND TAKING TROPHIES.
CAN YOUR GUY WHIP SIXTEEN CORPSES UP A FORTY-FOOT POLE IN SUBZERO TEMPERATURES?
SON-OF-A-!!!
STOP IT! STOP IT NOW!

LOOK, WE'VE BEEN FOLLOWING THE TRAIL OF THIS KILLER FROM LOS ANGELES THROUGH SAN FRANCISCO, PORTLAND AND THEN SEATTLE.

I CAN SEE WHERE THE SIMILARITIES ARE, AGENT FRENCH, BUT I HAVE TO AGREE WITH MY PARTNER...I SERIOUSLY DOUBT THIS IS THE WORK OF A SINGLE KILLER.

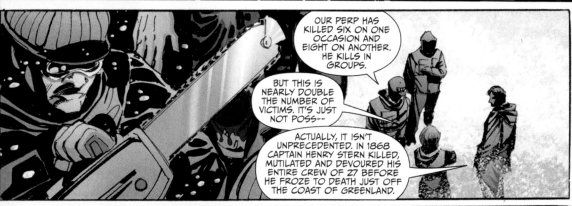

OUR PERP HAS KILLED SIX ON ONE OCCASION AND EIGHT ON ANOTHER. HE KILLS IN GROUPS.

BUT THIS IS NEARLY DOUBLE THE NUMBER OF VICTIMS. IT'S JUST NOT POSS--

ACTUALLY, IT ISN'T UNPRECEDENTED. IN 1868 CAPTAIN HENRY STERN KILLED, MUTILATED AND DEVOURED HIS ENTIRE CREW OF 27 BEFORE HE FROZE TO DEATH JUST OFF THE COAST OF GREENLAND.

ANYWAY...I'M SURE WE CAN ALL WORK WITHOUT GETTING IN EACH OTHERS' WAY.

I GUARANTEE IT. IN FACT, YOU CAN COUNT ON GETTING ABSOLUTELY NO HELP FROM ANY OF MY PEOPLE.

YOU HAVE A PROBLEM WITH US BEING HERE, TAKE IT UP WITH SKINNER.

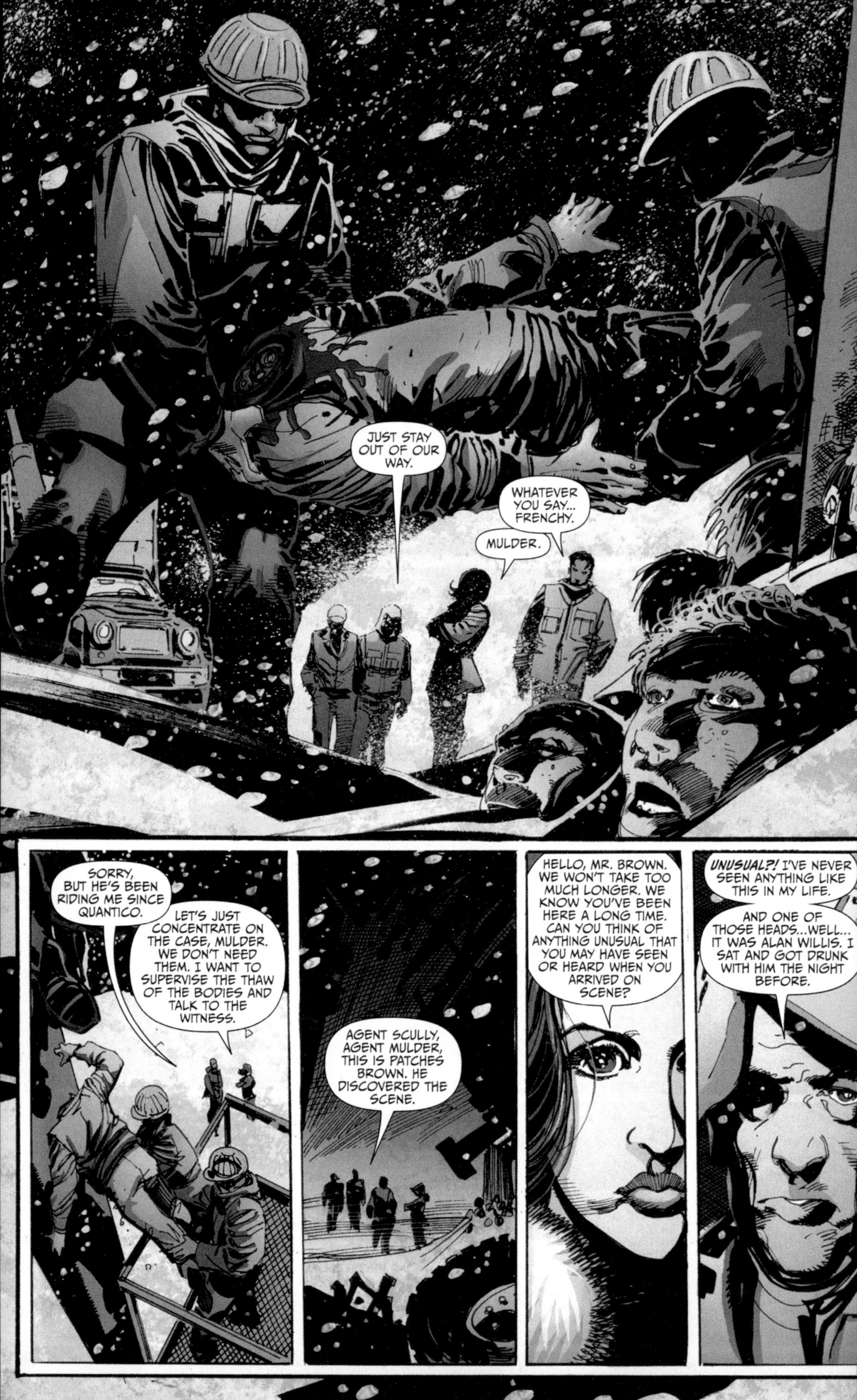
JUST STAY OUT OF OUR WAY.
WHATEVER YOU SAY... FRENCHY.
MULDER.
SORRY, BUT HE'S BEEN RIDING ME SINCE QUANTICO.
LET'S JUST CONCENTRATE ON THE CASE, MULDER. WE DON'T NEED THEM. I WANT TO SUPERVISE THE THAW OF THE BODIES AND TALK TO THE WITNESS.
AGENT SCULLY, AGENT MULDER, THIS IS PATCHES BROWN. HE DISCOVERED THE SCENE.
HELLO, MR. BROWN. WE WON'T TAKE TOO MUCH LONGER. WE KNOW YOU'VE BEEN HERE A LONG TIME. CAN YOU THINK OF ANYTHING UNUSUAL THAT YOU MAY HAVE SEEN OR HEARD WHEN YOU ARRIVED ON SCENE?
UNUSUAL?! I'VE NEVER SEEN ANYTHING LIKE THIS IN MY LIFE.
AND ONE OF THOSE HEADS...WELL... IT WAS ALAN WILLIS. I SAT AND GOT DRUNK WITH HIM THE NIGHT BEFORE.

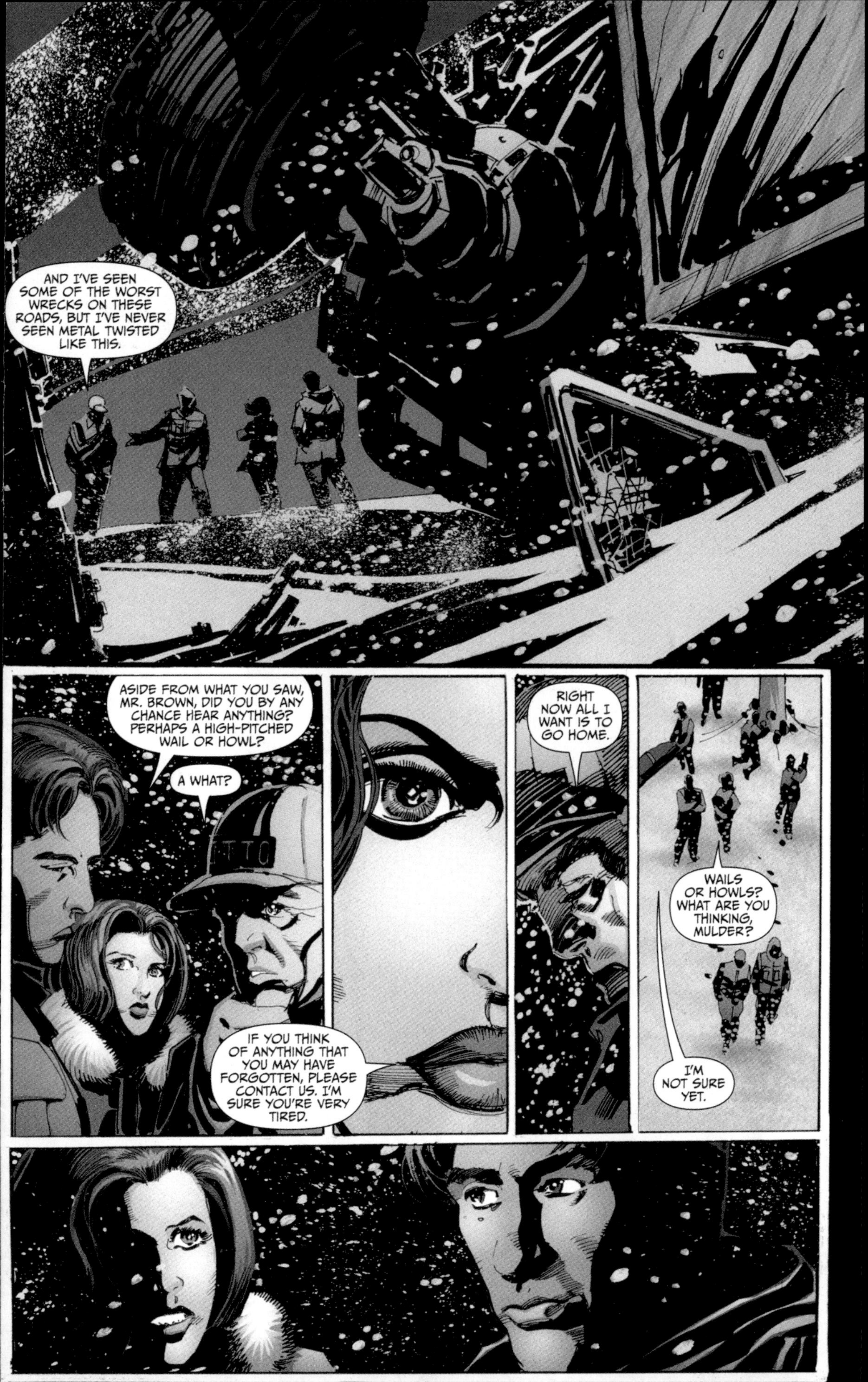
AND I'VE SEEN SOME OF THE WORST WRECKS ON THESE ROADS, BUT I'VE NEVER SEEN METAL TWISTED LIKE THIS.
ASIDE FROM WHAT YOU SAW, MR. BROWN, DID YOU BY ANY CHANCE HEAR ANYTHING? PERHAPS A HIGH-PITCHED WAIL OR HOWL?
A WHAT?
IF YOU THINK OF ANYTHING THAT YOU MAY HAVE FORGOTTEN, PLEASE CONTACT US. I'M SURE YOU'RE VERY TIRED.
RIGHT NOW ALL I WANT IS TO GO HOME.
WAILS OR HOWLS? WHAT ARE YOU THINKING, MULDER?
I'M NOT SURE YET.

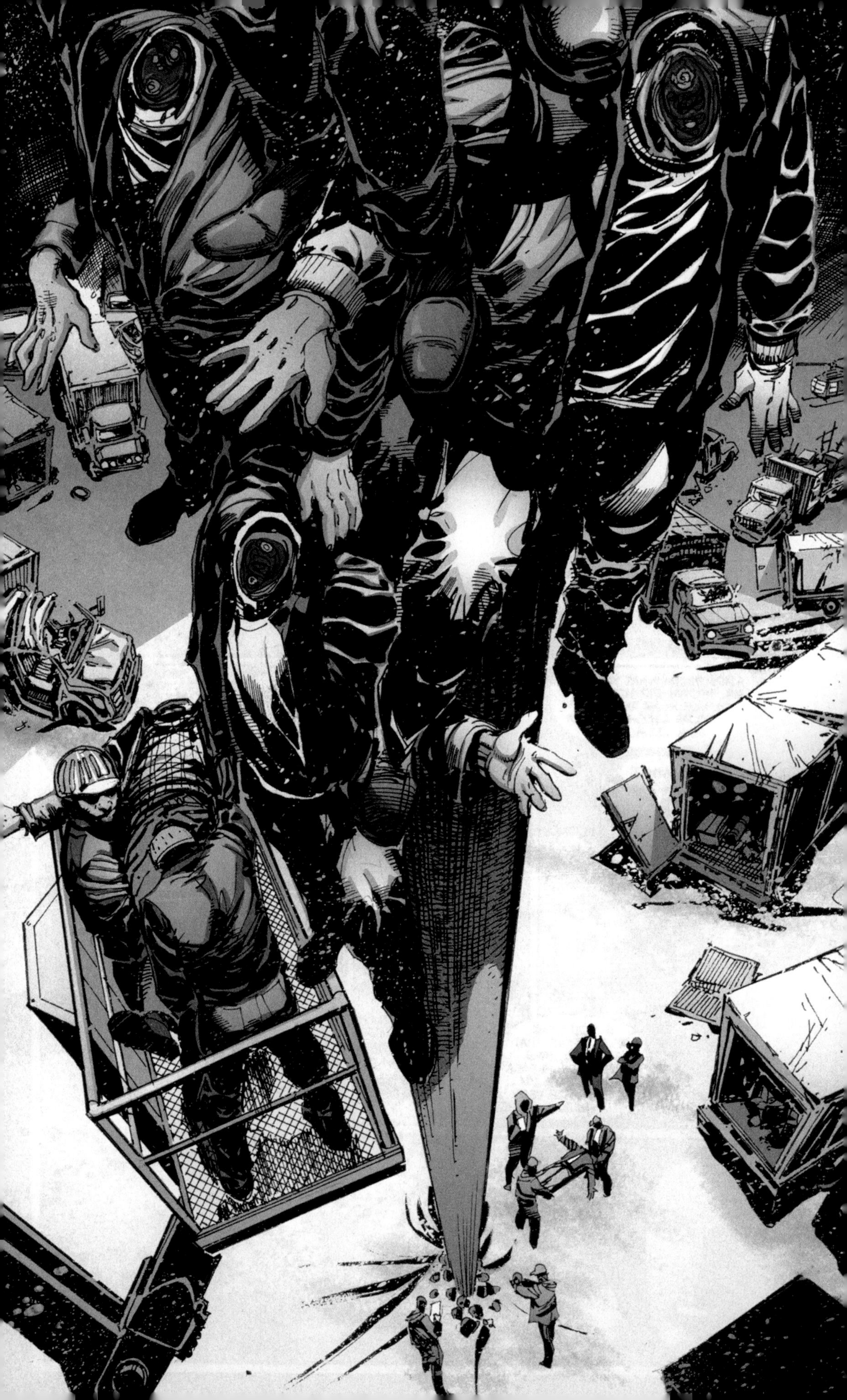

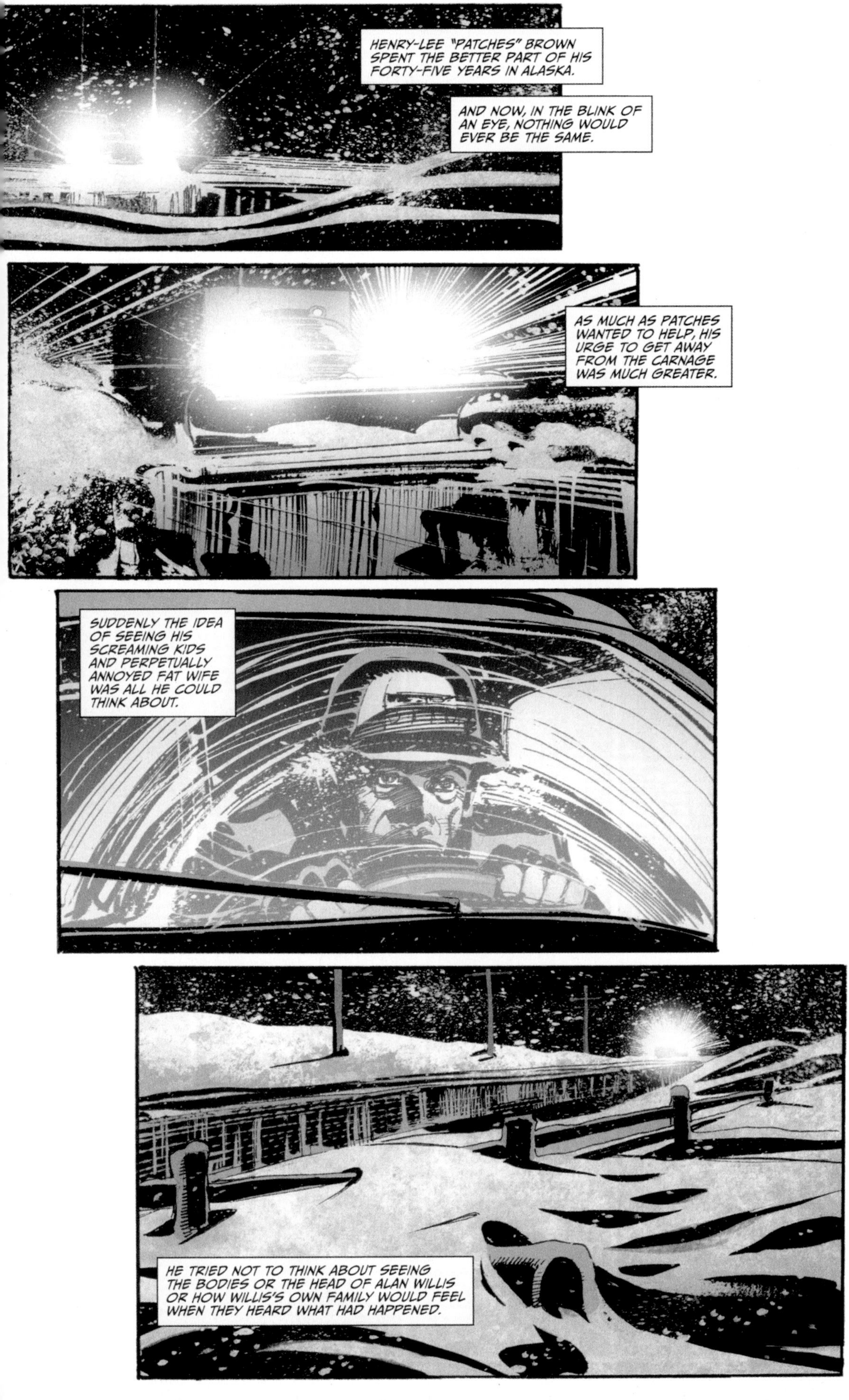
HENRY-LEE "PATCHES" BROWN SPENT THE BETTER PART OF HIS FORTY-FIVE YEARS IN ALASKA.
AND NOW, IN THE BLINK OF AN EYE, NOTHING WOULD EVER BE THE SAME.
AS MUCH AS PATCHES WANTED TO HELP, HIS URGE TO GET AWAY FROM THE CARNAGE WAS MUCH GREATER.
SUDDENLY THE IDEA OF SEEING HIS SCREAMING KIDS AND PERPETUALLY ANNOYED FAT WIFE WAS ALL HE COULD THINK ABOUT.
HE TRIED NOT TO THINK ABOUT SEEING THE BODIES OR THE HEAD OF ALAN WILLIS OR HOW WILLIS'S OWN FAMILY WOULD FEEL WHEN THEY HEARD WHAT HAD HAPPENED.

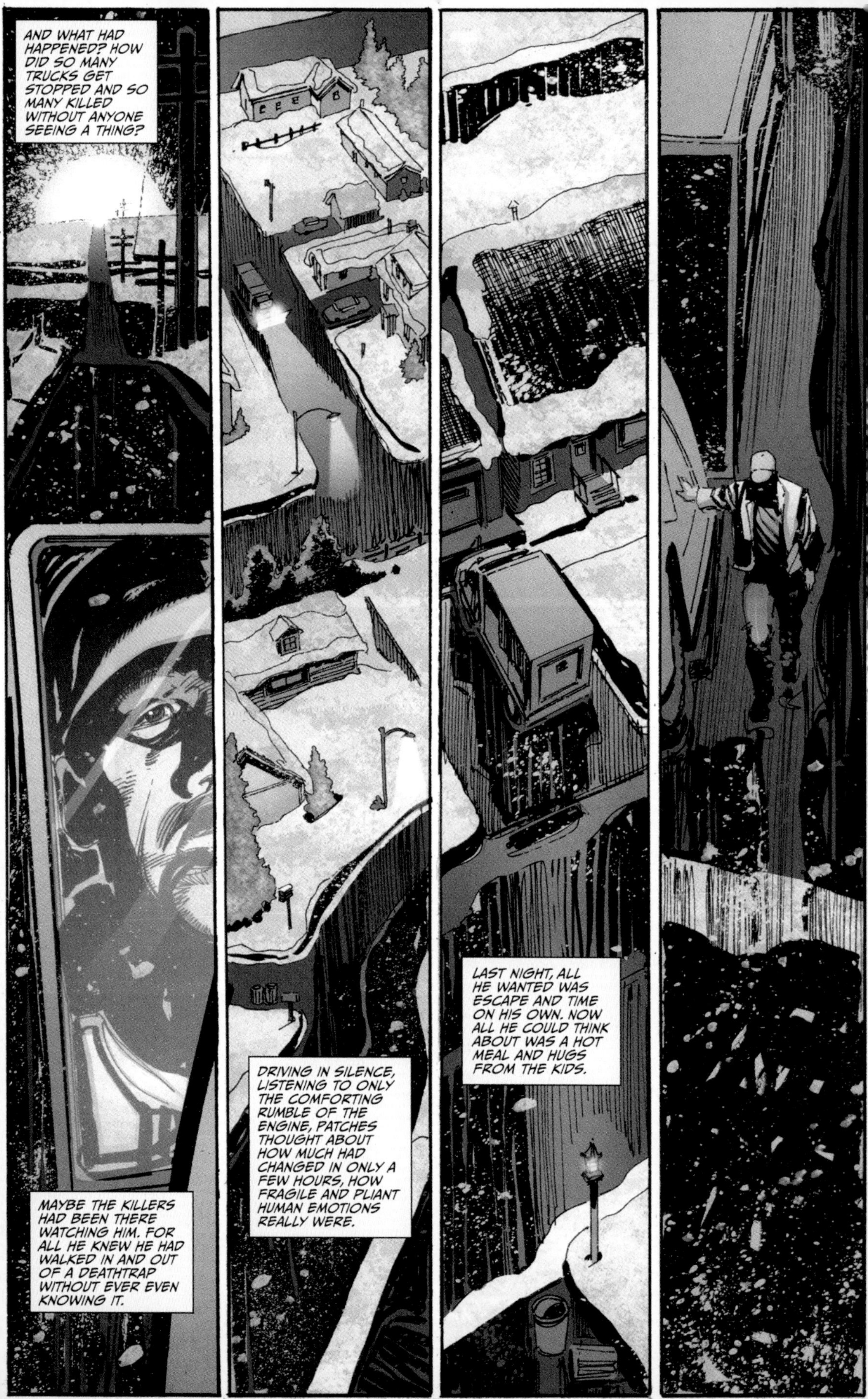
AND WHAT HAD HAPPENED? HOW DID SO MANY TRUCKS GET STOPPED AND SO MANY KILLED WITHOUT ANYONE SEEING A THING?
MAYBE THE KILLERS HAD BEEN THERE WATCHING HIM. FOR ALL HE KNEW HE HAD WALKED IN AND OUT OF A DEATHTRAP WITHOUT EVER EVEN KNOWING IT.
DRIVING IN SILENCE, LISTENING TO ONLY THE COMFORTING RUMBLE OF THE ENGINE, PATCHES THOUGHT ABOUT HOW MUCH HAD CHANGED IN ONLY A FEW HOURS, HOW FRAGILE AND PLIANT HUMAN EMOTIONS REALLY WERE.
LAST NIGHT, ALL HE WANTED WAS ESCAPE AND TIME ON HIS OWN. NOW ALL HE COULD THINK ABOUT WAS A HOT MEAL AND HUGS FROM THE KIDS.

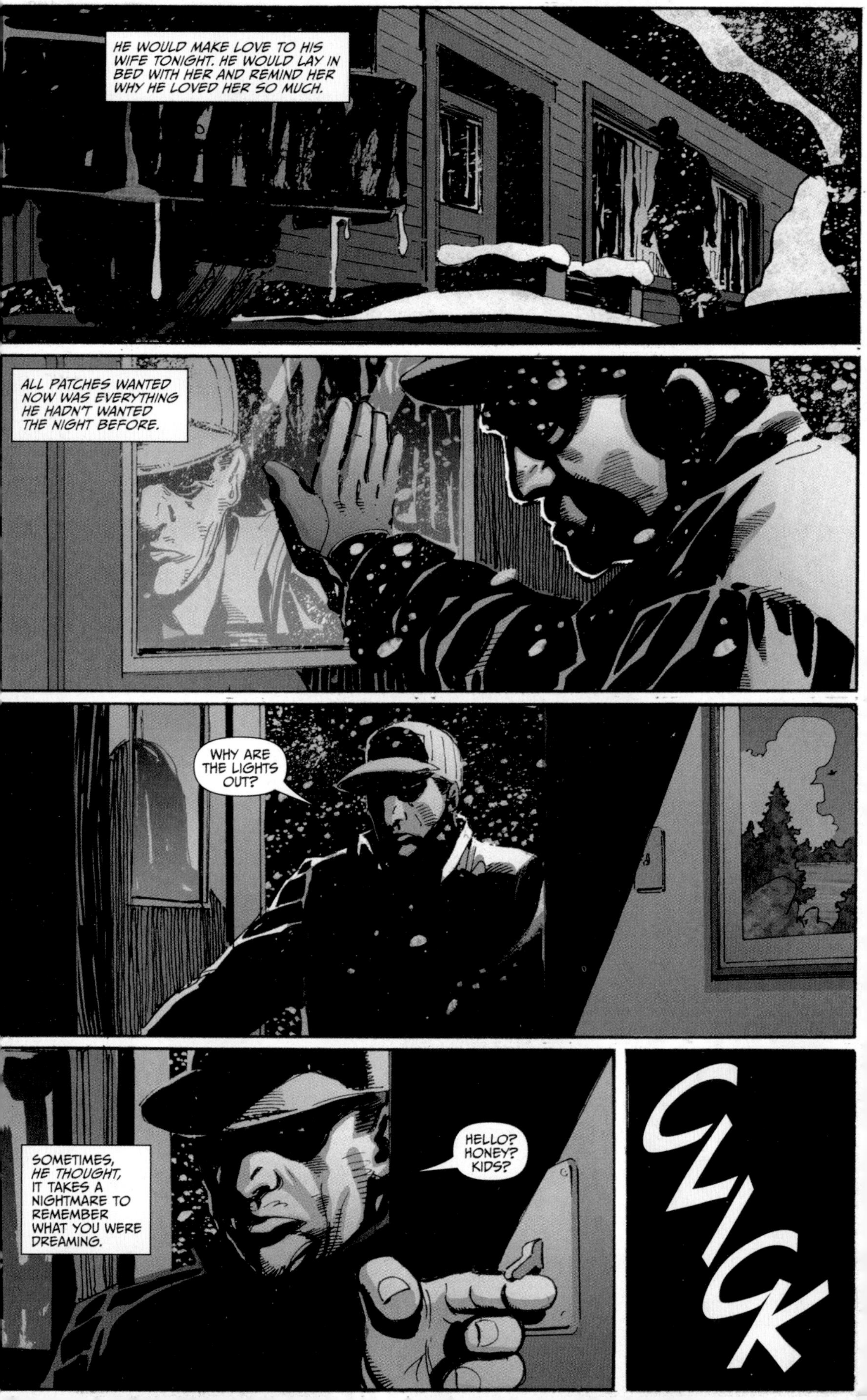
HE WOULD MAKE LOVE TO HIS WIFE TONIGHT. HE WOULD LAY IN BED WITH HER AND REMIND HER WHY HE LOVED HER SO MUCH.
ALL PATCHES WANTED NOW WAS EVERYTHING HE HADN'T WANTED THE NIGHT BEFORE.
WHY ARE THE LIGHTS OUT?
SOMETIMES, HE THOUGHT, IT TAKES A NIGHTMARE TO REMEMBER WHAT YOU WERE DREAMING.
HELLO? HONEY? KIDS?
CLICK

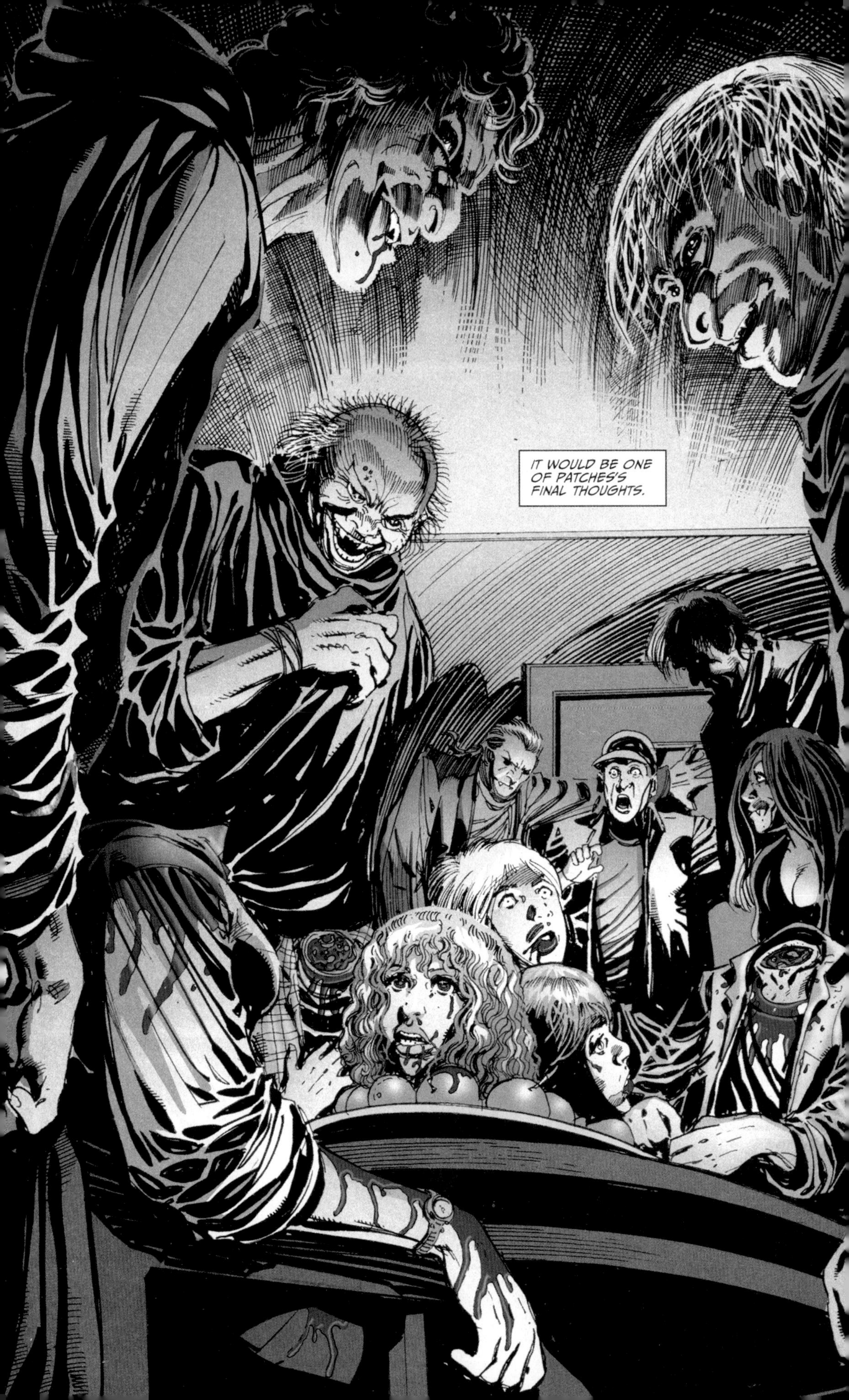
IT WOULD BE ONE
OF PATCHES'S
FINAL THOUGHTS.

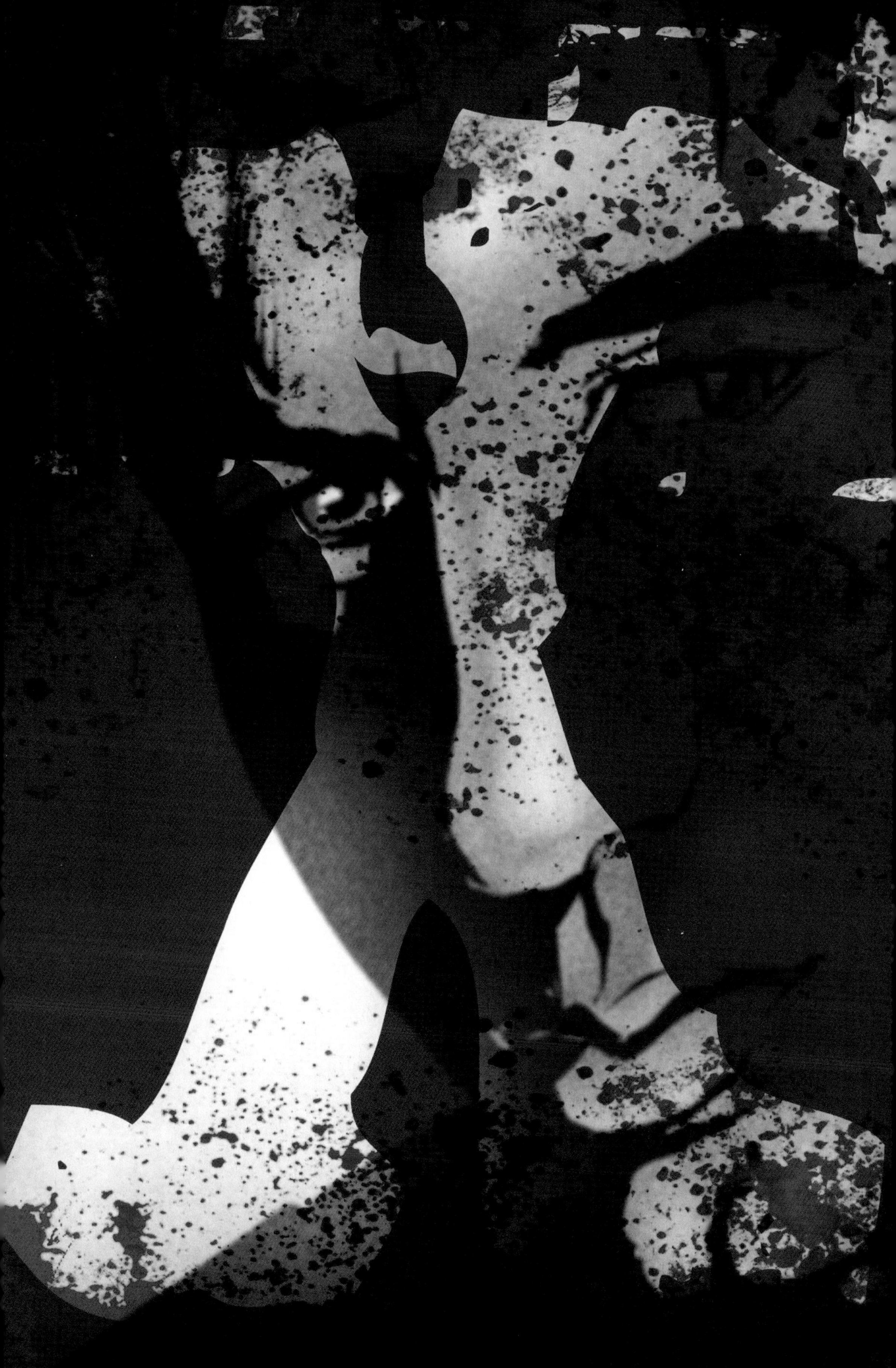

art by: Andrea Sorrentino

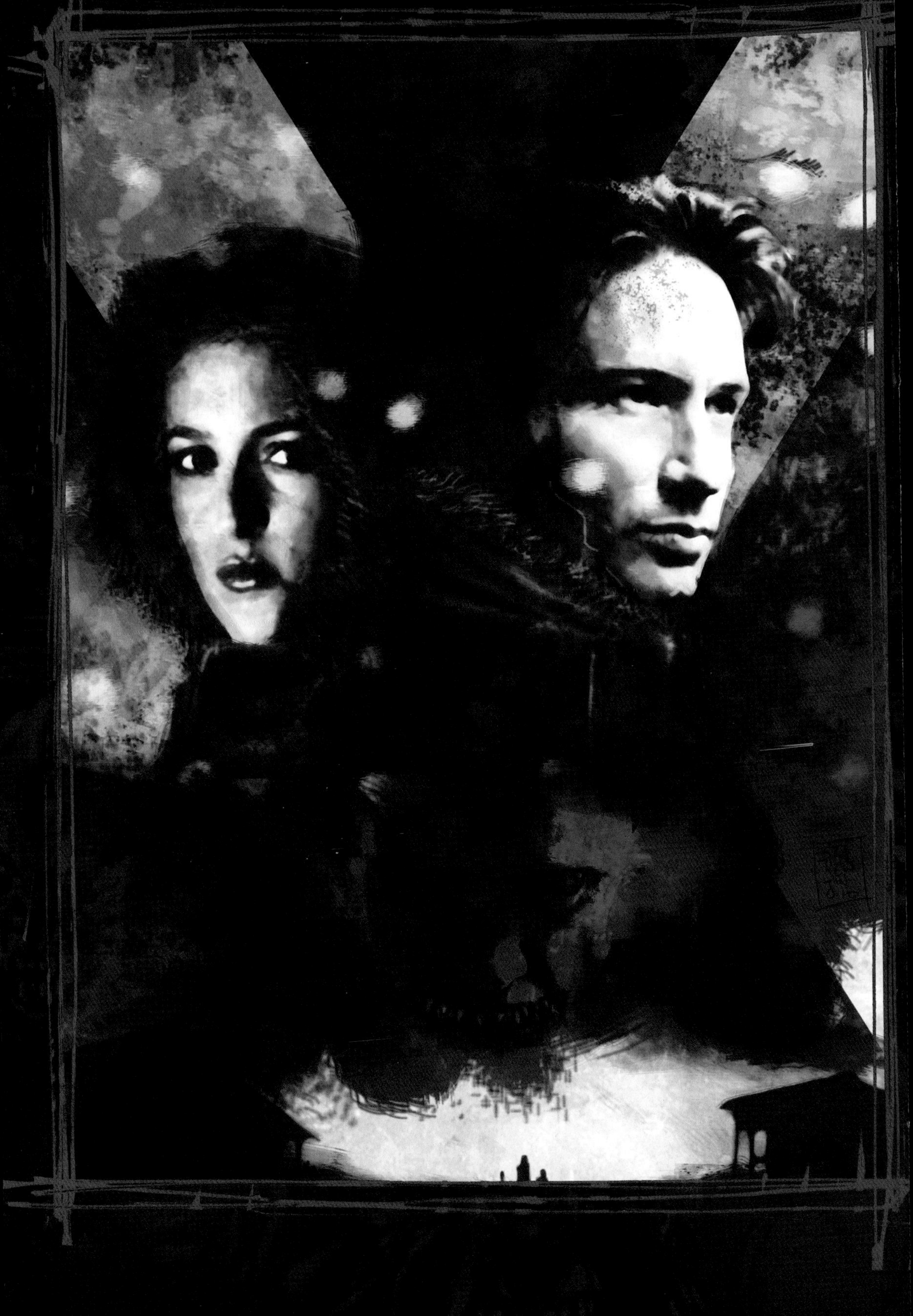

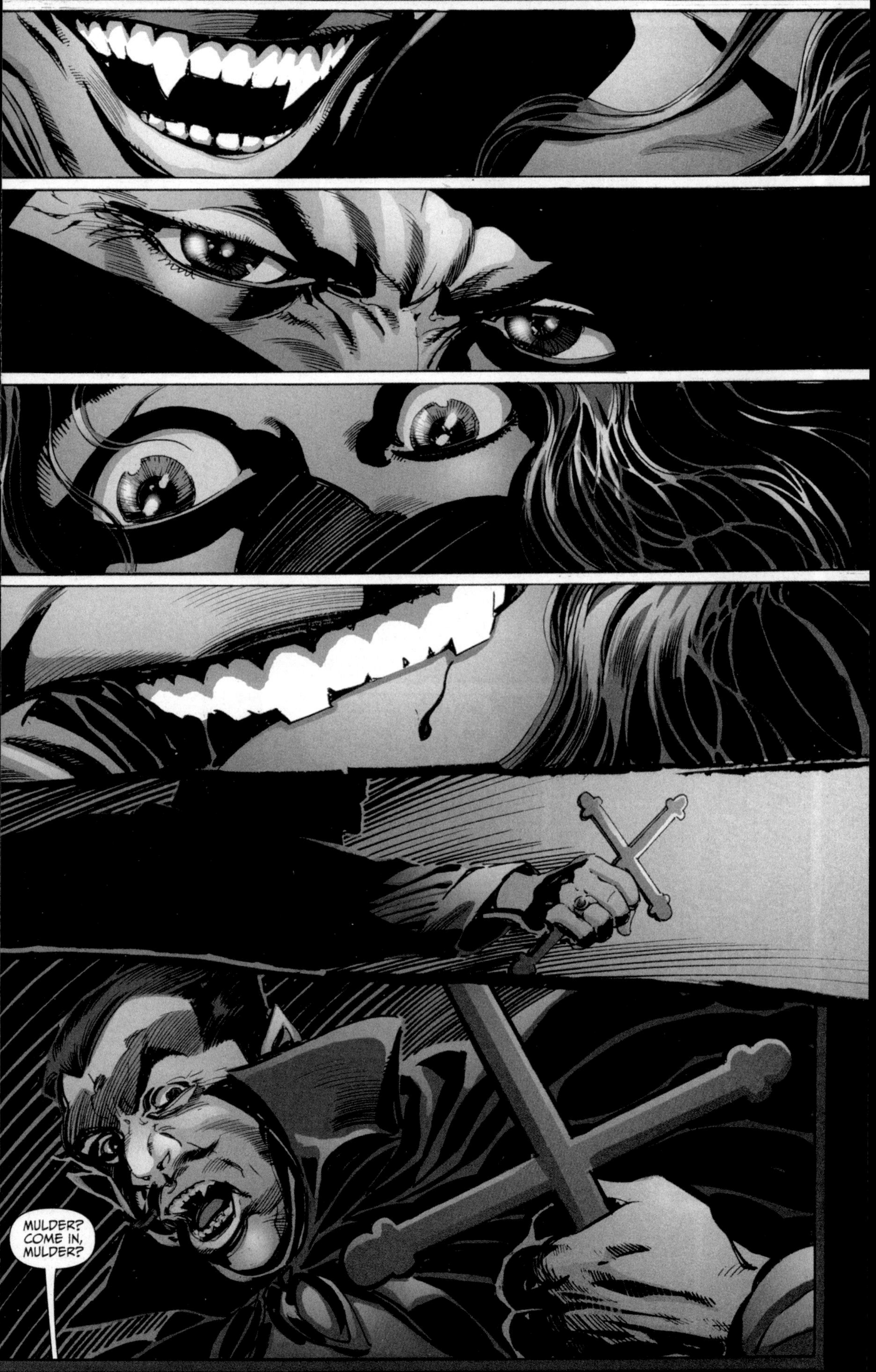
MULDER? COME IN, MULDER?

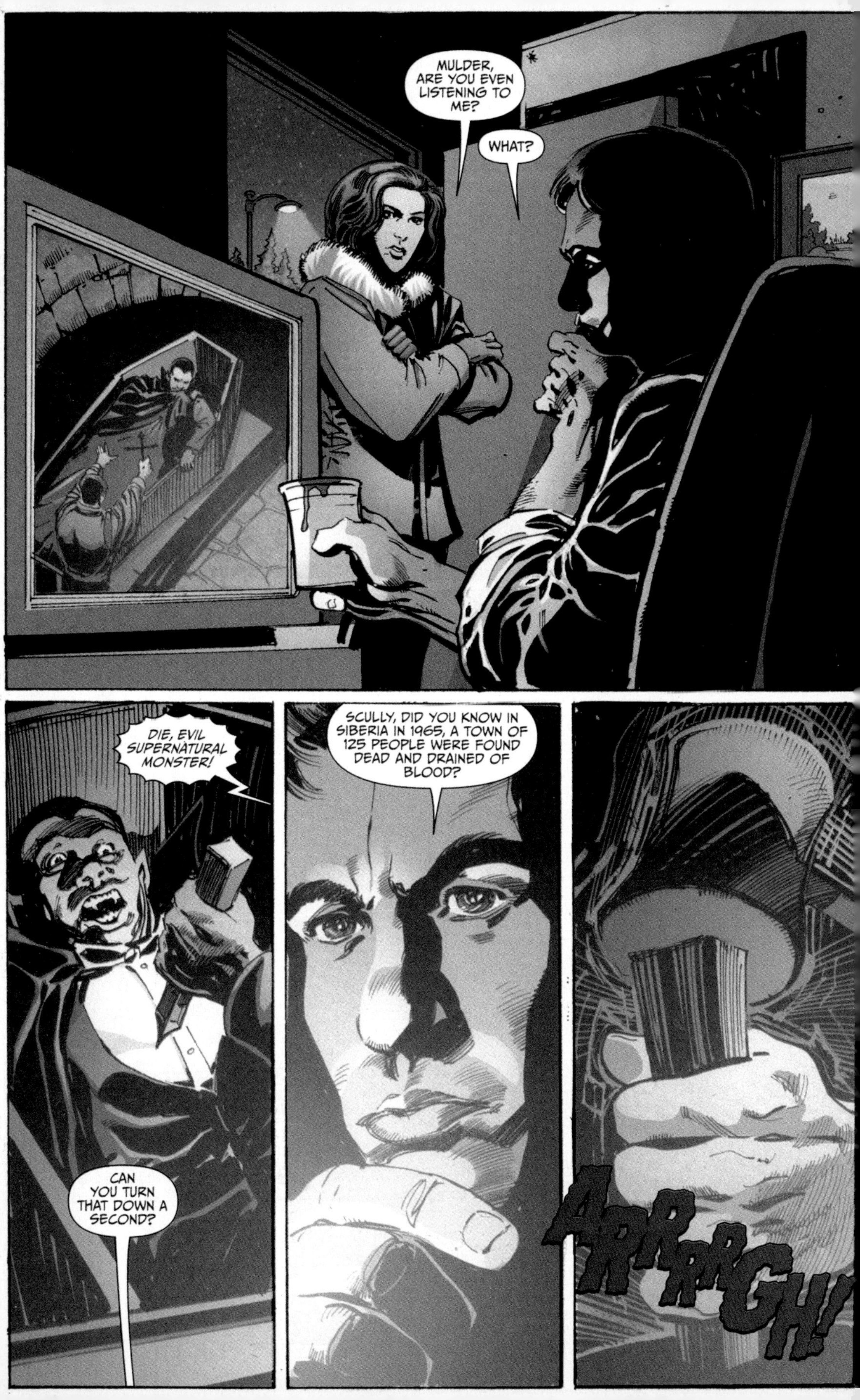
MULDER, ARE YOU EVEN LISTENING TO ME?
WHAT?
DIE, EVIL SUPERNATURAL MONSTER!
CAN YOU TURN THAT DOWN A SECOND?
SCULLY, DID YOU KNOW IN SIBERIA IN 1965, A TOWN OF 125 PEOPLE WERE FOUND DEAD AND DRAINED OF BLOOD?
ARRRRGH!!

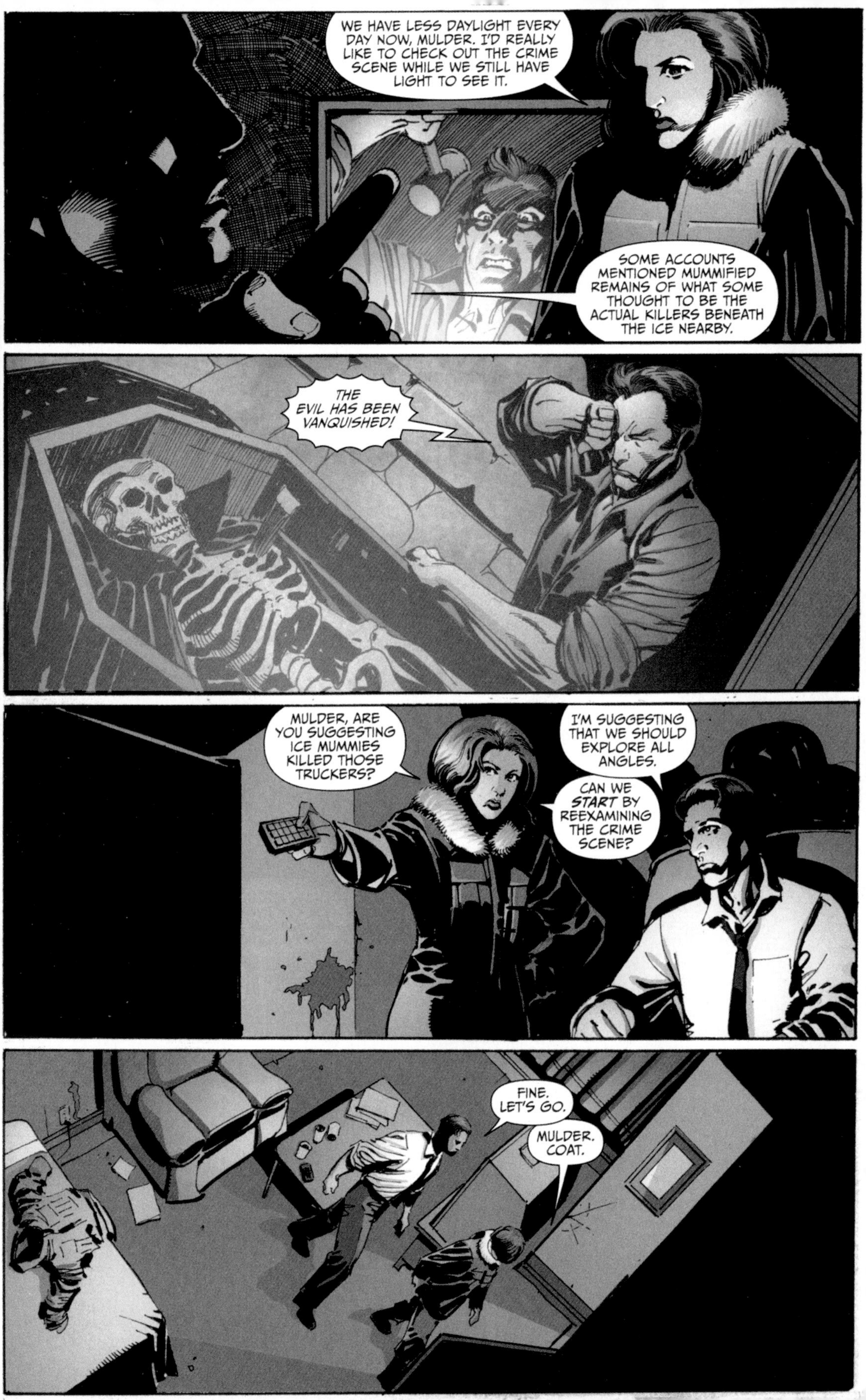
WE HAVE LESS DAYLIGHT EVERY DAY NOW, MULDER. I'D REALLY LIKE TO CHECK OUT THE CRIME SCENE WHILE WE STILL HAVE LIGHT TO SEE IT.
SOME ACCOUNTS MENTIONED MUMMIFIED REMAINS OF WHAT SOME THOUGHT TO BE THE ACTUAL KILLERS BENEATH THE ICE NEARBY.
THE EVIL HAS BEEN VANQUISHED!
MULDER, ARE YOU SUGGESTING ICE MUMMIES KILLED THOSE TRUCKERS?
I'M SUGGESTING THAT WE SHOULD EXPLORE ALL ANGLES.
CAN WE START BY REEXAMINING THE CRIME SCENE?
FINE. LET'S GO.
MULDER. COAT.

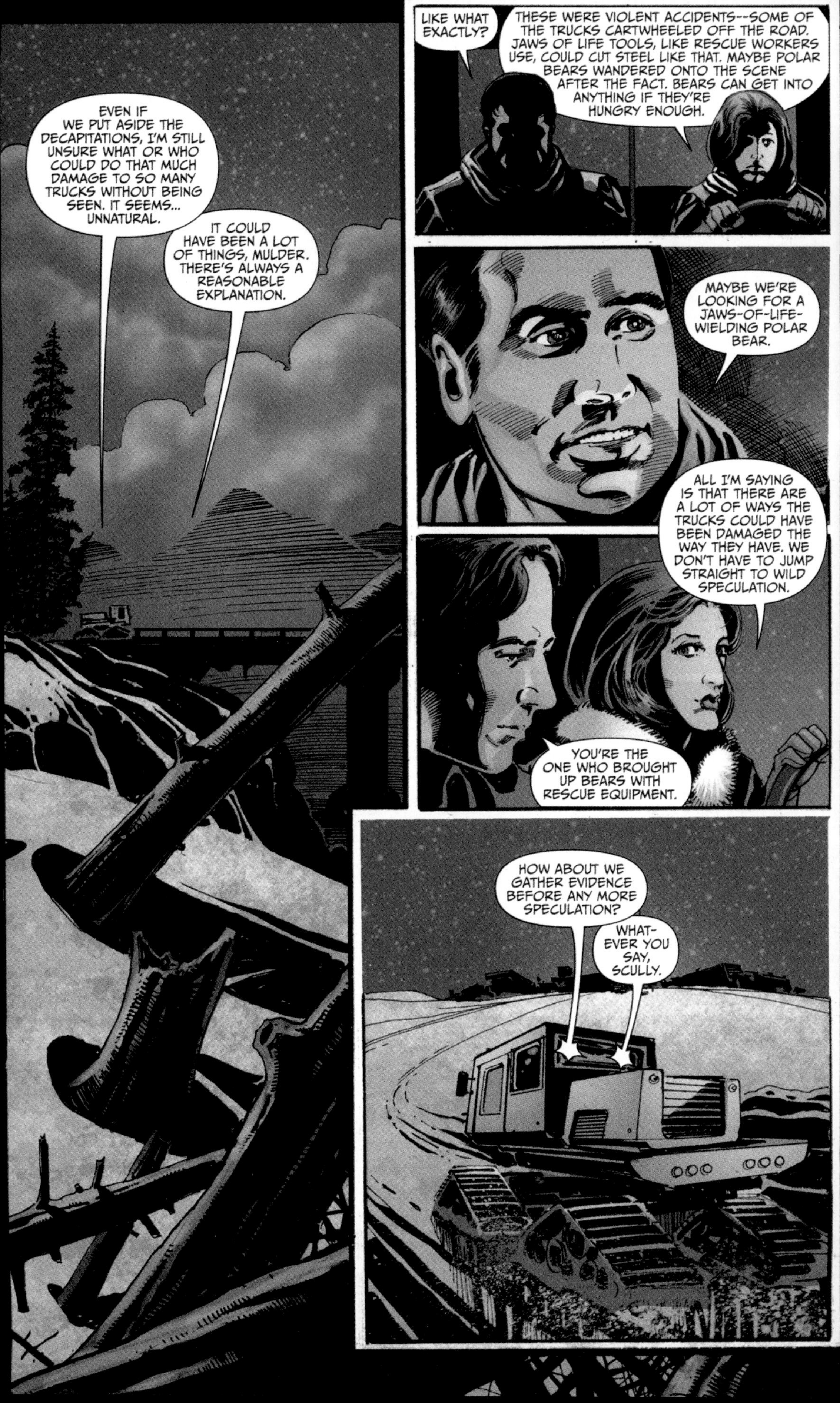
EVEN IF WE PUT ASIDE THE DECAPITATIONS, I'M STILL UNSURE WHAT OR WHO COULD DO THAT MUCH DAMAGE TO SO MANY TRUCKS WITHOUT BEING SEEN. IT SEEMS... UNNATURAL.
IT COULD HAVE BEEN A LOT OF THINGS, MULDER. THERE'S ALWAYS A REASONABLE EXPLANATION.
LIKE WHAT EXACTLY?
THESE WERE VIOLENT ACCIDENTS--SOME OF THE TRUCKS CARTWHEELED OFF THE ROAD. JAWS OF LIFE TOOLS, LIKE RESCUE WORKERS USE, COULD CUT STEEL LIKE THAT. MAYBE POLAR BEARS WANDERED ONTO THE SCENE AFTER THE FACT. BEARS CAN GET INTO ANYTHING IF THEY'RE HUNGRY ENOUGH.
MAYBE WE'RE LOOKING FOR A JAWS-OF-LIFE-WIELDING POLAR BEAR.
ALL I'M SAYING IS THAT THERE ARE A LOT OF WAYS THE TRUCKS COULD HAVE BEEN DAMAGED THE WAY THEY HAVE. WE DON'T HAVE TO JUMP STRAIGHT TO WILD SPECULATION.
YOU'RE THE ONE WHO BROUGHT UP BEARS WITH RESCUE EQUIPMENT.
HOW ABOUT WE GATHER EVIDENCE BEFORE ANY MORE SPECULATION?
WHAT-EVER YOU SAY, SCULLY.

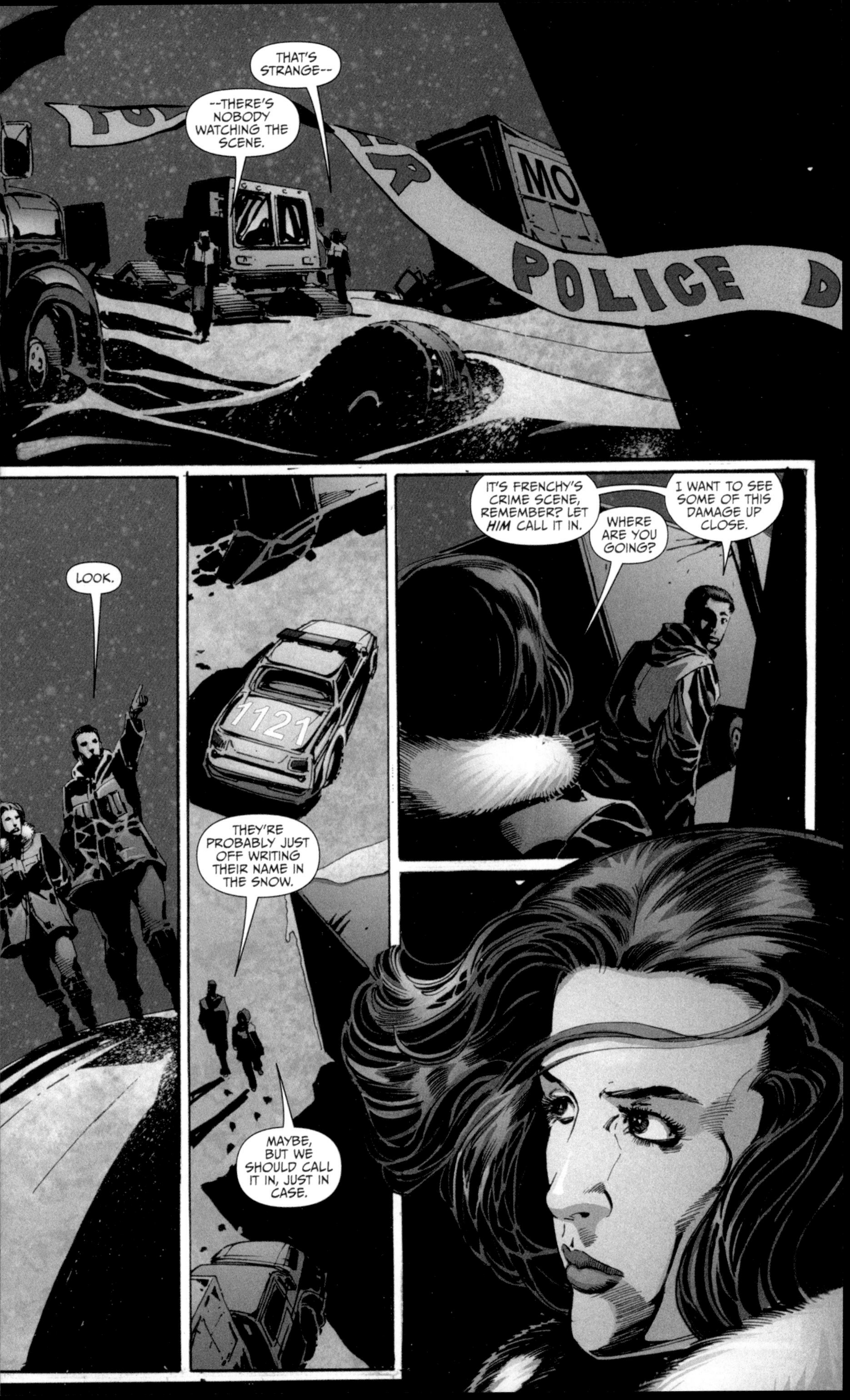
THAT'S STRANGE--
--THERE'S NOBODY WATCHING THE SCENE.
POLICE
LOOK.
THEY'RE PROBABLY JUST OFF WRITING THEIR NAME IN THE SNOW.
MAYBE, BUT WE SHOULD CALL IT IN, JUST IN CASE.
IT'S FRENCHY'S CRIME SCENE, REMEMBER? LET HIM CALL IT IN.
I WANT TO SEE SOME OF THIS DAMAGE UP CLOSE.
WHERE ARE YOU GOING?

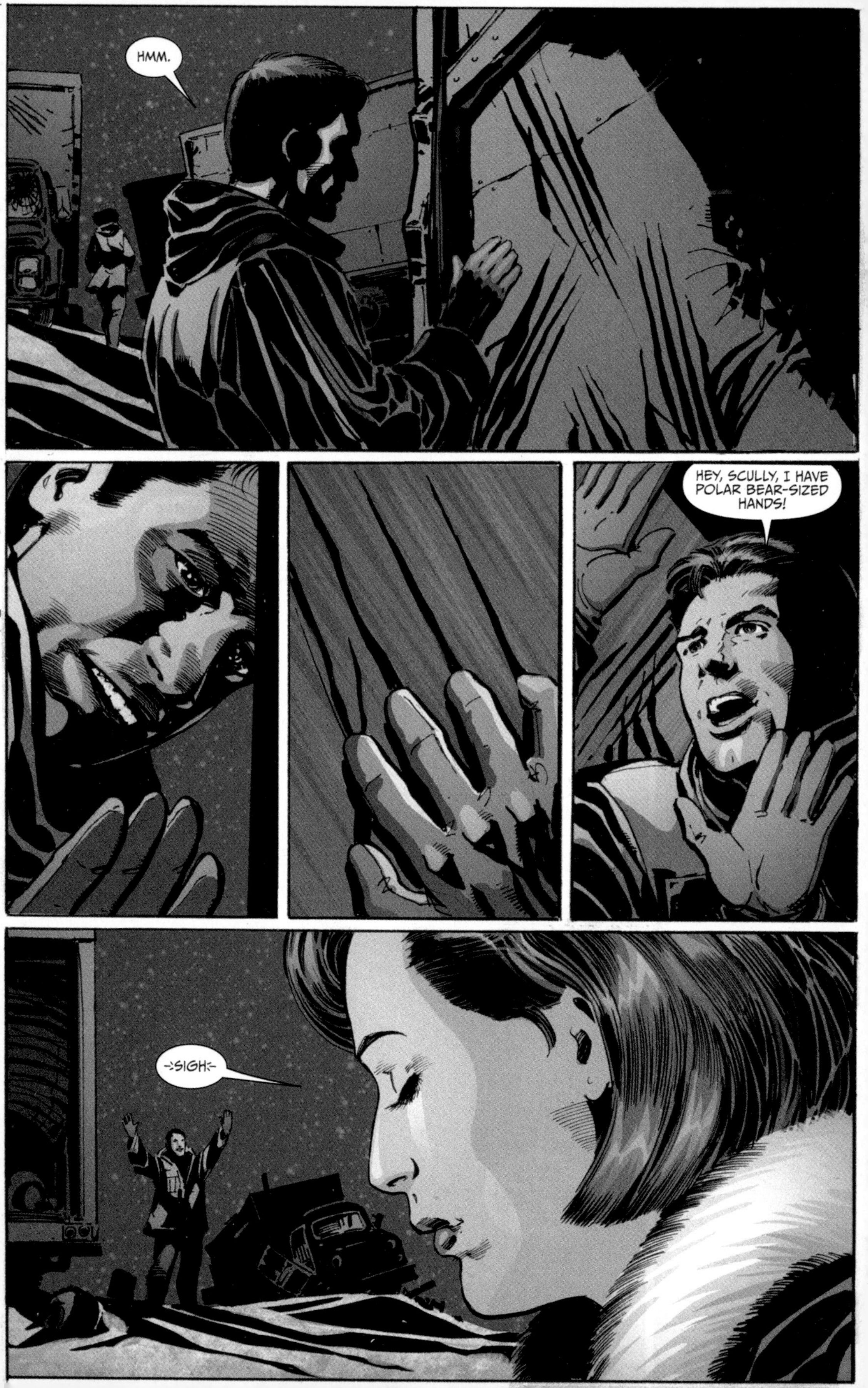
HMM.
HEY, SCULLY, I HAVE POLAR BEAR-SIZED HANDS!
-SIGH-

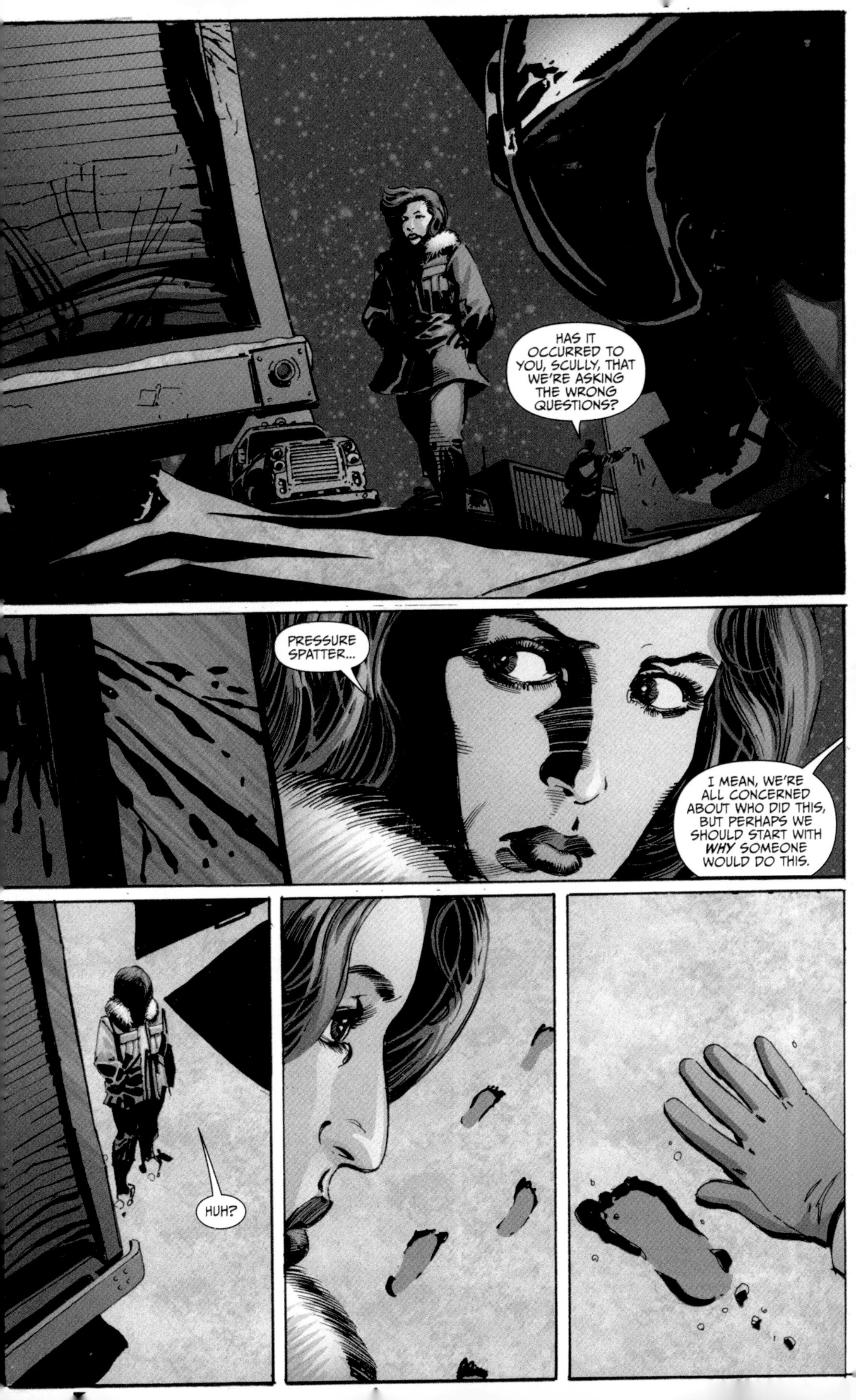
HAS IT OCCURRED TO YOU, SCULLY, THAT WE'RE ASKING THE WRONG QUESTIONS?
PRESSURE SPATTER...
I MEAN, WE'RE ALL CONCERNED ABOUT WHO DID THIS, BUT PERHAPS WE SHOULD START WITH ***WHY*** SOMEONE WOULD DO THIS.
HUH?

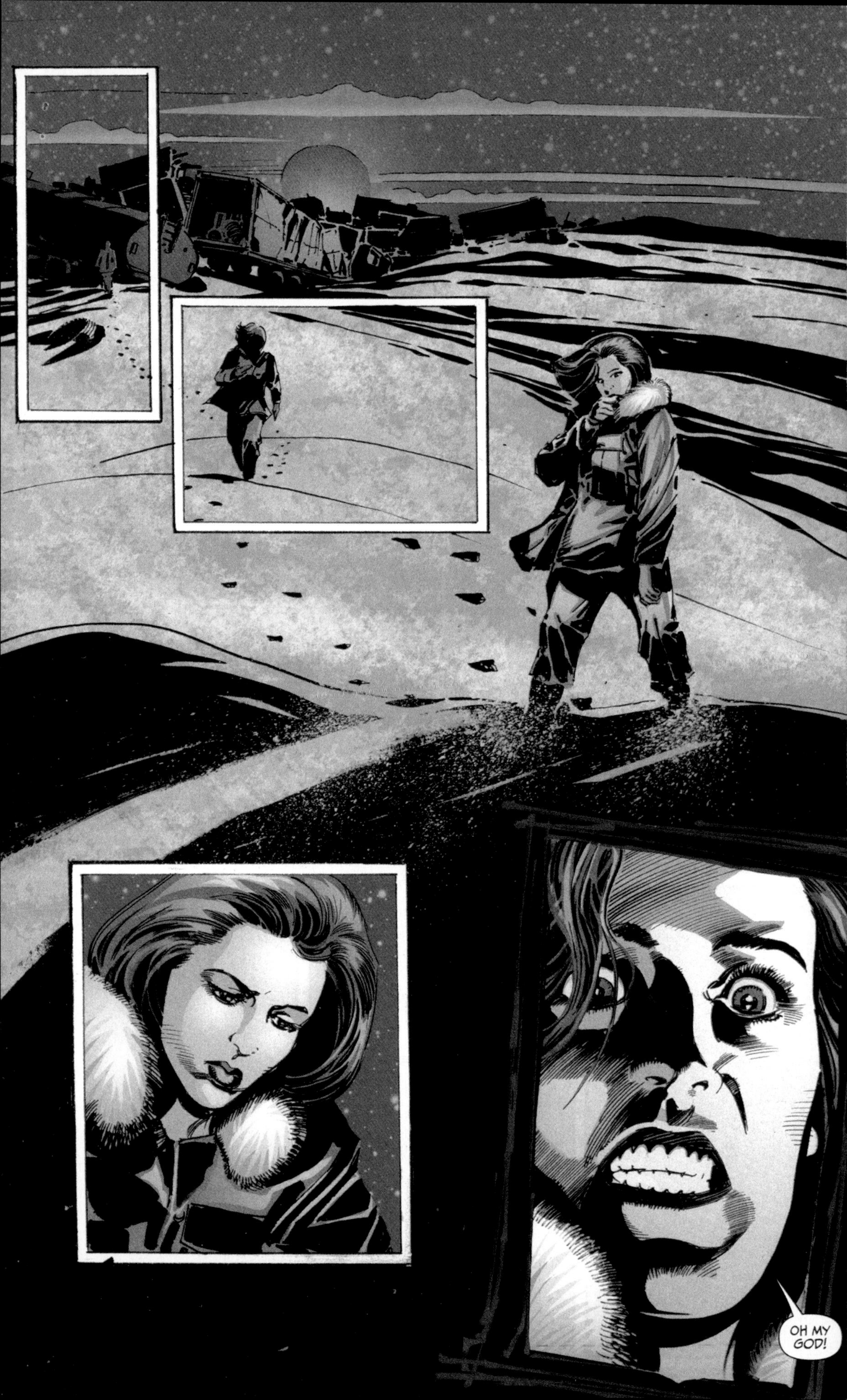
OH MY GOD!

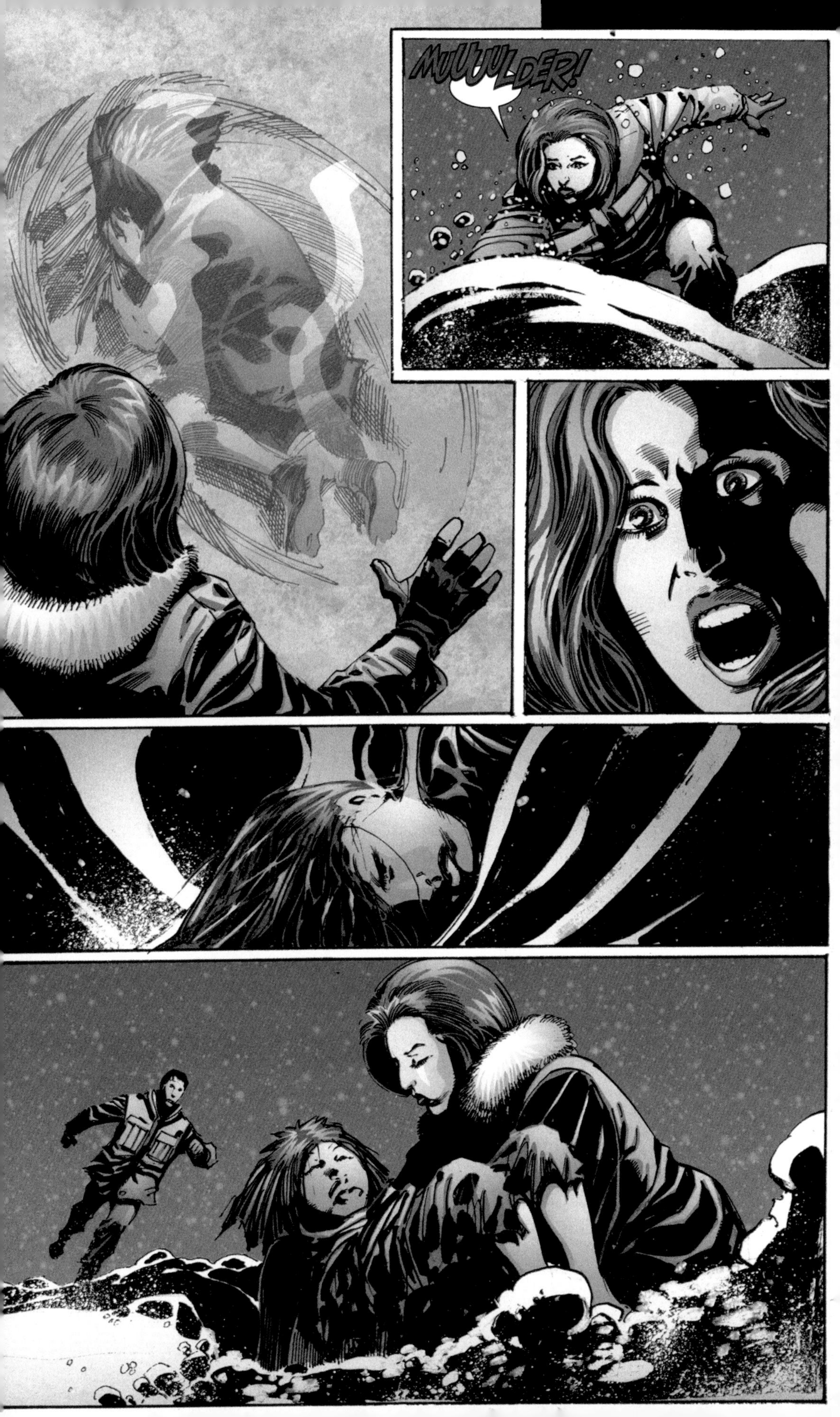
MUUUULDER!

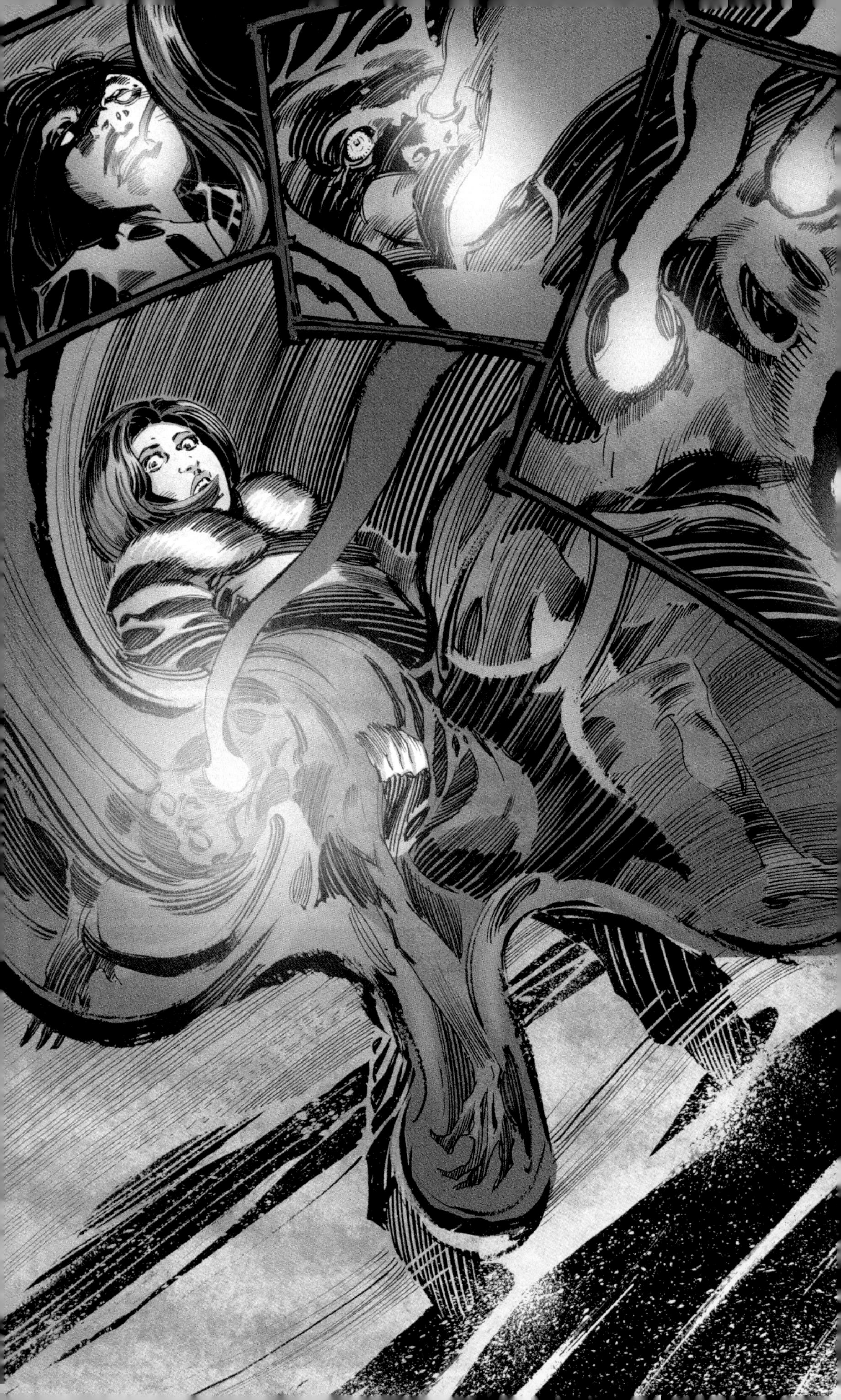

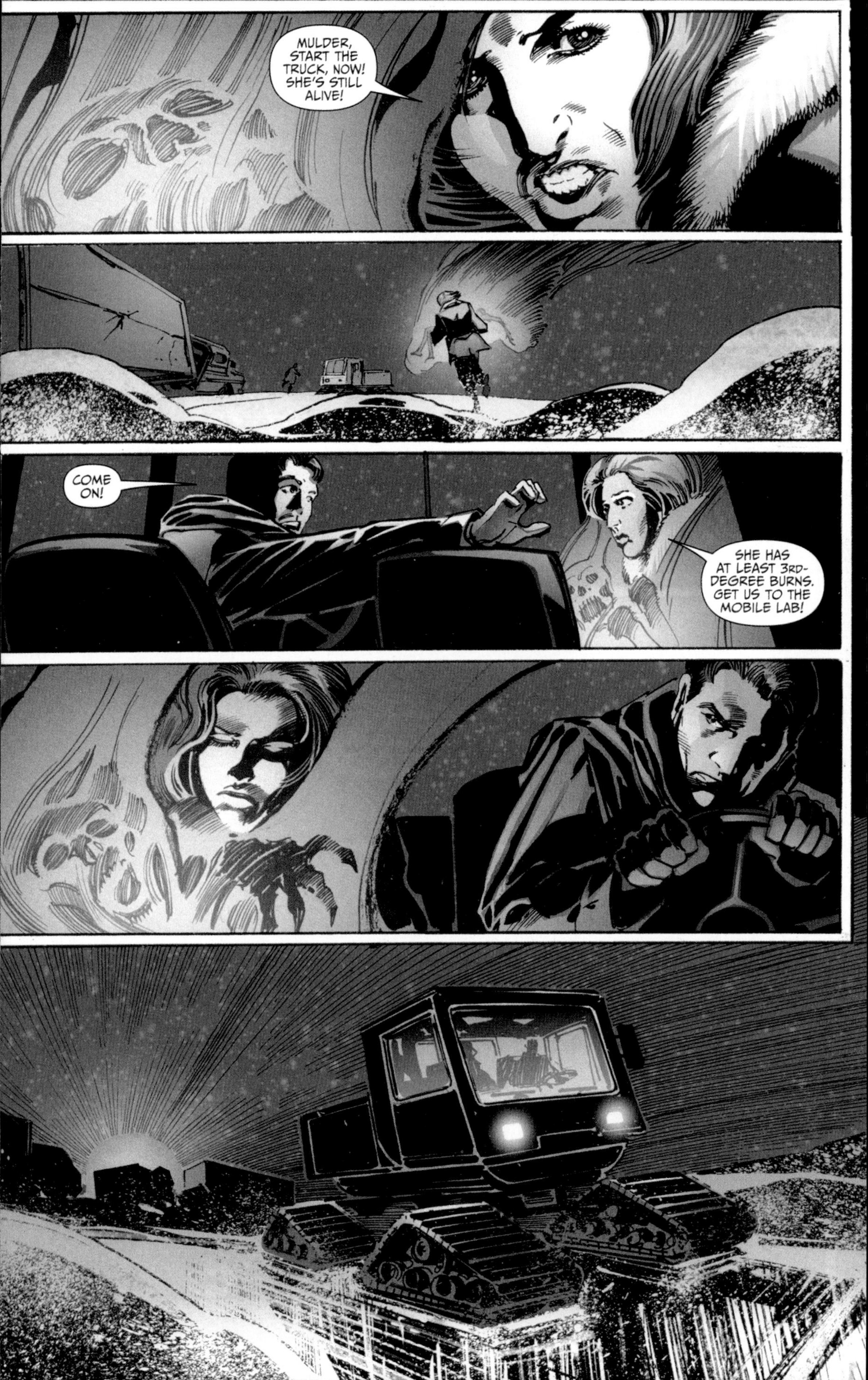

MULDER, START THE TRUCK, NOW! SHE'S STILL ALIVE!
COME ON!
SHE HAS AT LEAST 3RD-DEGREE BURNS. GET US TO THE MOBILE LAB!

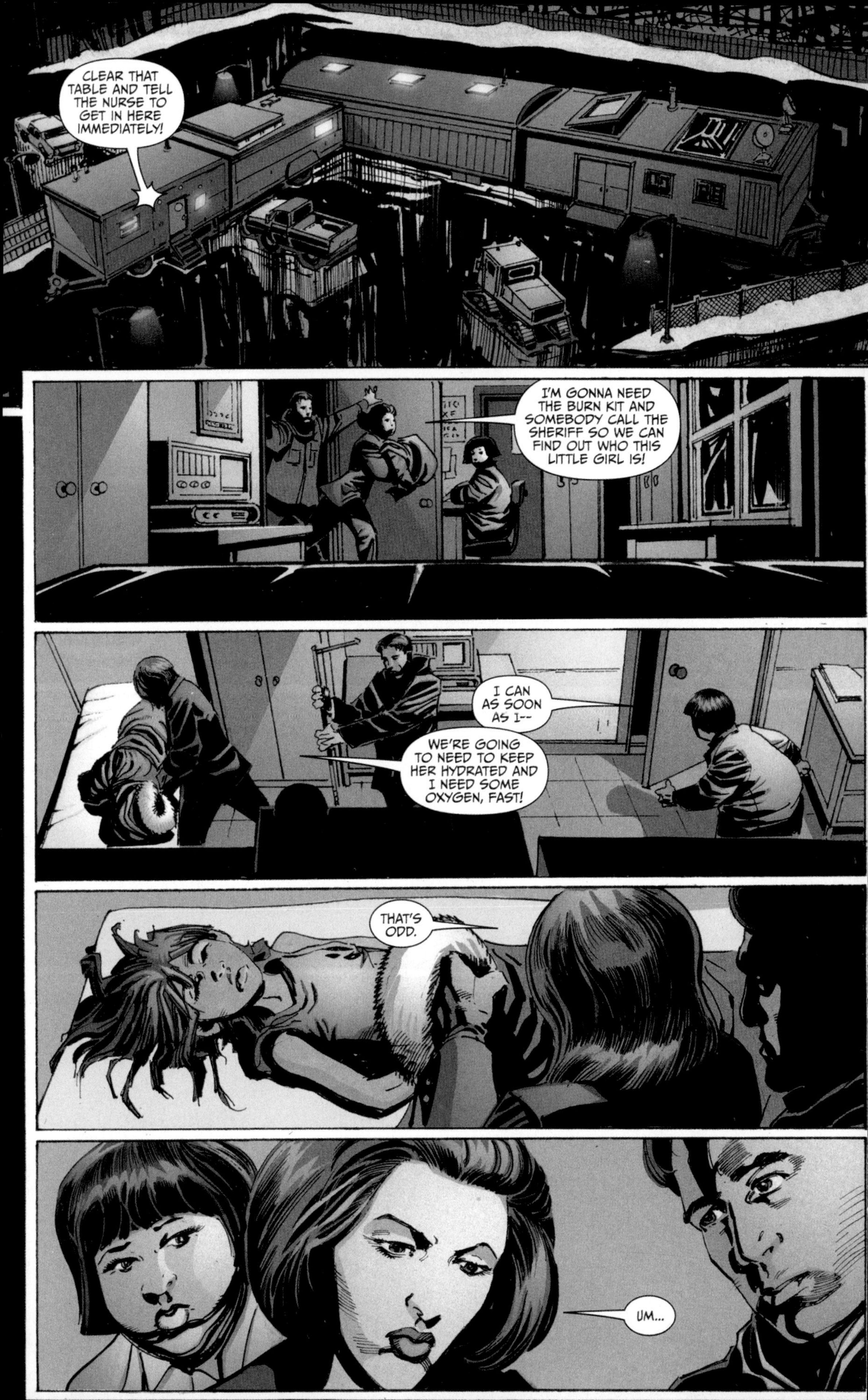
CLEAR THAT TABLE AND TELL THE NURSE TO GET IN HERE IMMEDIATELY!
I'M GONNA NEED THE BURN KIT AND SOMEBODY CALL THE SHERIFF SO WE CAN FIND OUT WHO THIS LITTLE GIRL IS!
I CAN AS SOON AS I--
WE'RE GOING TO NEED TO KEEP HER HYDRATED AND I NEED SOME OXYGEN, FAST!
THAT'S ODD.
UM...

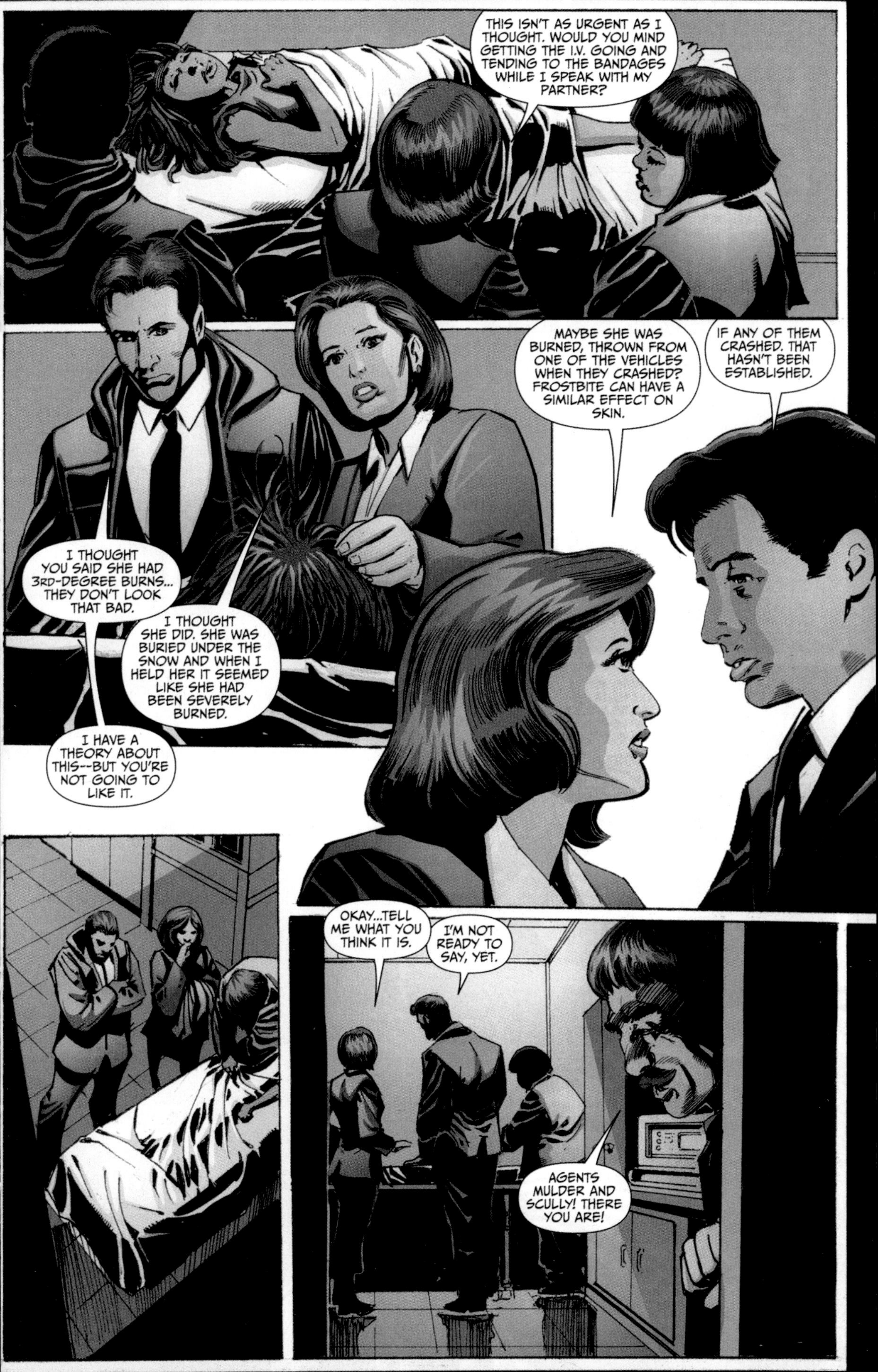
THIS ISN'T AS URGENT AS I THOUGHT. WOULD YOU MIND GETTING THE I.V. GOING AND TENDING TO THE BANDAGES WHILE I SPEAK WITH MY PARTNER?
I THOUGHT YOU SAID SHE HAD 3RD-DEGREE BURNS... THEY DON'T LOOK THAT BAD.
I THOUGHT SHE DID. SHE WAS BURIED UNDER THE SNOW AND WHEN I HELD HER IT SEEMED LIKE SHE HAD BEEN SEVERELY BURNED.
MAYBE SHE WAS BURNED, THROWN FROM ONE OF THE VEHICLES WHEN THEY CRASHED? FROSTBITE CAN HAVE A SIMILAR EFFECT ON SKIN.
IF ANY OF THEM CRASHED. THAT HASN'T BEEN ESTABLISHED.
I HAVE A THEORY ABOUT THIS--BUT YOU'RE NOT GOING TO LIKE IT.
OKAY...TELL ME WHAT YOU THINK IT IS.
I'M NOT READY TO SAY, YET.
AGENTS MULDER AND SCULLY! THERE YOU ARE!

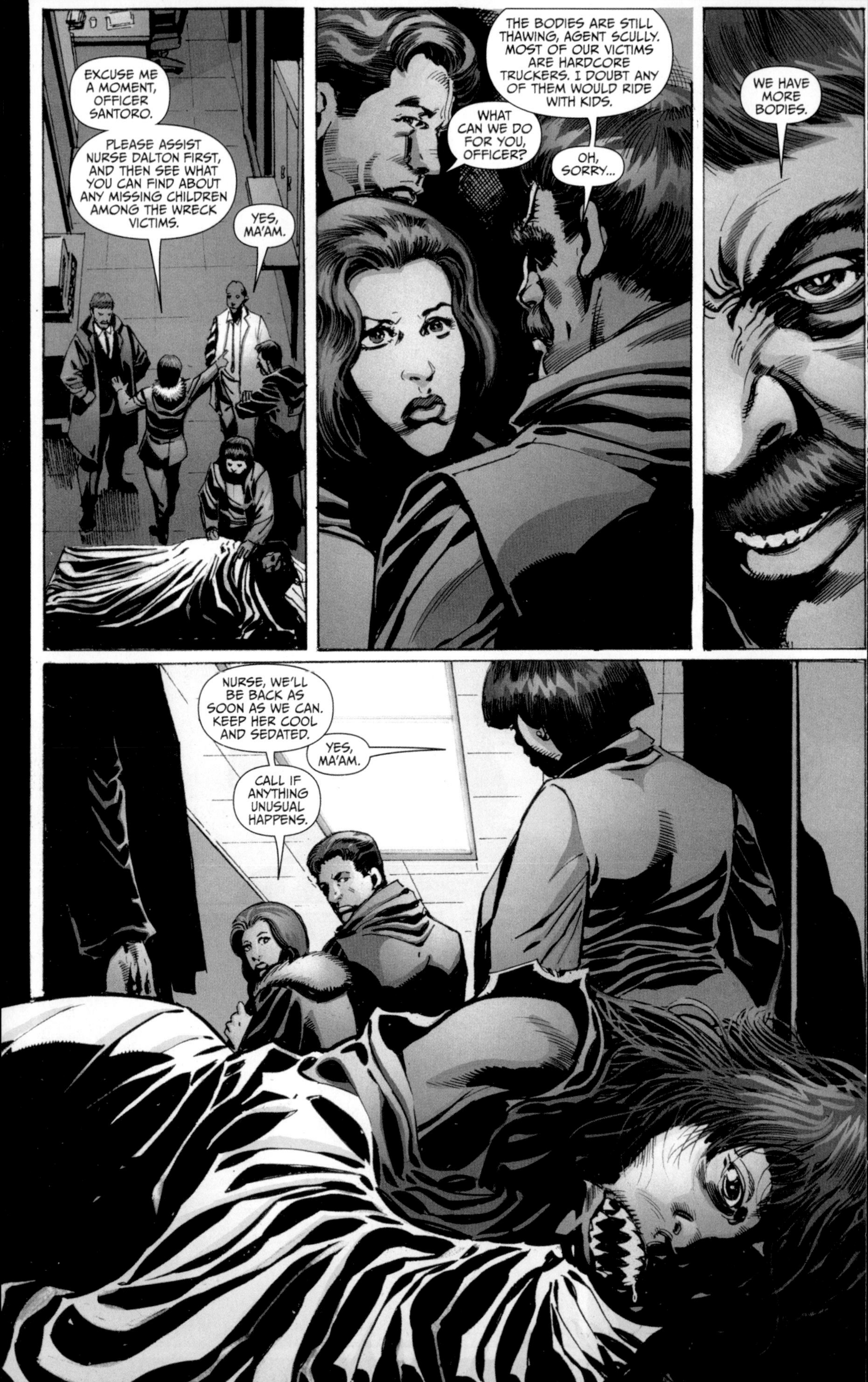
EXCUSE ME A MOMENT, OFFICER SANTORO.
PLEASE ASSIST NURSE DALTON FIRST, AND THEN SEE WHAT YOU CAN FIND ABOUT ANY MISSING CHILDREN AMONG THE WRECK VICTIMS.
YES, MA'AM.
THE BODIES ARE STILL THAWING, AGENT SCULLY. MOST OF OUR VICTIMS ARE HARDCORE TRUCKERS. I DOUBT ANY OF THEM WOULD RIDE WITH KIDS.
WHAT CAN WE DO FOR YOU, OFFICER?
OH, SORRY...
WE HAVE MORE BODIES.
NURSE, WE'LL BE BACK AS SOON AS WE CAN. KEEP HER COOL AND SEDATED.
YES, MA'AM.
CALL IF ANYTHING UNUSUAL HAPPENS.

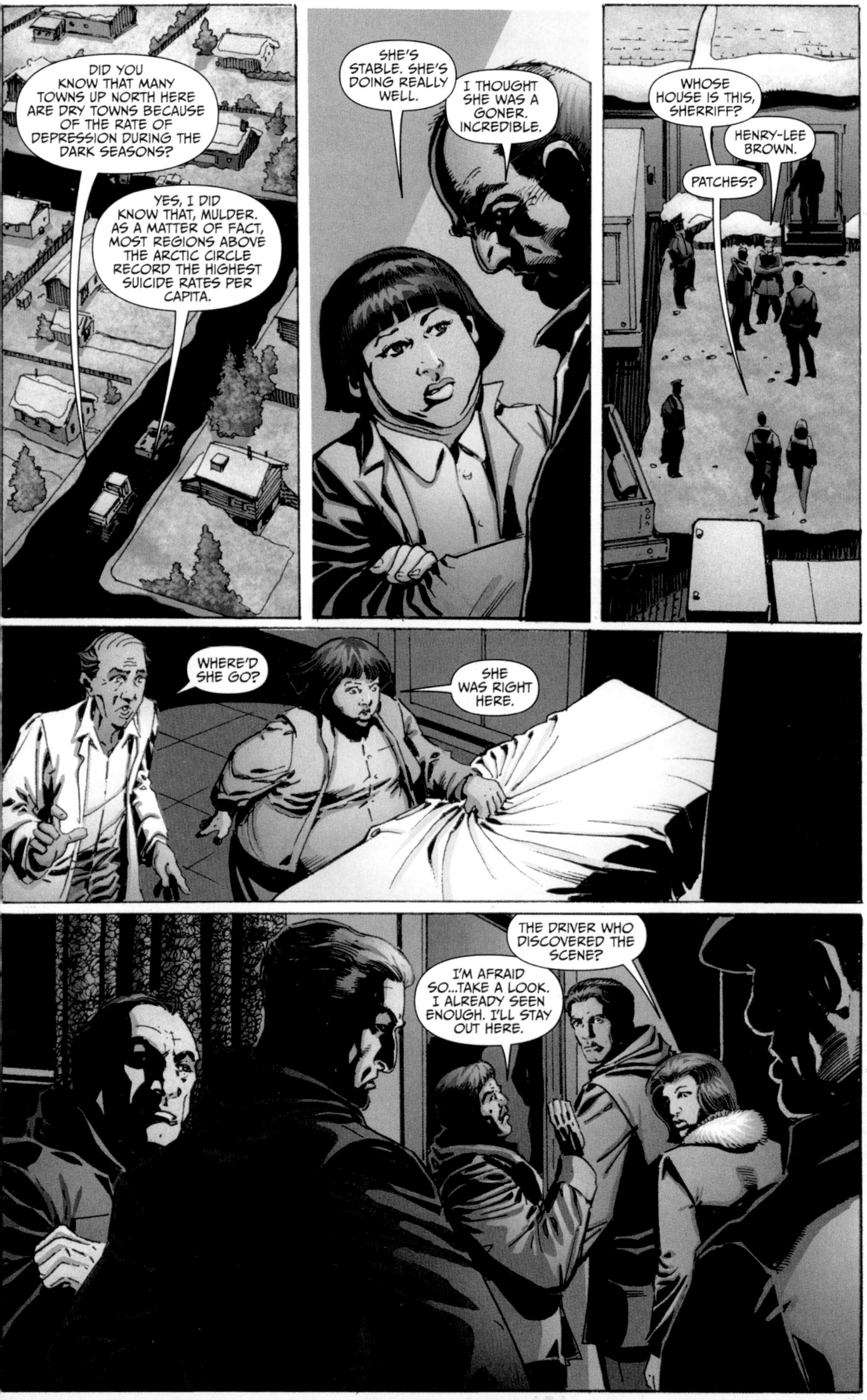
DID YOU KNOW THAT MANY TOWNS UP NORTH HERE ARE DRY TOWNS BECAUSE OF THE RATE OF DEPRESSION DURING THE DARK SEASONS?
YES, I DID KNOW THAT, MULDER. AS A MATTER OF FACT, MOST REGIONS ABOVE THE ARCTIC CIRCLE RECORD THE HIGHEST SUICIDE RATES PER CAPITA.
SHE'S STABLE. SHE'S DOING REALLY WELL.
I THOUGHT SHE WAS A GONER. INCREDIBLE.
WHOSE HOUSE IS THIS, SHERRIFF?
HENRY-LEE BROWN.
PATCHES?
WHERE'D SHE GO?
SHE WAS RIGHT HERE.
THE DRIVER WHO DISCOVERED THE SCENE?
I'M AFRAID SO...TAKE A LOOK. I ALREADY SEEN ENOUGH. I'LL STAY OUT HERE.

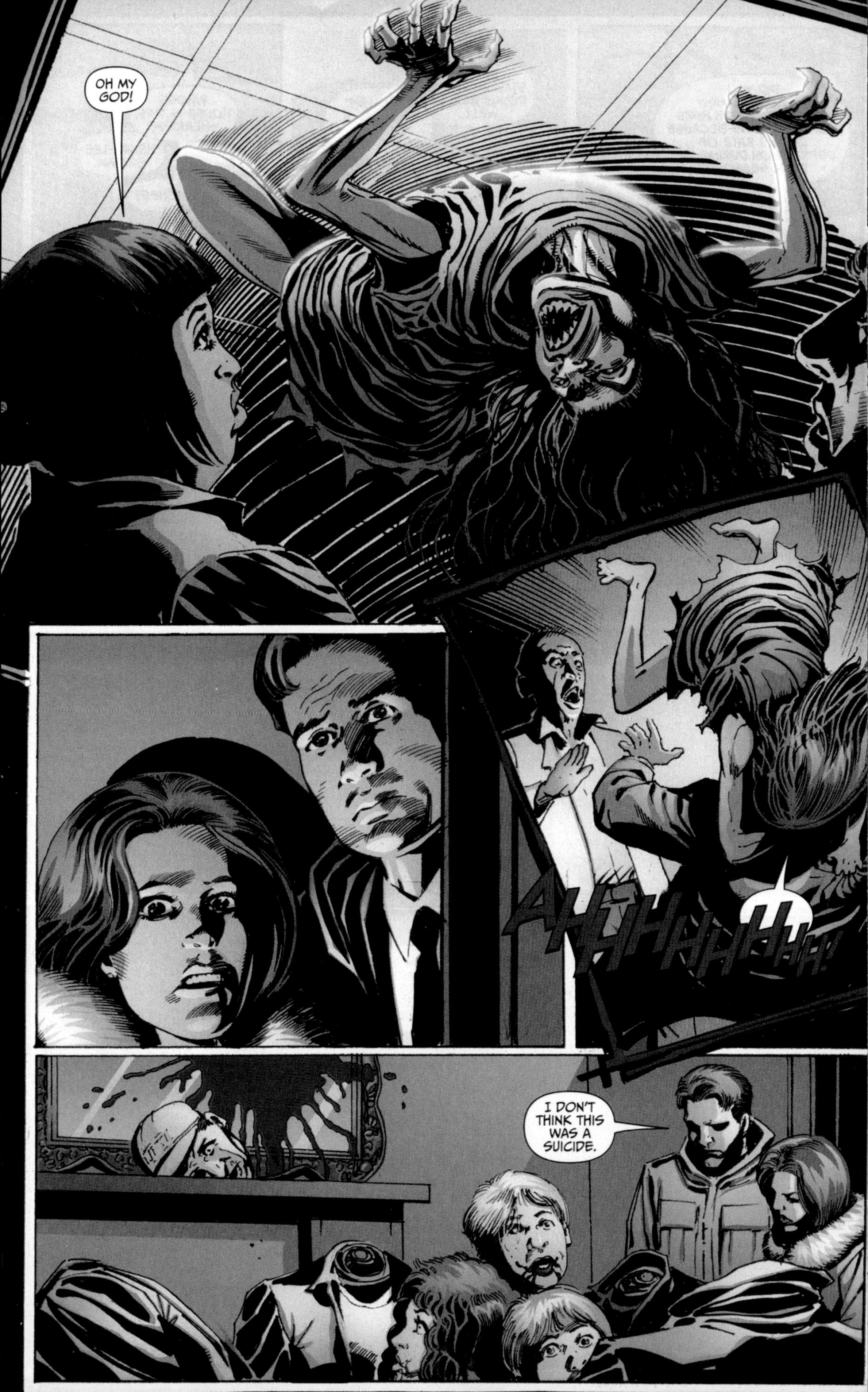
OH MY GOD!
AHHHHHHHHH!
I DON'T THINK THIS WAS A SUICIDE.

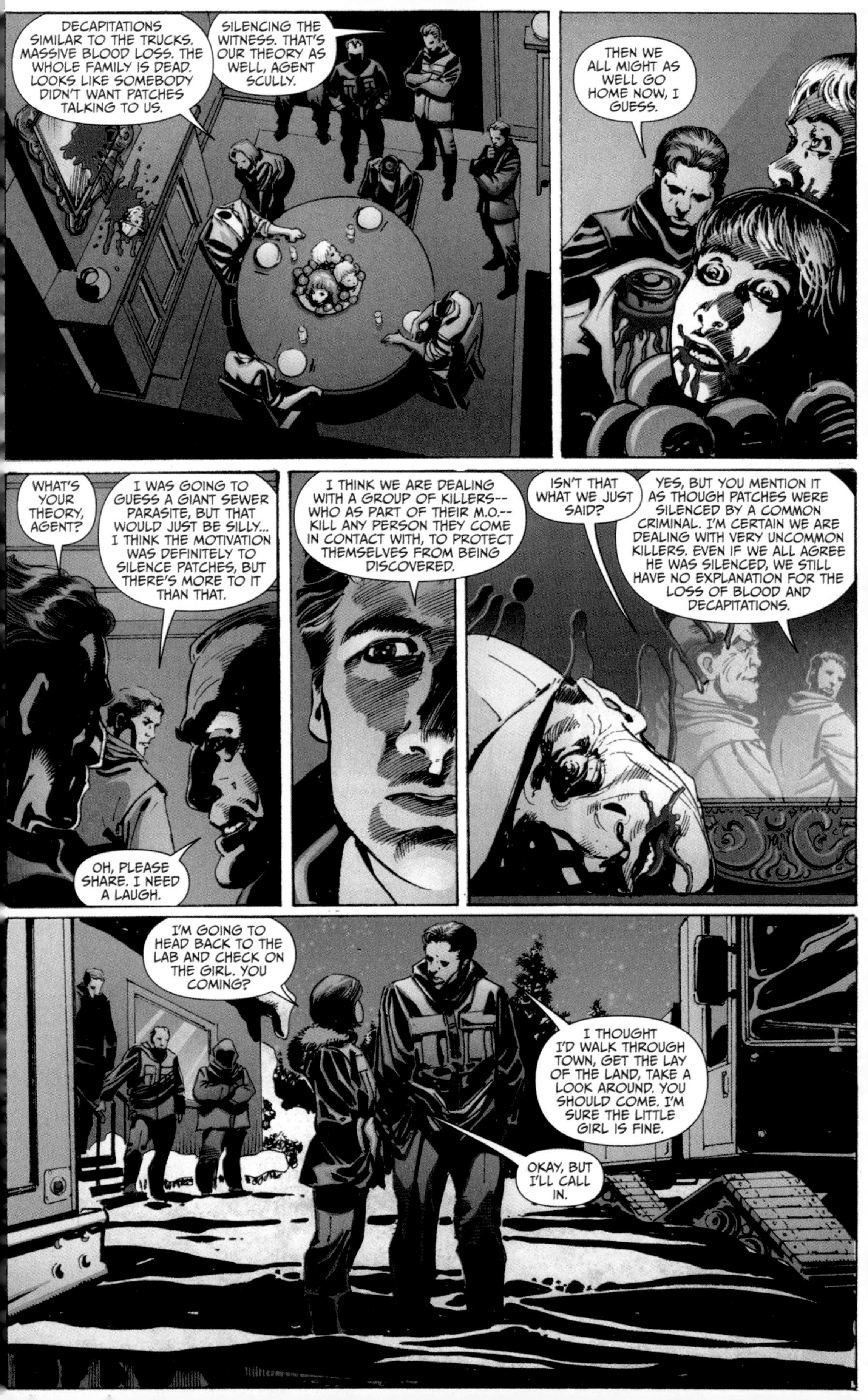
DECAPITATIONS SIMILAR TO THE TRUCKS. MASSIVE BLOOD LOSS. THE WHOLE FAMILY IS DEAD. LOOKS LIKE SOMEBODY DIDN'T WANT PATCHES TALKING TO US.
SILENCING THE WITNESS. THAT'S OUR THEORY AS WELL, AGENT SCULLY.
THEN WE ALL MIGHT AS WELL GO HOME NOW, I GUESS.
WHAT'S YOUR THEORY, AGENT?
I WAS GOING TO GUESS A GIANT SEWER PARASITE, BUT THAT WOULD JUST BE SILLY... I THINK THE MOTIVATION WAS DEFINITELY TO SILENCE PATCHES, BUT THERE'S MORE TO IT THAN THAT.
OH, PLEASE SHARE. I NEED A LAUGH.
I THINK WE ARE DEALING WITH A GROUP OF KILLERS-- WHO AS PART OF THEIR M.O.-- KILL ANY PERSON THEY COME IN CONTACT WITH, TO PROTECT THEMSELVES FROM BEING DISCOVERED.
ISN'T THAT WHAT WE JUST SAID?
YES, BUT YOU MENTION IT AS THOUGH PATCHES WERE SILENCED BY A COMMON CRIMINAL. I'M CERTAIN WE ARE DEALING WITH VERY UNCOMMON KILLERS. EVEN IF WE ALL AGREE HE WAS SILENCED, WE STILL HAVE NO EXPLANATION FOR THE LOSS OF BLOOD AND DECAPITATIONS.
I'M GOING TO HEAD BACK TO THE LAB AND CHECK ON THE GIRL. YOU COMING?
I THOUGHT I'D WALK THROUGH TOWN, GET THE LAY OF THE LAND, TAKE A LOOK AROUND. YOU SHOULD COME. I'M SURE THE LITTLE GIRL IS FINE.
OKAY, BUT I'LL CALL IN.

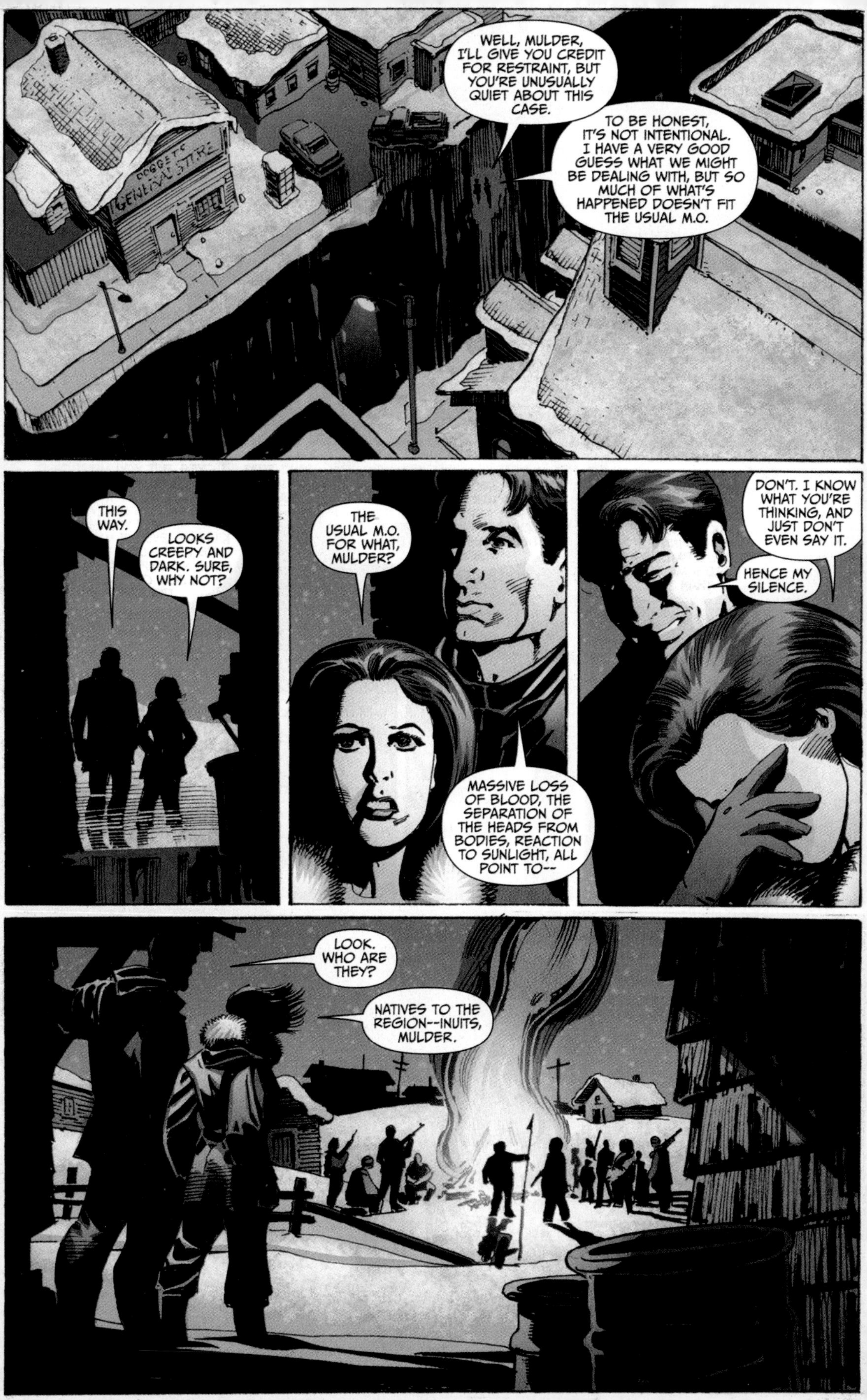
DOGGET'S GENERAL STORE
WELL, MULDER, I'LL GIVE YOU CREDIT FOR RESTRAINT, BUT YOU'RE UNUSUALLY QUIET ABOUT THIS CASE.
TO BE HONEST, IT'S NOT INTENTIONAL. I HAVE A VERY GOOD GUESS WHAT WE MIGHT BE DEALING WITH, BUT SO MUCH OF WHAT'S HAPPENED DOESN'T FIT THE USUAL M.O.
THIS WAY.
LOOKS CREEPY AND DARK. SURE, WHY NOT?
THE USUAL M.O. FOR WHAT, MULDER?
MASSIVE LOSS OF BLOOD, THE SEPARATION OF THE HEADS FROM BODIES, REACTION TO SUNLIGHT, ALL POINT TO--
DON'T. I KNOW WHAT YOU'RE THINKING, AND JUST DON'T EVEN SAY IT.
HENCE MY SILENCE.
LOOK. WHO ARE THEY?
NATIVES TO THE REGION--INUITS, MULDER.

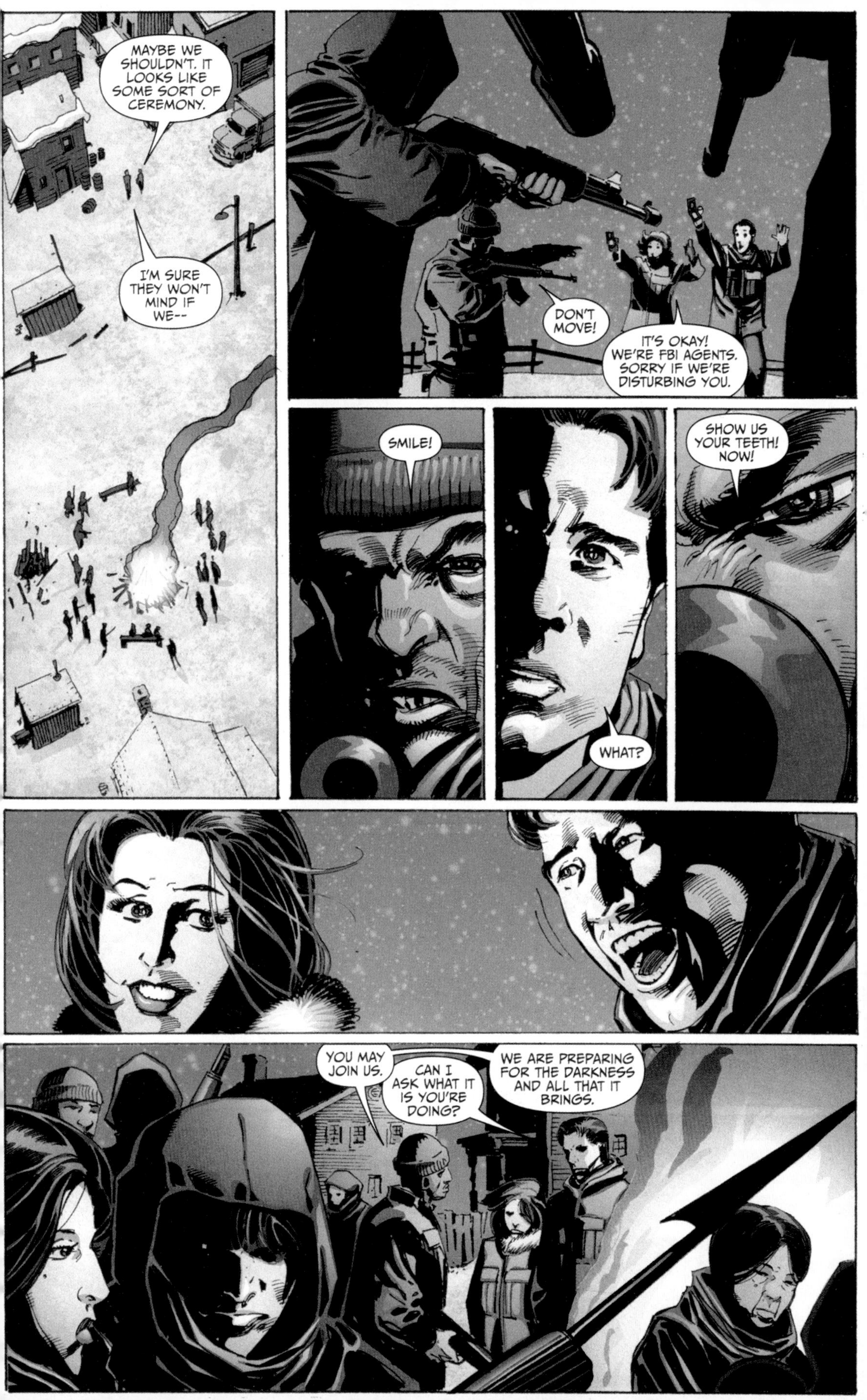
MAYBE WE SHOULDN'T. IT LOOKS LIKE SOME SORT OF CEREMONY.
I'M SURE THEY WON'T MIND IF WE--
DON'T MOVE!
IT'S OKAY! WE'RE FBI AGENTS. SORRY IF WE'RE DISTURBING YOU.
SMILE!
WHAT?
SHOW US YOUR TEETH! NOW!
YOU MAY JOIN US.
CAN I ASK WHAT IT IS YOU'RE DOING?
WE ARE PREPARING FOR THE DARKNESS AND ALL THAT IT BRINGS.

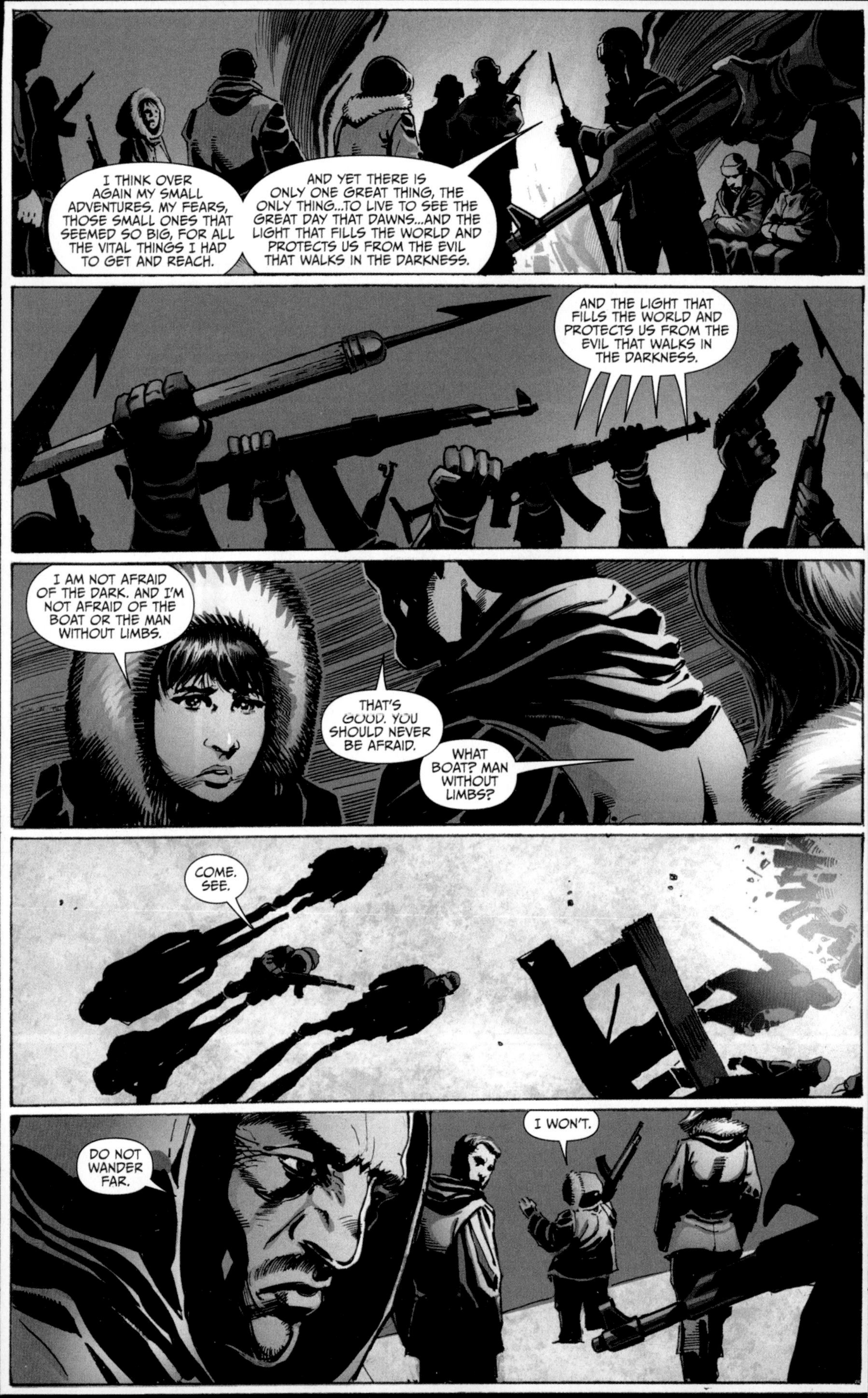
I THINK OVER AGAIN MY SMALL ADVENTURES. MY FEARS, THOSE SMALL ONES THAT SEEMED SO BIG, FOR ALL THE VITAL THINGS I HAD TO GET AND REACH.
AND YET THERE IS ONLY ONE GREAT THING, THE ONLY THING...TO LIVE TO SEE THE GREAT DAY THAT DAWNS...AND THE LIGHT THAT FILLS THE WORLD AND PROTECTS US FROM THE EVIL THAT WALKS IN THE DARKNESS.
AND THE LIGHT THAT FILLS THE WORLD AND PROTECTS US FROM THE EVIL THAT WALKS IN THE DARKNESS.
I AM NOT AFRAID OF THE DARK. AND I'M NOT AFRAID OF THE BOAT OR THE MAN WITHOUT LIMBS.
THAT'S GOOD. YOU SHOULD NEVER BE AFRAID.
WHAT BOAT? MAN WITHOUT LIMBS?
COME. SEE.
DO NOT WANDER FAR.
I WON'T.

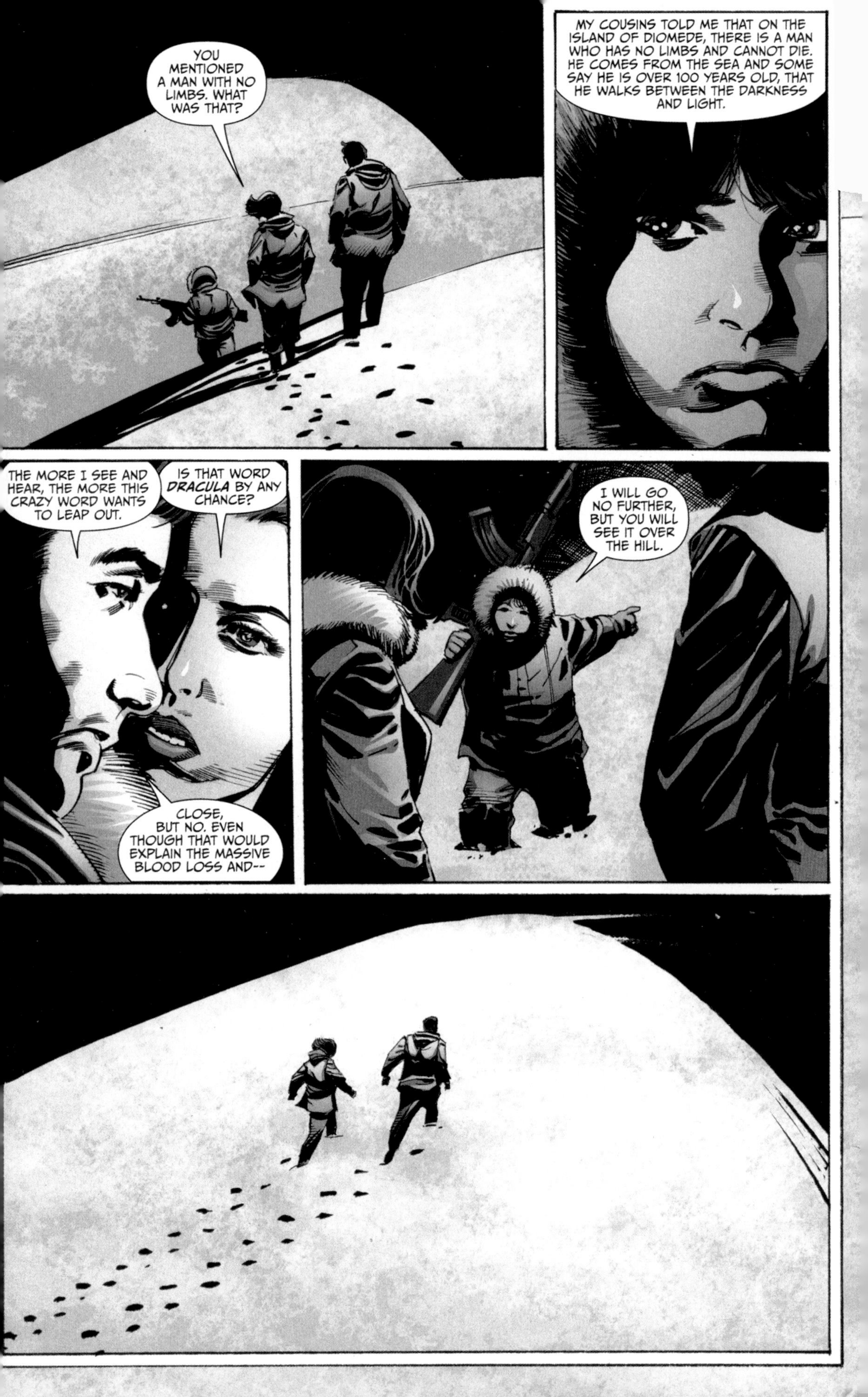
YOU MENTIONED A MAN WITH NO LIMBS. WHAT WAS THAT?
MY COUSINS TOLD ME THAT ON THE ISLAND OF DIOMEDE, THERE IS A MAN WHO HAS NO LIMBS AND CANNOT DIE. HE COMES FROM THE SEA AND SOME SAY HE IS OVER 100 YEARS OLD, THAT HE WALKS BETWEEN THE DARKNESS AND LIGHT.
THE MORE I SEE AND HEAR, THE MORE THIS CRAZY WORD WANTS TO LEAP OUT.
IS THAT WORD *DRACULA* BY ANY CHANCE?
CLOSE, BUT NO. EVEN THOUGH THAT WOULD EXPLAIN THE MASSIVE BLOOD LOSS AND--
I WILL GO NO FURTHER, BUT YOU WILL SEE IT OVER THE HILL.

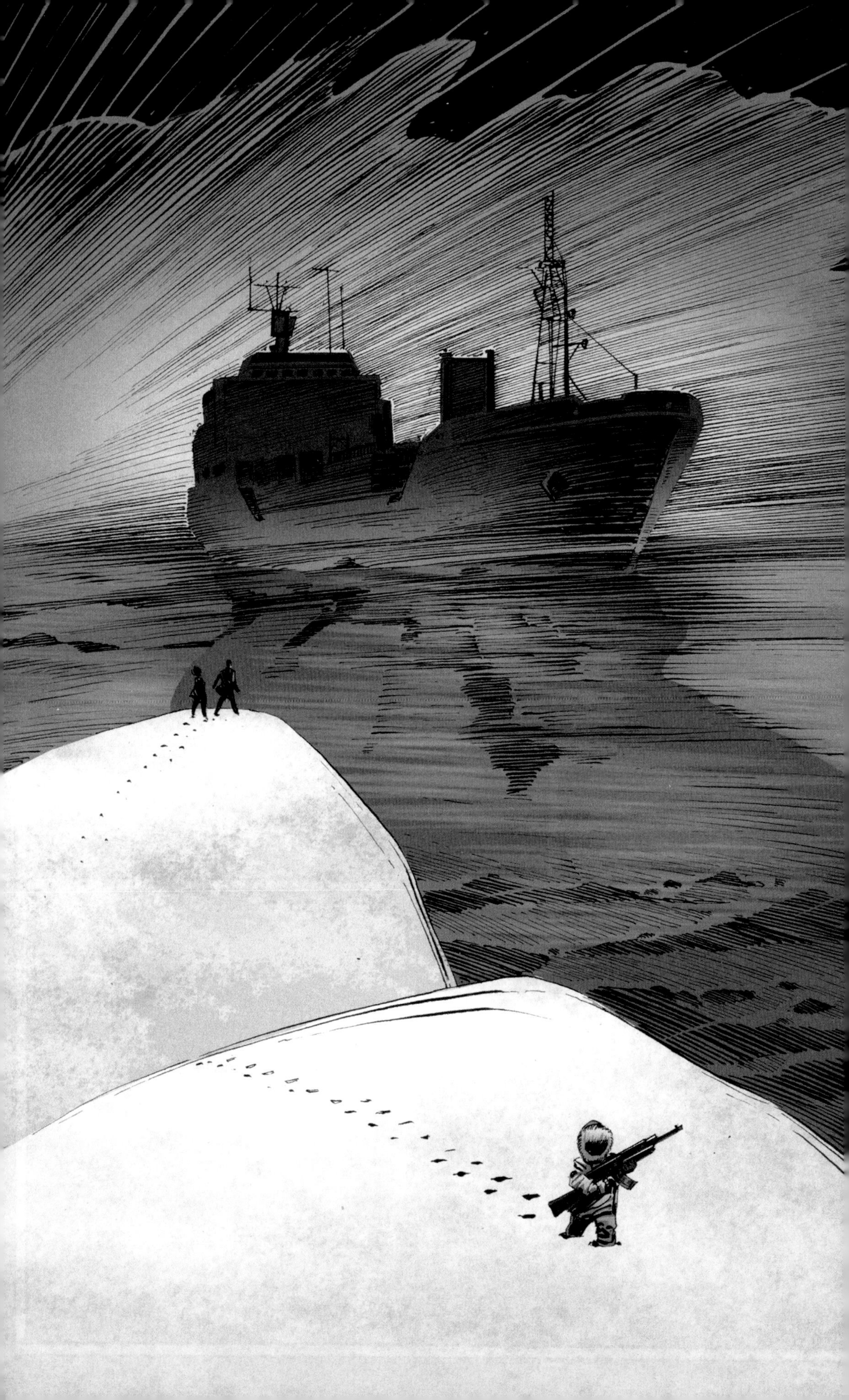

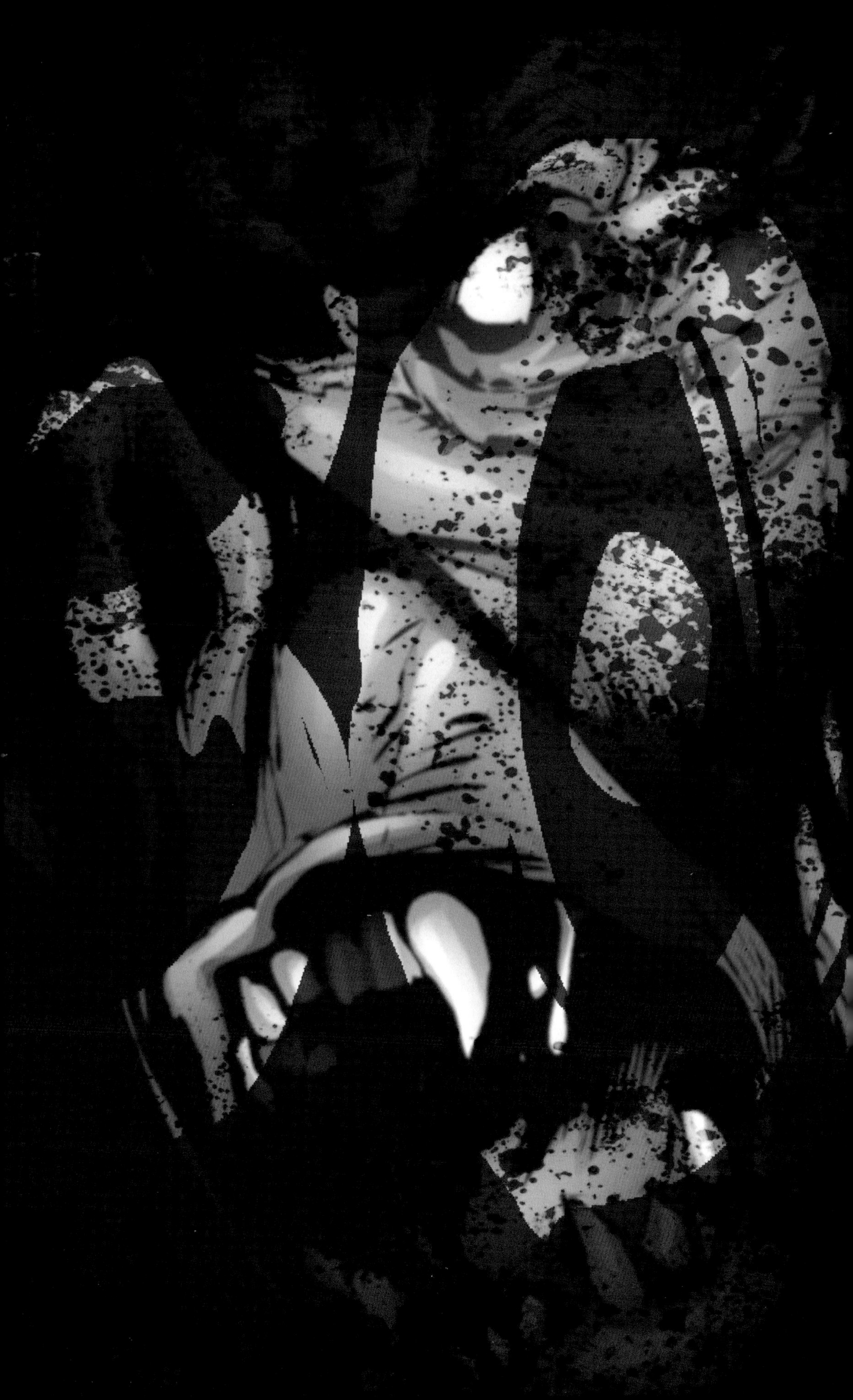

art by: Andrea Sorrentino

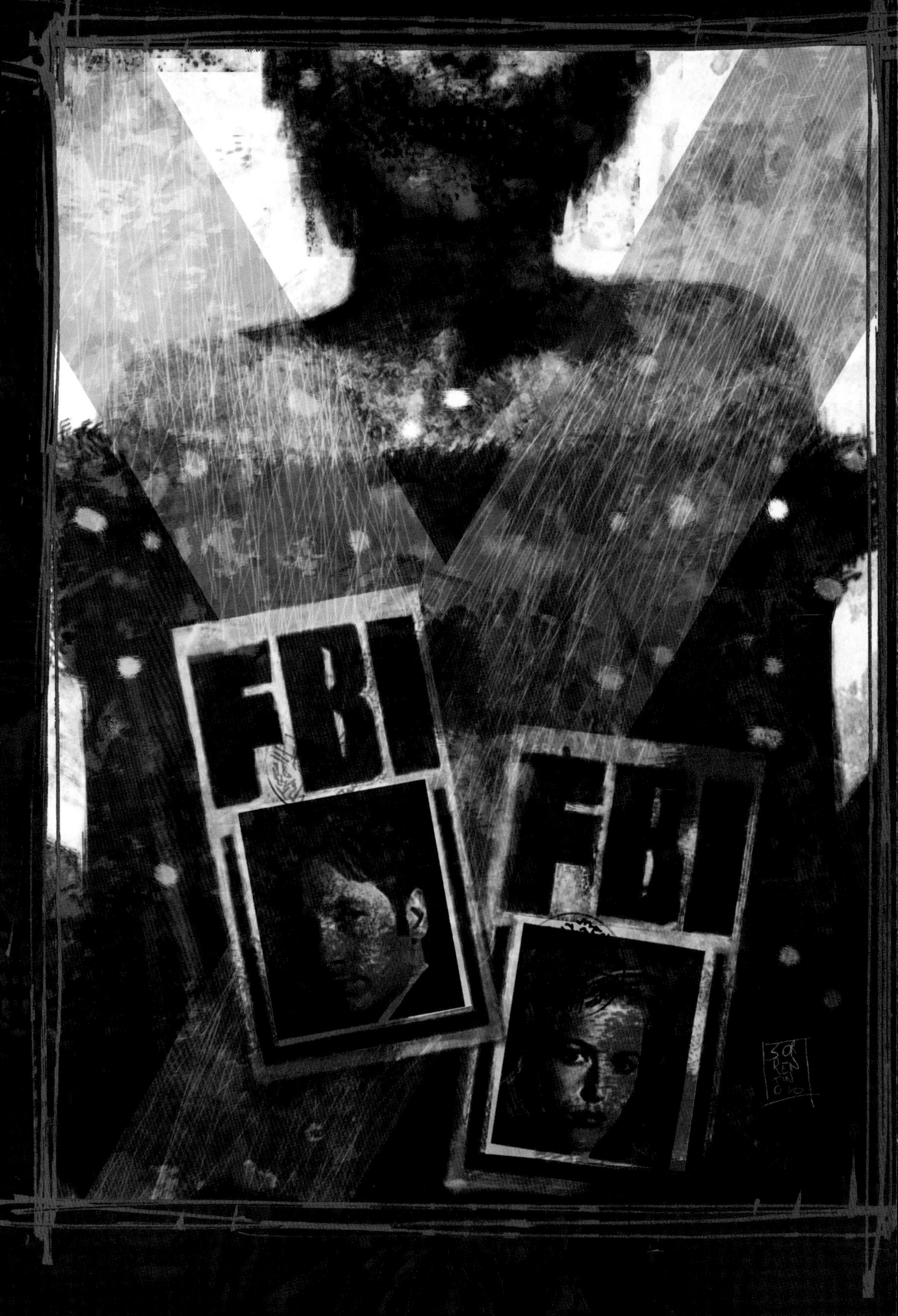
FBI
FBI

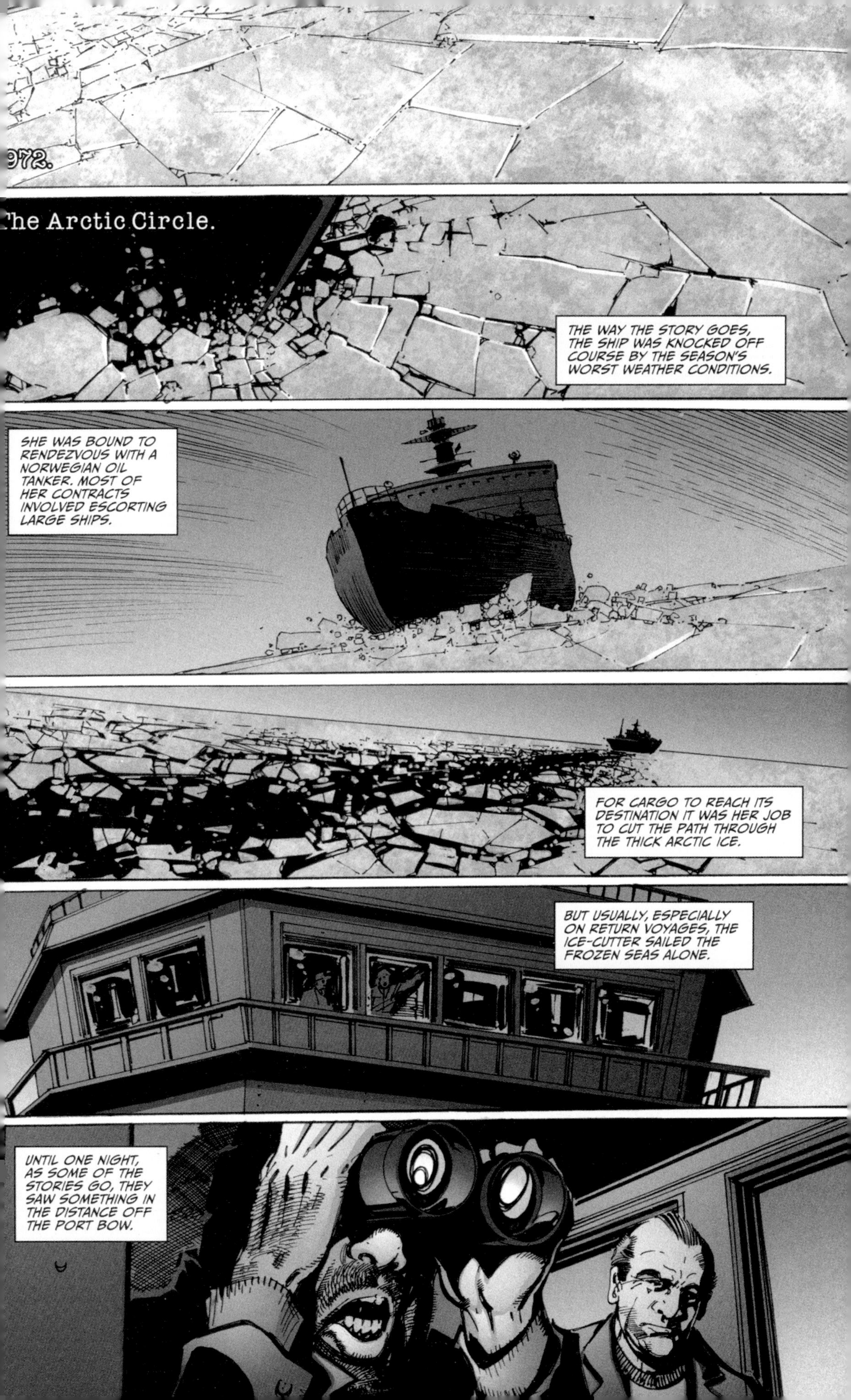
972.
The Arctic Circle.
THE WAY THE STORY GOES, THE SHIP WAS KNOCKED OFF COURSE BY THE SEASON'S WORST WEATHER CONDITIONS.
SHE WAS BOUND TO RENDEZVOUS WITH A NORWEGIAN OIL TANKER. MOST OF HER CONTRACTS INVOLVED ESCORTING LARGE SHIPS.
FOR CARGO TO REACH ITS DESTINATION IT WAS HER JOB TO CUT THE PATH THROUGH THE THICK ARCTIC ICE.
BUT USUALLY, ESPECIALLY ON RETURN VOYAGES, THE ICE-CUTTER SAILED THE FROZEN SEAS ALONE.
UNTIL ONE NIGHT, AS SOME OF THE STORIES GO, THEY SAW SOMETHING IN THE DISTANCE OFF THE PORT BOW.

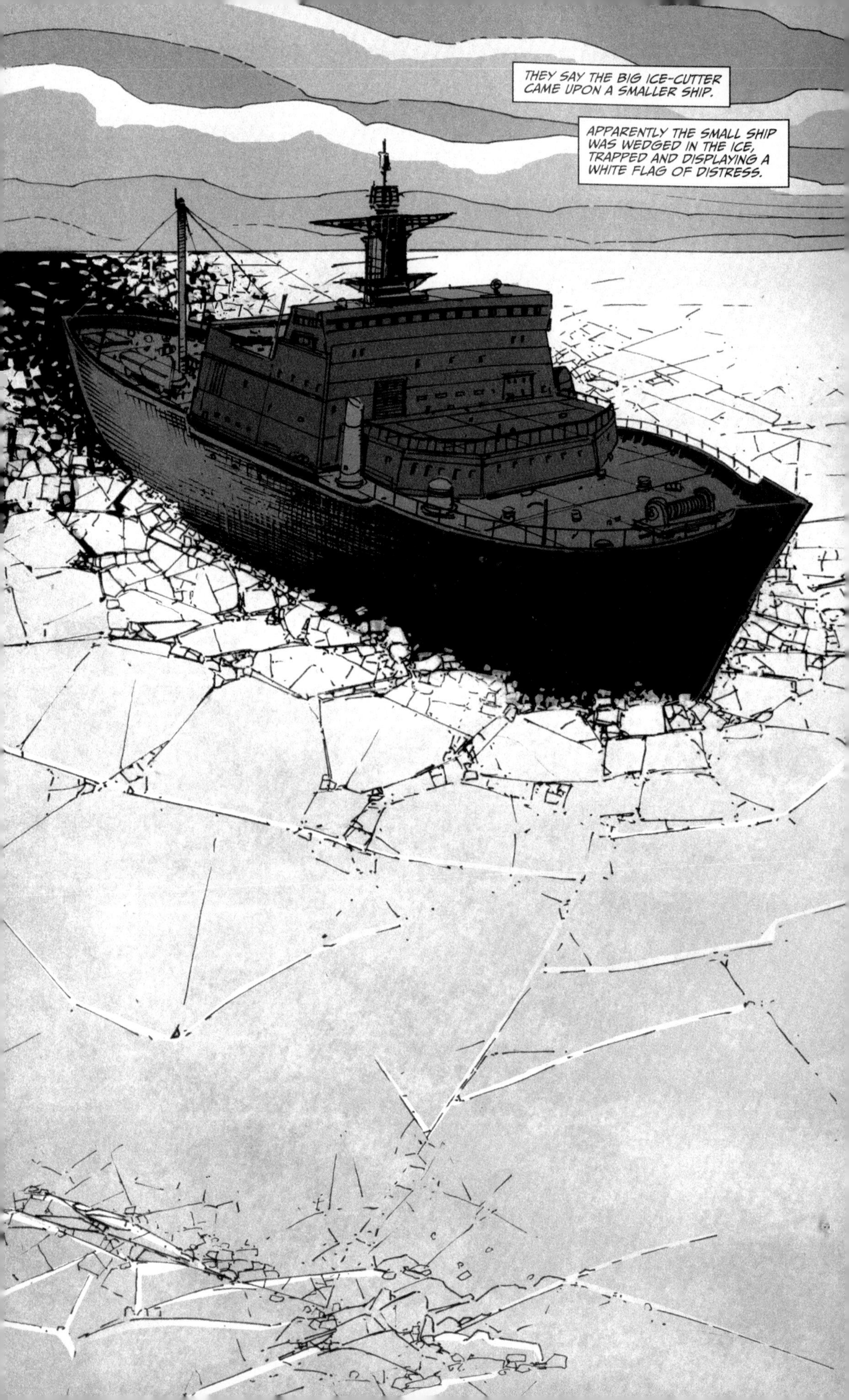
THEY SAY THE BIG ICE-CUTTER CAME UPON A SMALLER SHIP.
APPARENTLY THE SMALL SHIP WAS WEDGED IN THE ICE, TRAPPED AND DISPLAYING A WHITE FLAG OF DISTRESS.

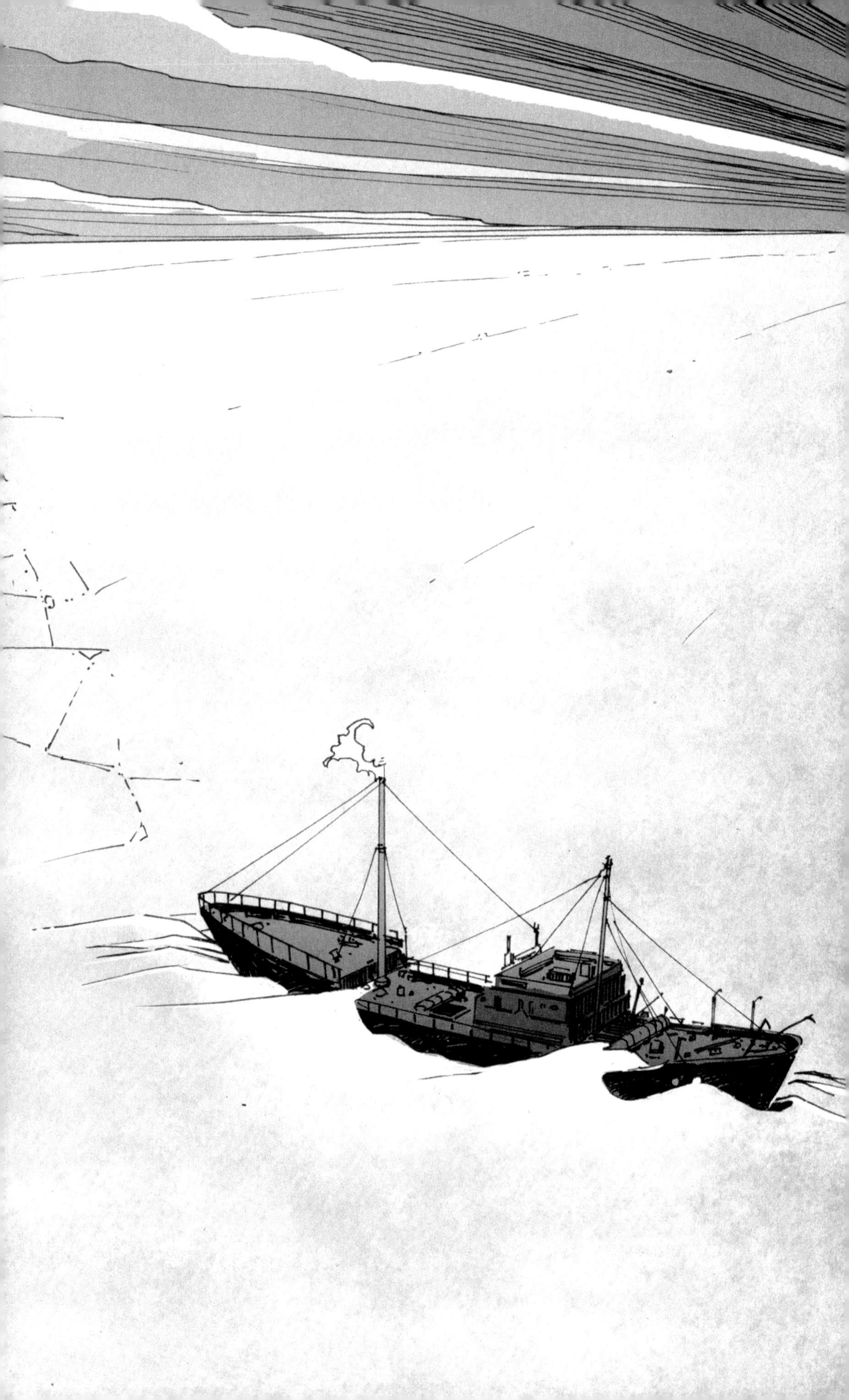

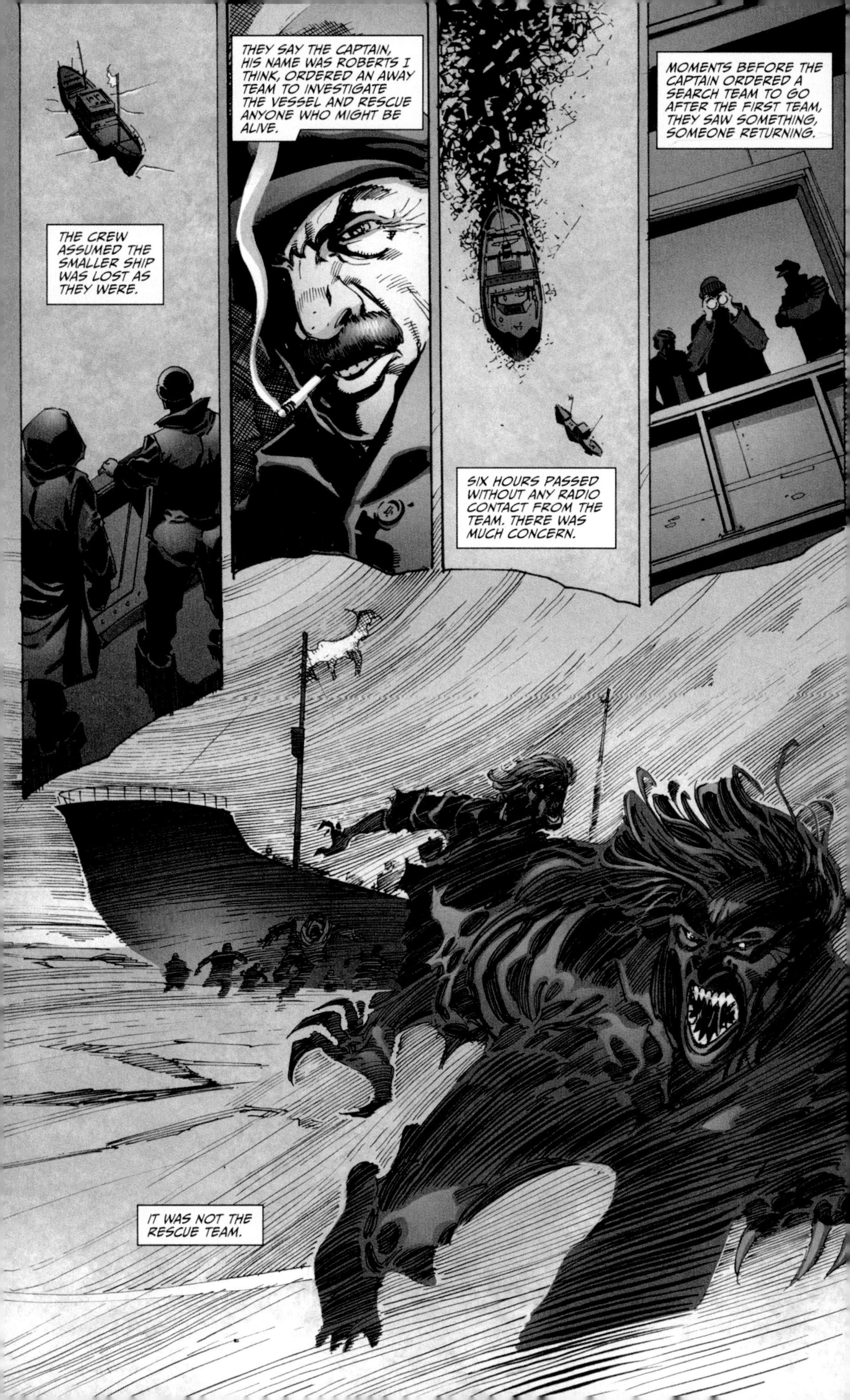
THE CREW ASSUMED THE SMALLER SHIP WAS LOST AS THEY WERE.
THEY SAY THE CAPTAIN, HIS NAME WAS ROBERTS I THINK, ORDERED AN AWAY TEAM TO INVESTIGATE THE VESSEL AND RESCUE ANYONE WHO MIGHT BE ALIVE.
SIX HOURS PASSED WITHOUT ANY RADIO CONTACT FROM THE TEAM. THERE WAS MUCH CONCERN.
MOMENTS BEFORE THE CAPTAIN ORDERED A SEARCH TEAM TO GO AFTER THE FIRST TEAM, THEY SAW SOMETHING, SOMEONE RETURNING.
IT WAS NOT THE RESCUE TEAM.

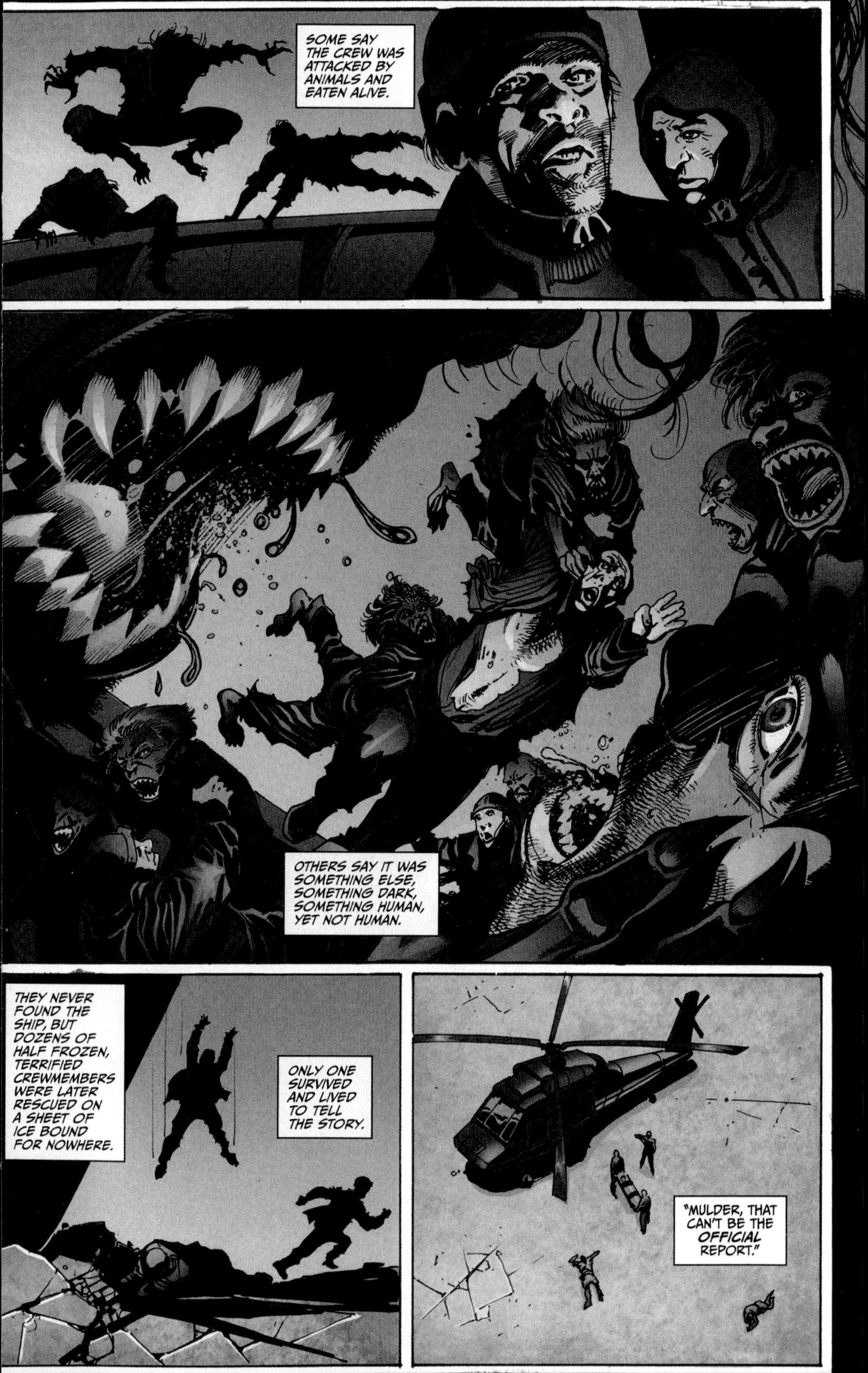
SOME SAY THE CREW WAS ATTACKED BY ANIMALS AND EATEN ALIVE.
OTHERS SAY IT WAS SOMETHING ELSE, SOMETHING DARK, SOMETHING HUMAN, YET NOT HUMAN.
THEY NEVER FOUND THE SHIP, BUT DOZENS OF HALF FROZEN, TERRIFIED CREWMEMBERS WERE LATER RESCUED ON A SHEET OF ICE BOUND FOR NOWHERE.
ONLY ONE SURVIVED AND LIVED TO TELL THE STORY.
"MULDER, THAT CAN'T BE THE OFFICIAL REPORT."

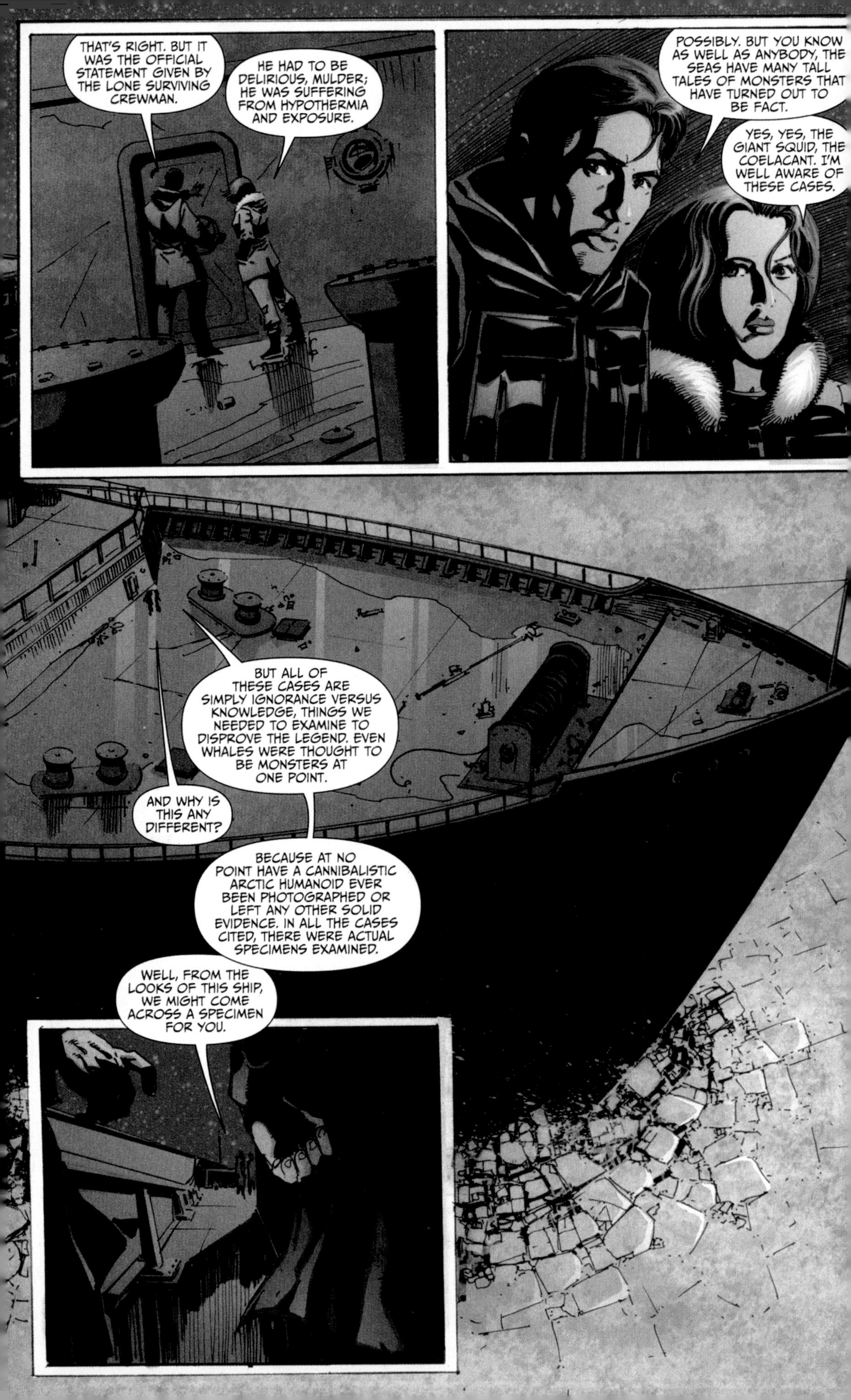
THAT'S RIGHT. BUT IT WAS THE OFFICIAL STATEMENT GIVEN BY THE LONE SURVIVING CREWMAN.
HE HAD TO BE DELIRIOUS, MULDER; HE WAS SUFFERING FROM HYPOTHERMIA AND EXPOSURE.
POSSIBLY. BUT YOU KNOW AS WELL AS ANYBODY, THE SEAS HAVE MANY TALL TALES OF MONSTERS THAT HAVE TURNED OUT TO BE FACT.
YES, YES, THE GIANT SQUID, THE COELACANT. I'M WELL AWARE OF THESE CASES.
BUT ALL OF THESE CASES ARE SIMPLY IGNORANCE VERSUS KNOWLEDGE, THINGS WE NEEDED TO EXAMINE TO DISPROVE THE LEGEND. EVEN WHALES WERE THOUGHT TO BE MONSTERS AT ONE POINT.
AND WHY IS THIS ANY DIFFERENT?
BECAUSE AT NO POINT HAVE A CANNIBALISTIC ARCTIC HUMANOID EVER BEEN PHOTOGRAPHED OR LEFT ANY OTHER SOLID EVIDENCE. IN ALL THE CASES CITED, THERE WERE ACTUAL SPECIMENS EXAMINED.
WELL, FROM THE LOOKS OF THIS SHIP, WE MIGHT COME ACROSS A SPECIMEN FOR YOU.

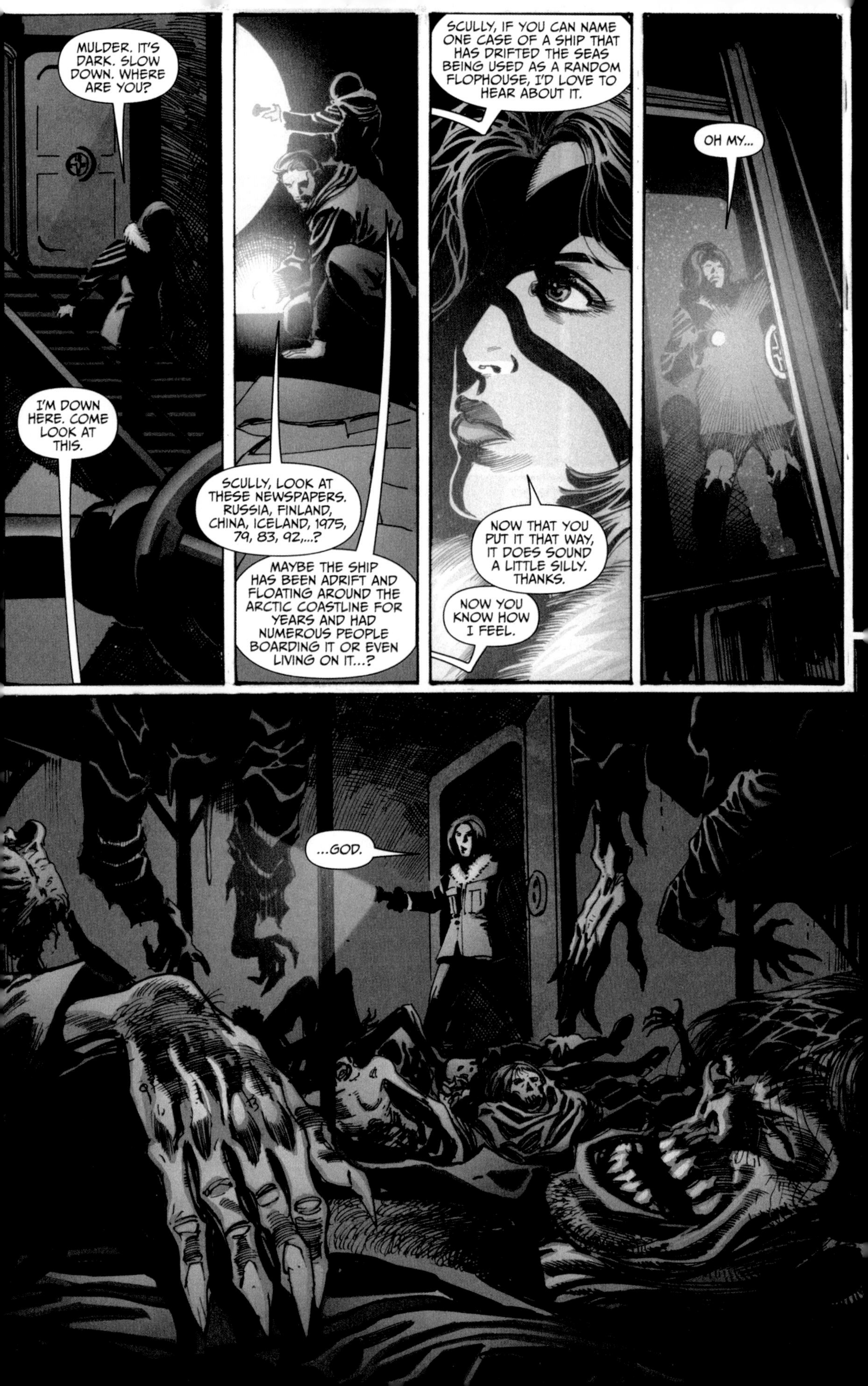
MULDER. IT'S DARK. SLOW DOWN. WHERE ARE YOU?
I'M DOWN HERE. COME LOOK AT THIS.
SCULLY, LOOK AT THESE NEWSPAPERS. RUSSIA, FINLAND, CHINA, ICELAND, 1975, 79, 83, 92,...?
MAYBE THE SHIP HAS BEEN ADRIFT AND FLOATING AROUND THE ARCTIC COASTLINE FOR YEARS AND HAD NUMEROUS PEOPLE BOARDING IT OR EVEN LIVING ON IT...?
SCULLY, IF YOU CAN NAME ONE CASE OF A SHIP THAT HAS DRIFTED THE SEAS BEING USED AS A RANDOM FLOPHOUSE, I'D LOVE TO HEAR ABOUT IT.
NOW THAT YOU PUT IT THAT WAY, IT DOES SOUND A LITTLE SILLY. THANKS.
NOW YOU KNOW HOW I FEEL.
OH MY...
...GOD.

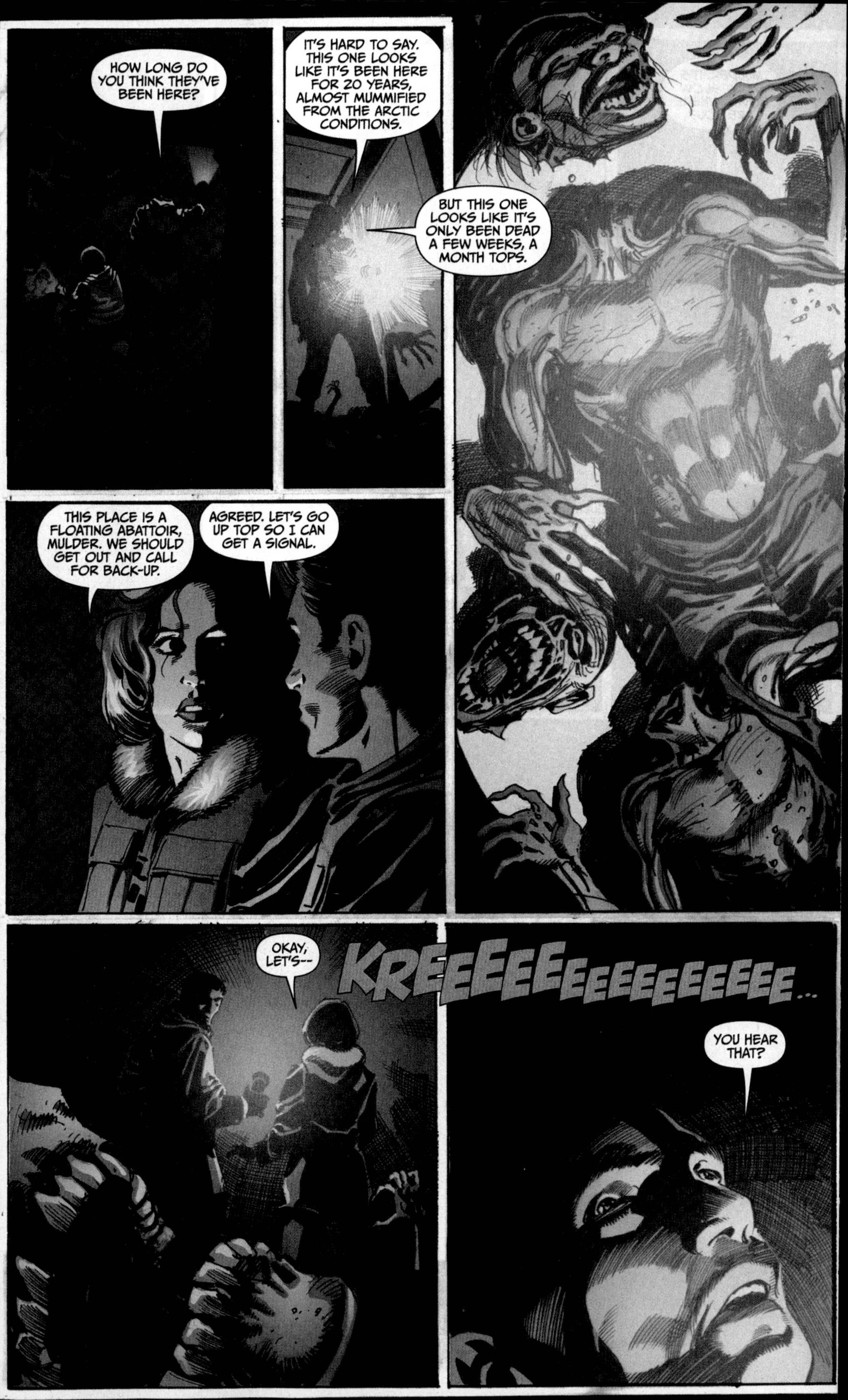
HOW LONG DO YOU THINK THEY'VE BEEN HERE?
IT'S HARD TO SAY. THIS ONE LOOKS LIKE IT'S BEEN HERE FOR 20 YEARS, ALMOST MUMMIFIED FROM THE ARCTIC CONDITIONS.
BUT THIS ONE LOOKS LIKE IT'S ONLY BEEN DEAD A FEW WEEKS, A MONTH TOPS.
THIS PLACE IS A FLOATING ABATTOIR, MULDER. WE SHOULD GET OUT AND CALL FOR BACK-UP.
AGREED. LET'S GO UP TOP SO I CAN GET A SIGNAL.
OKAY, LET'S--
KREEEEEEEEEEEEEEEE...
YOU HEAR THAT?

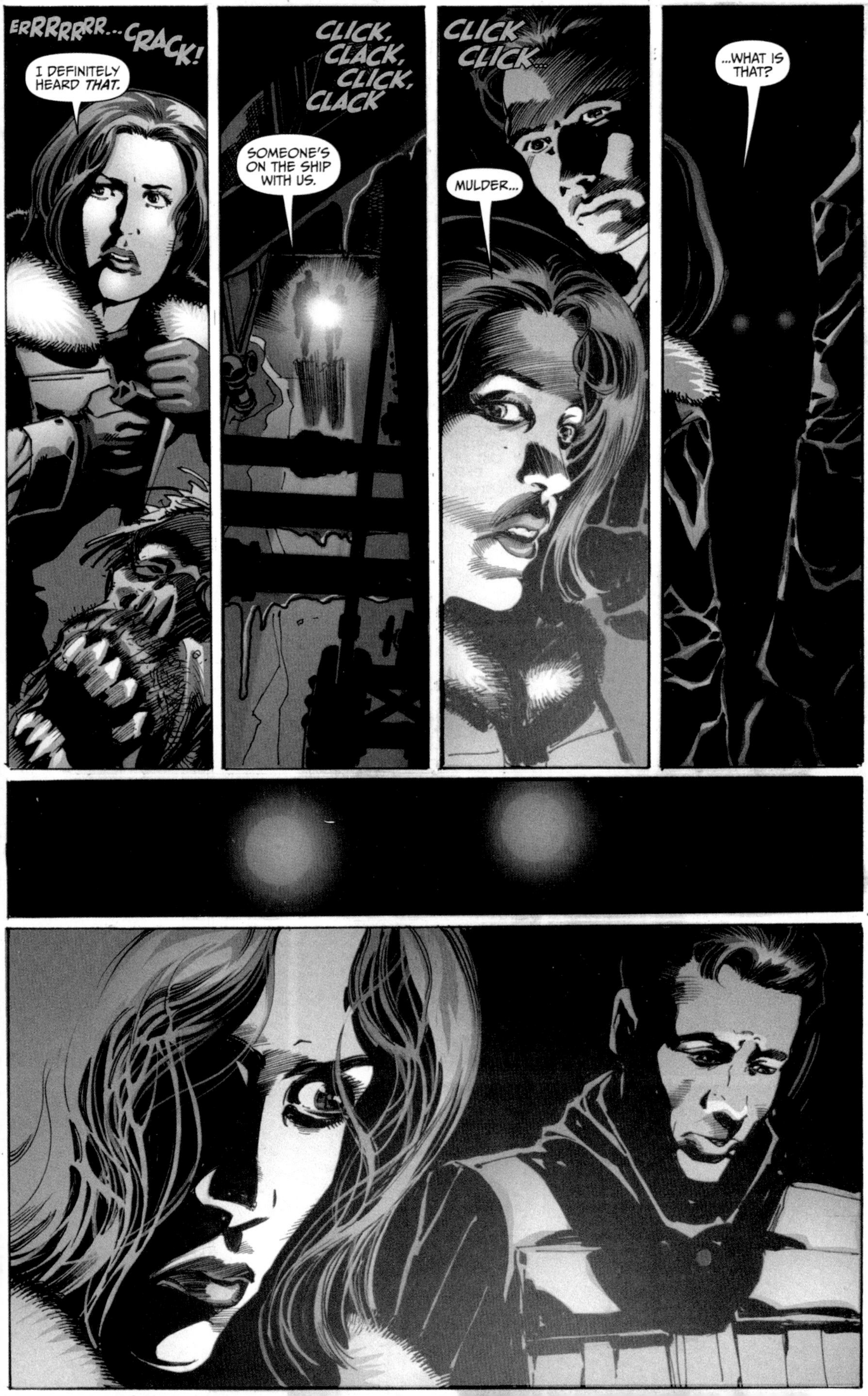
ERRRRRRR... CRACK!
I DEFINITELY HEARD THAT.
CLICK, CLACK, CLICK, CLACK
SOMEONE'S ON THE SHIP WITH US.
CLICK CLICK...
MULDER...
...WHAT IS THAT?

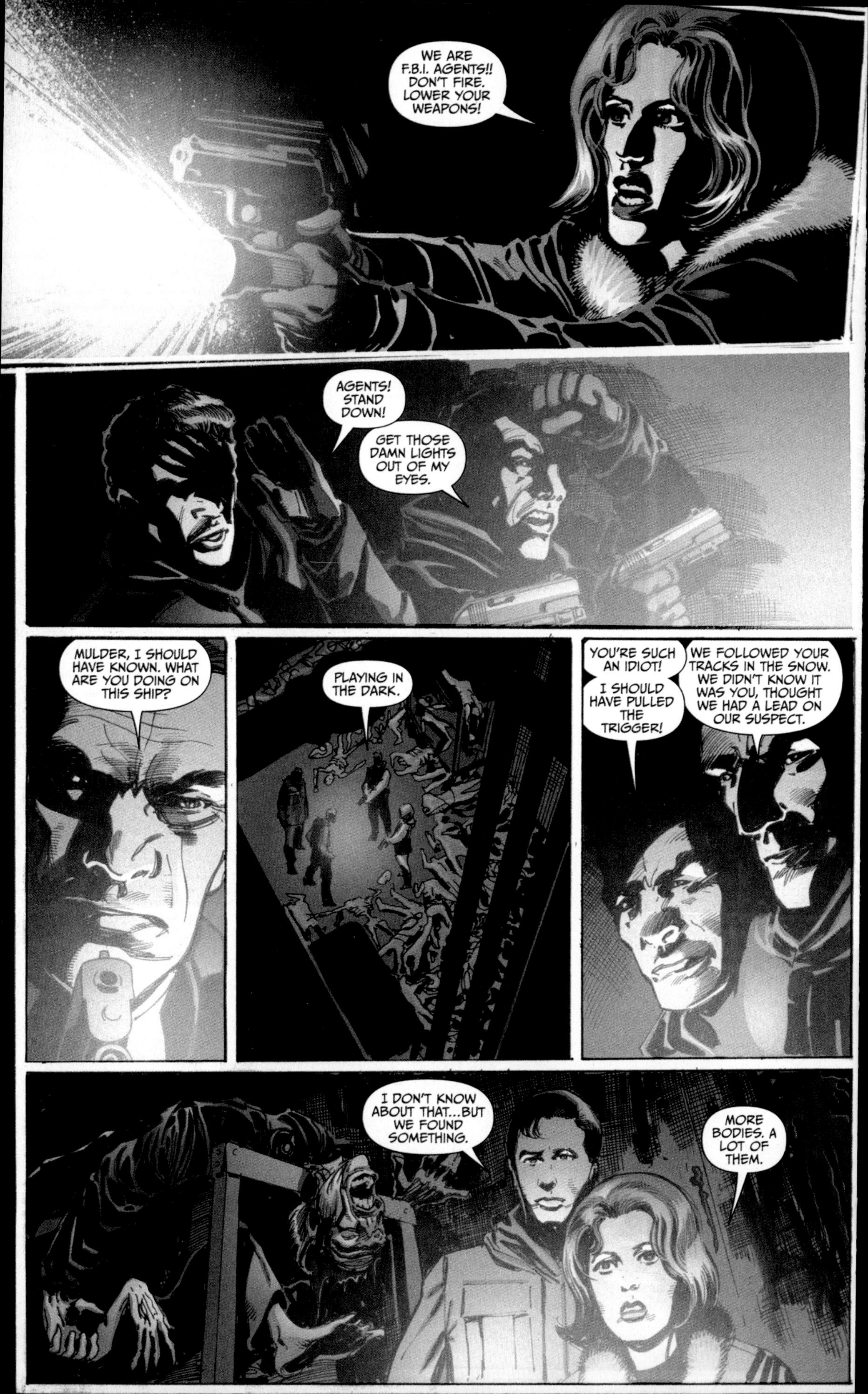
WE ARE F.B.I. AGENTS!! DON'T FIRE. LOWER YOUR WEAPONS!
AGENTS! STAND DOWN!
GET THOSE DAMN LIGHTS OUT OF MY EYES.
MULDER, I SHOULD HAVE KNOWN. WHAT ARE YOU DOING ON THIS SHIP?
PLAYING IN THE DARK.
YOU'RE SUCH AN IDIOT!
I SHOULD HAVE PULLED THE TRIGGER!
WE FOLLOWED YOUR TRACKS IN THE SNOW. WE DIDN'T KNOW IT WAS YOU, THOUGHT WE HAD A LEAD ON OUR SUSPECT.
I DON'T KNOW ABOUT THAT...BUT WE FOUND SOMETHING.
MORE BODIES. A LOT OF THEM.

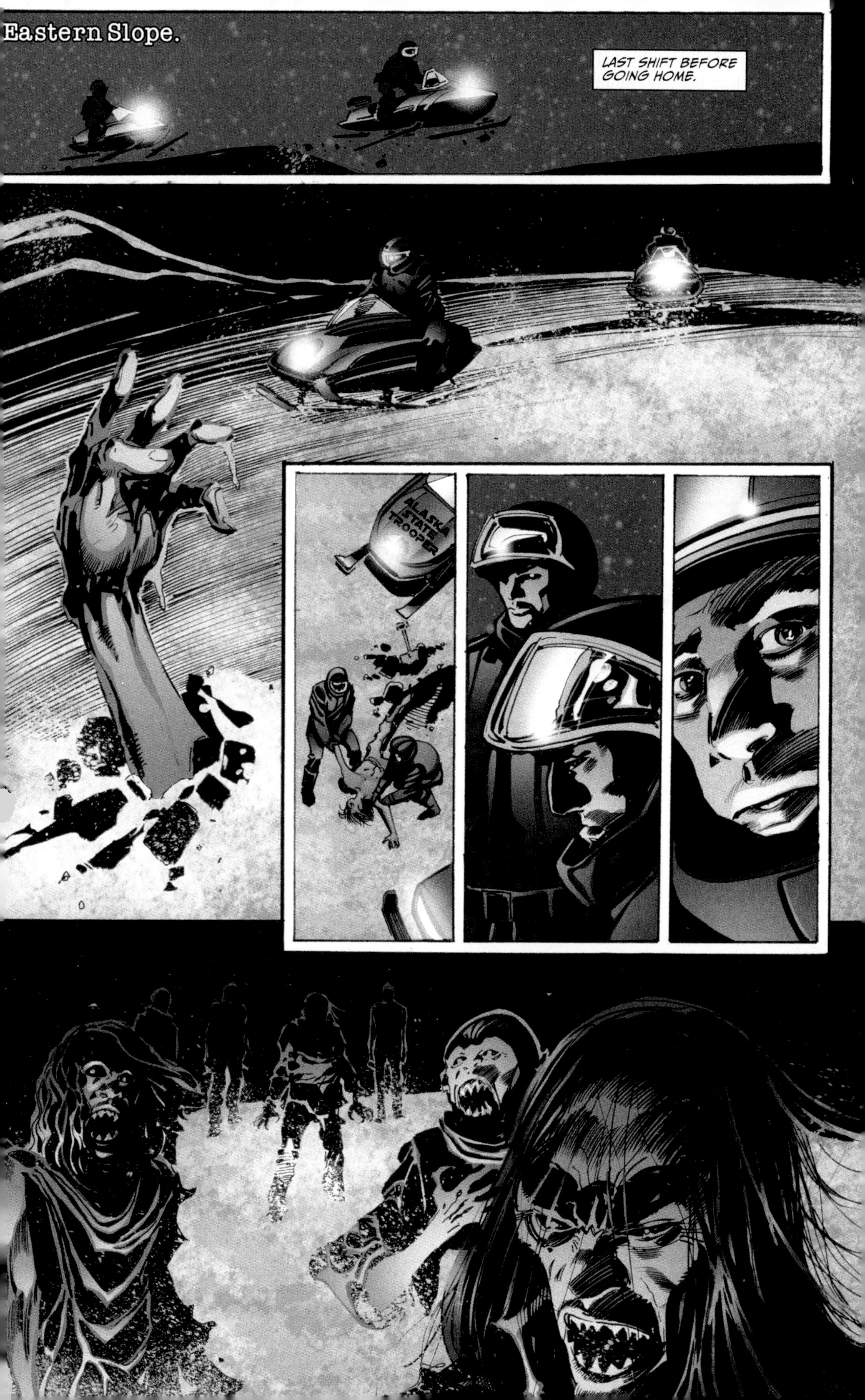
Eastern Slope.
LAST SHIFT BEFORE GOING HOME.
ALASKA STATE TROOPER

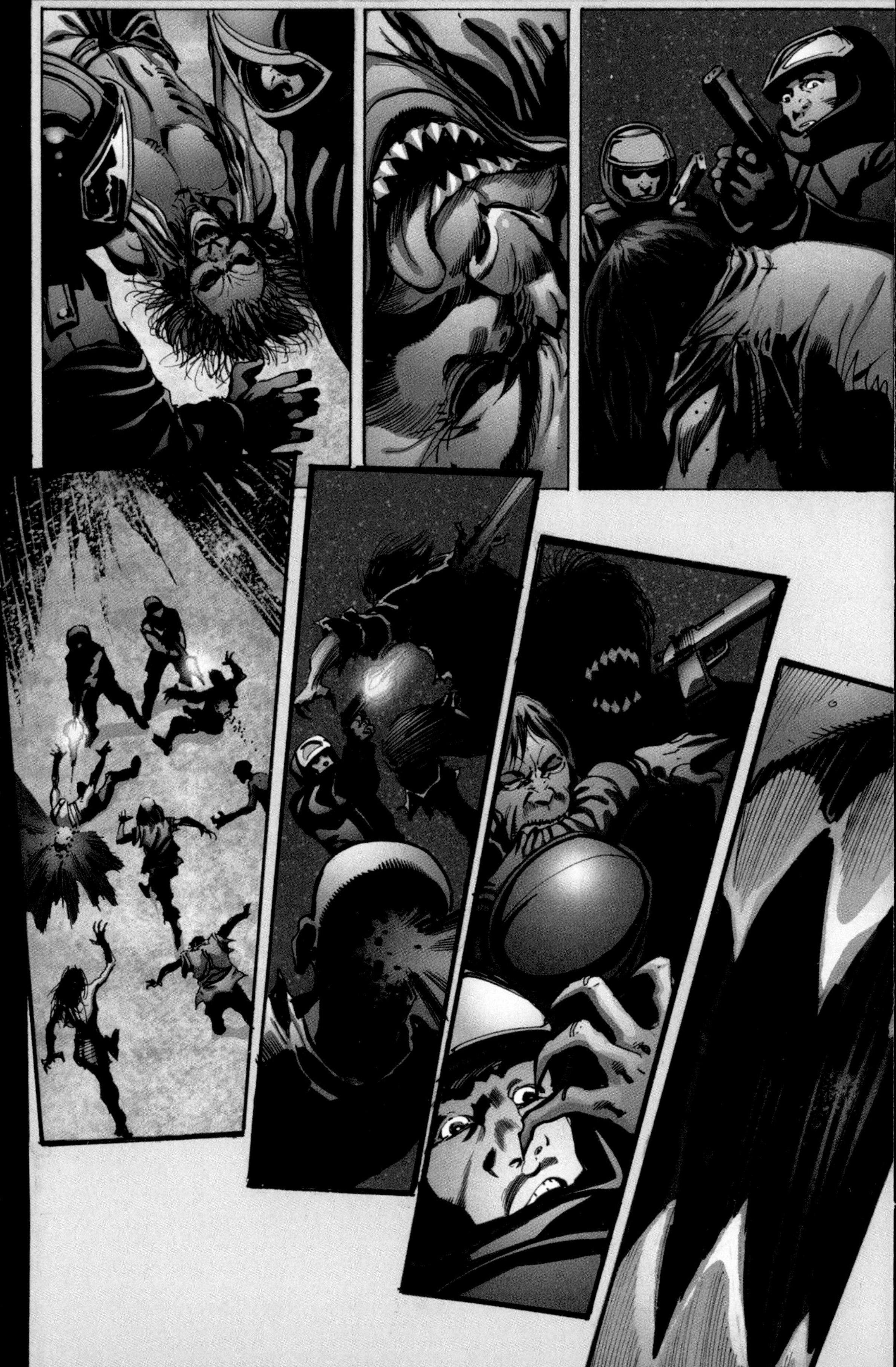

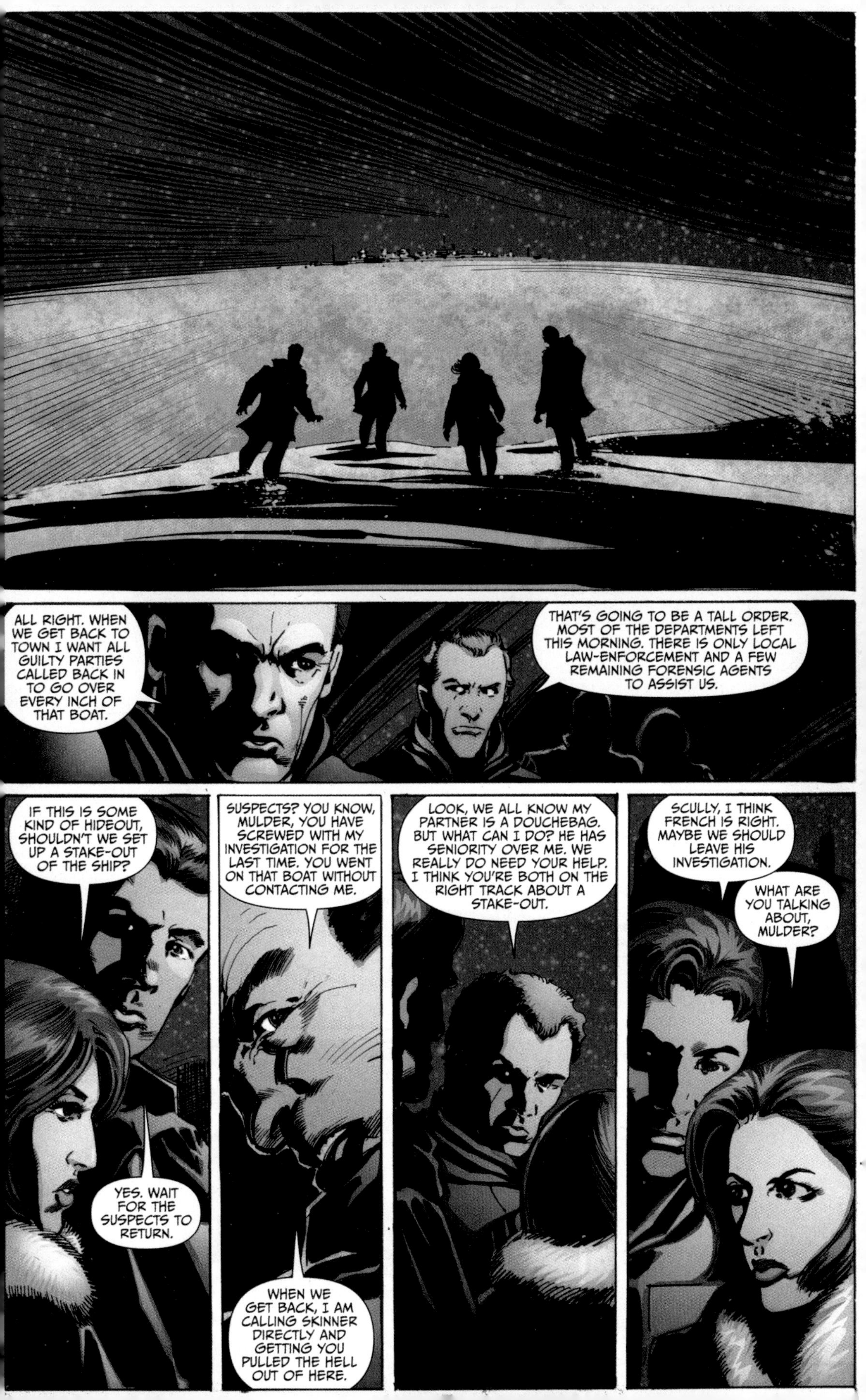
ALL RIGHT. WHEN WE GET BACK TO TOWN I WANT ALL GUILTY PARTIES CALLED BACK IN TO GO OVER EVERY INCH OF THAT BOAT.
THAT'S GOING TO BE A TALL ORDER. MOST OF THE DEPARTMENTS LEFT THIS MORNING. THERE IS ONLY LOCAL LAW-ENFORCEMENT AND A FEW REMAINING FORENSIC AGENTS TO ASSIST US.
IF THIS IS SOME KIND OF HIDEOUT, SHOULDN'T WE SET UP A STAKE-OUT OF THE SHIP?
YES. WAIT FOR THE SUSPECTS TO RETURN.
SUSPECTS? YOU KNOW, MULDER, YOU HAVE SCREWED WITH MY INVESTIGATION FOR THE LAST TIME. YOU WENT ON THAT BOAT WITHOUT CONTACTING ME.
WHEN WE GET BACK, I AM CALLING SKINNER DIRECTLY AND GETTING YOU PULLED THE HELL OUT OF HERE.
LOOK, WE ALL KNOW MY PARTNER IS A DOUCHEBAG. BUT WHAT CAN I DO? HE HAS SENIORITY OVER ME. WE REALLY DO NEED YOUR HELP. I THINK YOU'RE BOTH ON THE RIGHT TRACK ABOUT A STAKE-OUT.
SCULLY, I THINK FRENCH IS RIGHT. MAYBE WE SHOULD LEAVE HIS INVESTIGATION.
WHAT ARE YOU TALKING ABOUT, MULDER?

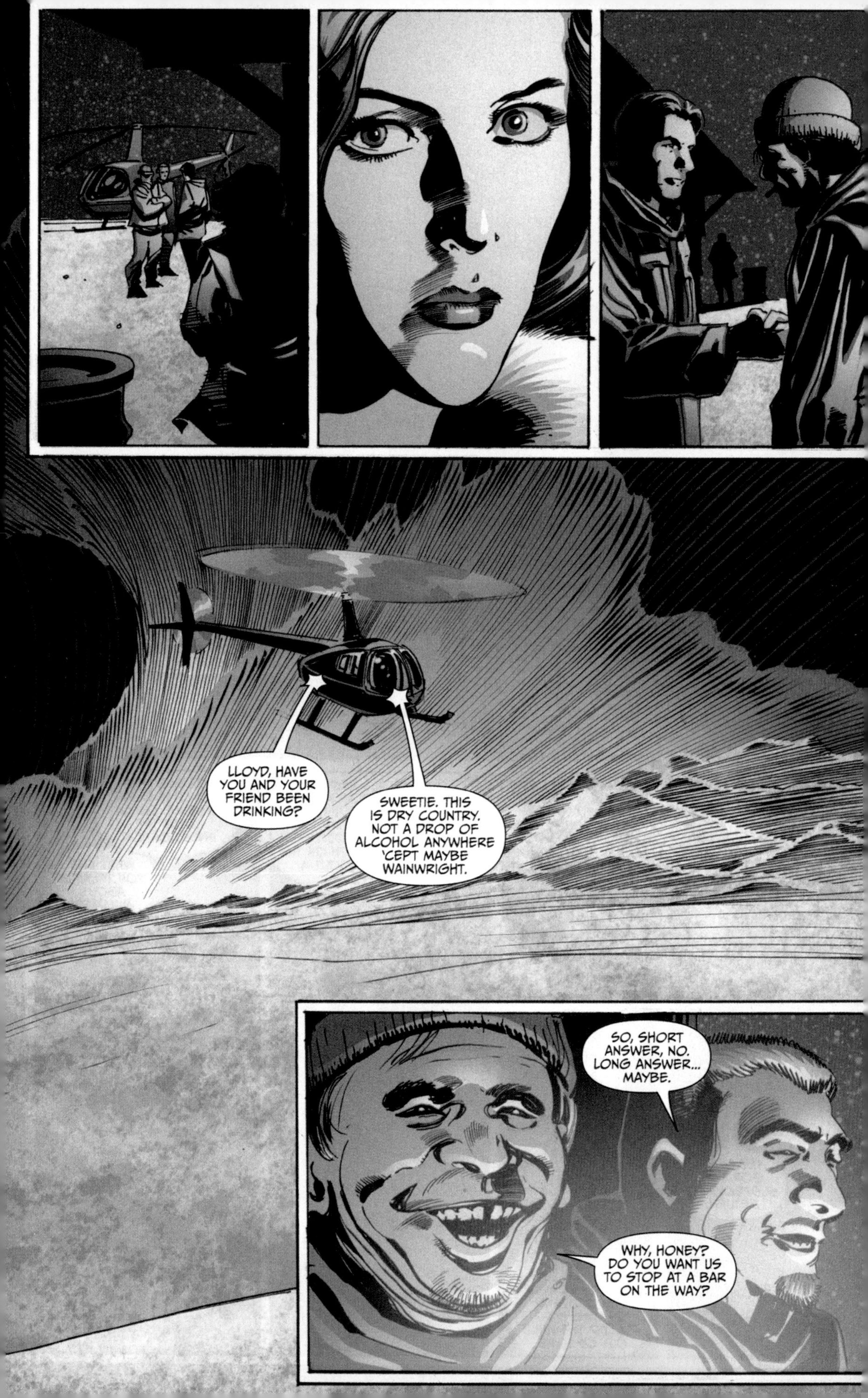
LLOYD, HAVE YOU AND YOUR FRIEND BEEN DRINKING?
SWEETIE. THIS IS DRY COUNTRY. NOT A DROP OF ALCOHOL ANYWHERE 'CEPT MAYBE WAINWRIGHT.
SO, SHORT ANSWER, NO. LONG ANSWER... MAYBE.
WHY, HONEY? DO YOU WANT US TO STOP AT A BAR ON THE WAY?

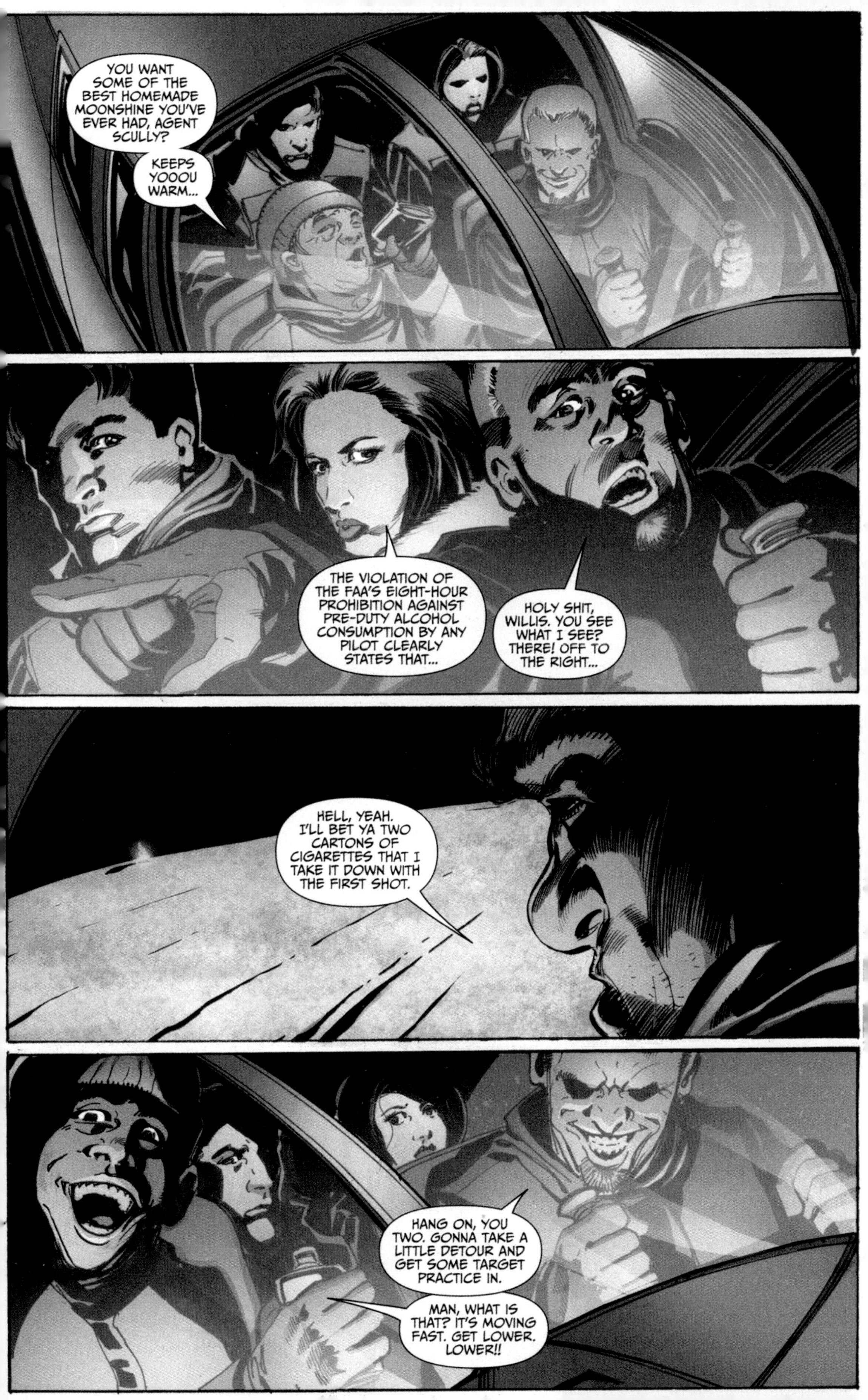
YOU WANT SOME OF THE BEST HOMEMADE MOONSHINE YOU'VE EVER HAD, AGENT SCULLY?
KEEPS YOOOU WARM...
THE VIOLATION OF THE FAA'S EIGHT-HOUR PROHIBITION AGAINST PRE-DUTY ALCOHOL CONSUMPTION BY ANY PILOT CLEARLY STATES THAT...
HOLY SHIT, WILLIS. YOU SEE WHAT I SEE? THERE! OFF TO THE RIGHT...
HELL, YEAH. I'LL BET YA TWO CARTONS OF CIGARETTES THAT I TAKE IT DOWN WITH THE FIRST SHOT.
HANG ON, YOU TWO. GONNA TAKE A LITTLE DETOUR AND GET SOME TARGET PRACTICE IN.
MAN, WHAT IS THAT? IT'S MOVING FAST. GET LOWER. LOWER!!

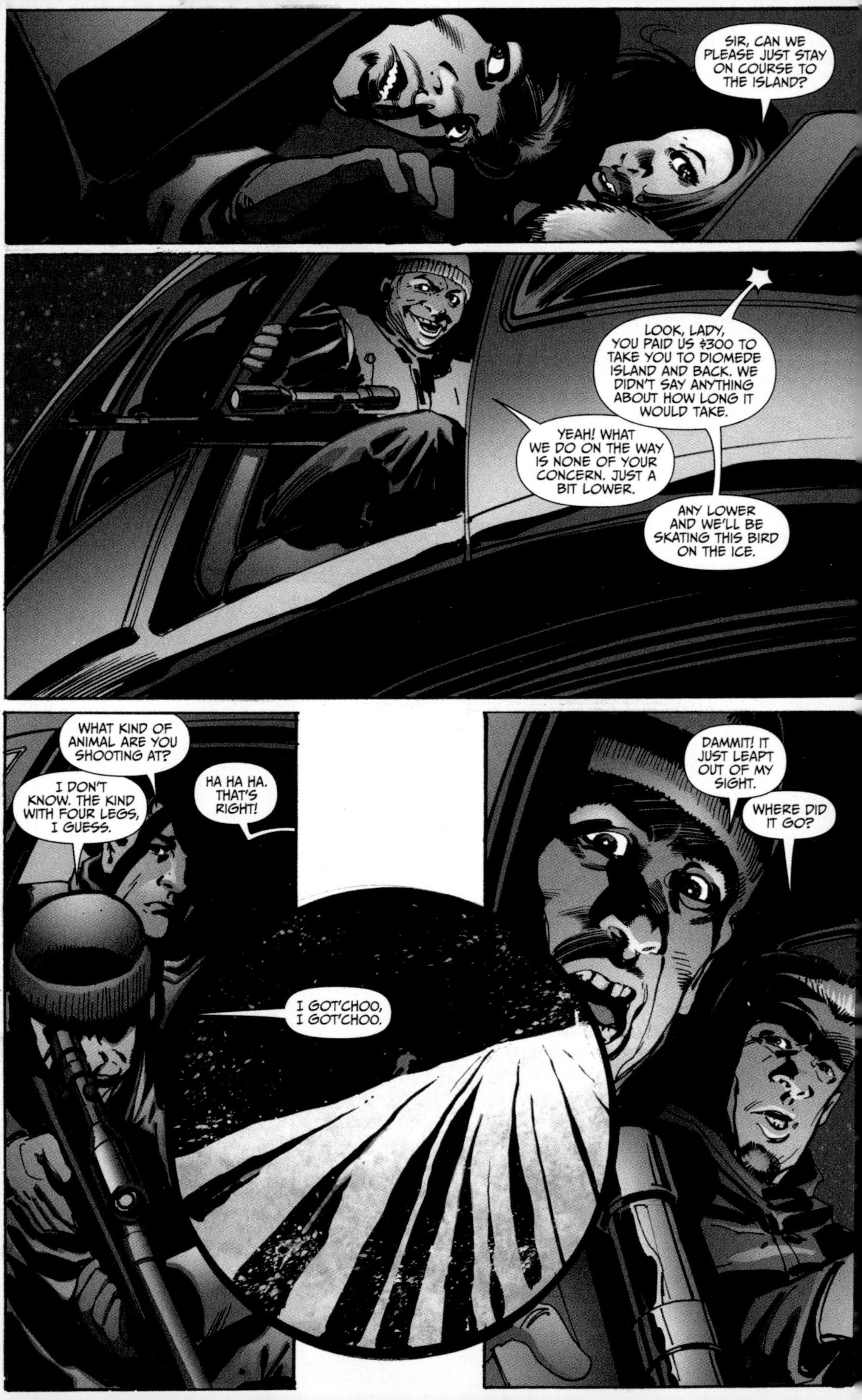
SIR, CAN WE PLEASE JUST STAY ON COURSE TO THE ISLAND?
LOOK, LADY, YOU PAID US $300 TO TAKE YOU TO DIOMEDE ISLAND AND BACK. WE DIDN'T SAY ANYTHING ABOUT HOW LONG IT WOULD TAKE.
YEAH! WHAT WE DO ON THE WAY IS NONE OF YOUR CONCERN. JUST A BIT LOWER.
ANY LOWER AND WE'LL BE SKATING THIS BIRD ON THE ICE.
WHAT KIND OF ANIMAL ARE YOU SHOOTING AT?
I DON'T KNOW. THE KIND WITH FOUR LEGS, I GUESS.
HA HA HA. THAT'S RIGHT!
I GOT'CHOO, I GOT'CHOO.
DAMMIT! IT JUST LEAPT OUT OF MY SIGHT.
WHERE DID IT GO?

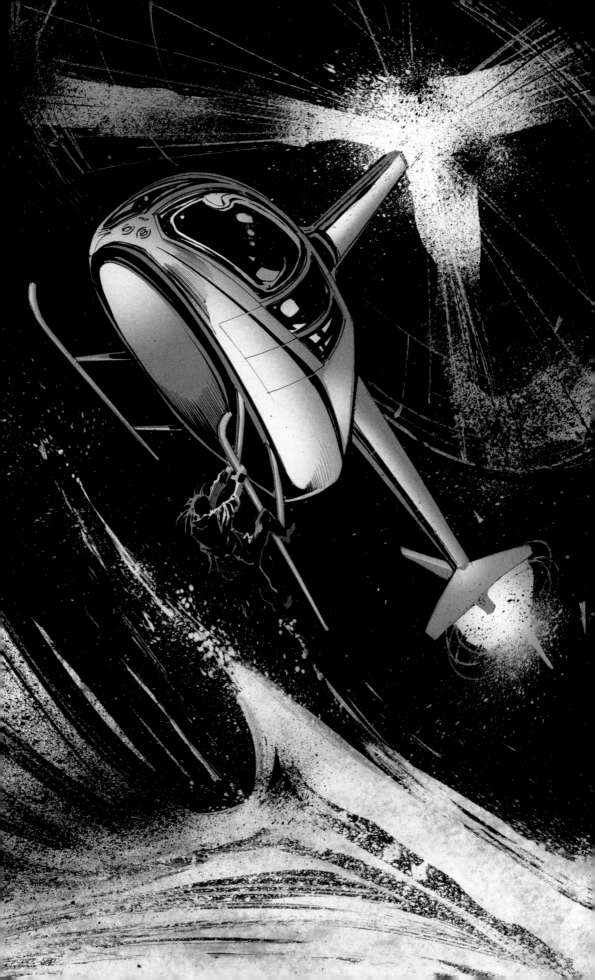

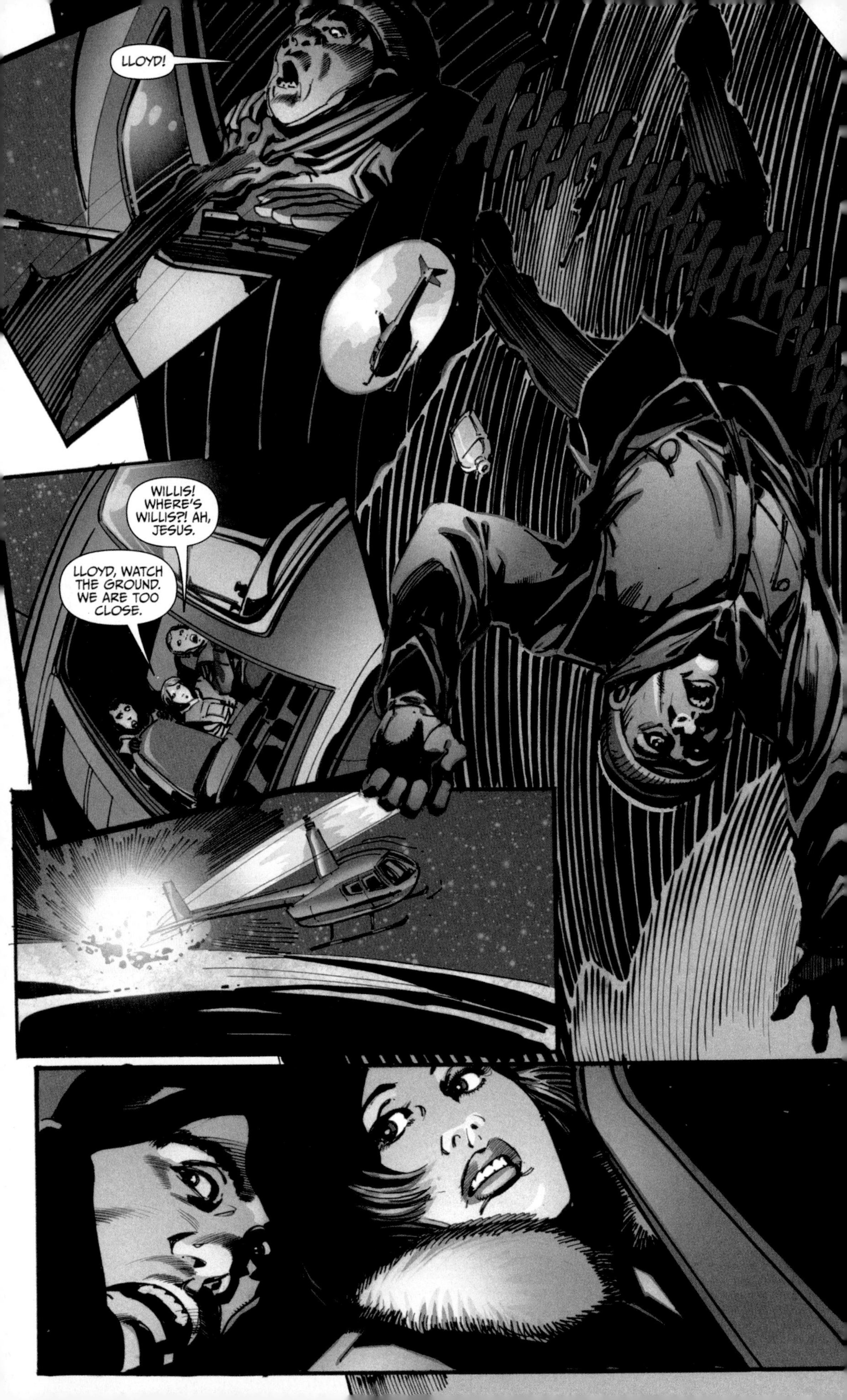
LLOYD!
AHHHHHHHHHHHHHHHHH
WILLIS! WHERE'S WILLIS?! AH, JESUS.
LLOYD, WATCH THE GROUND. WE ARE TOO CLOSE.

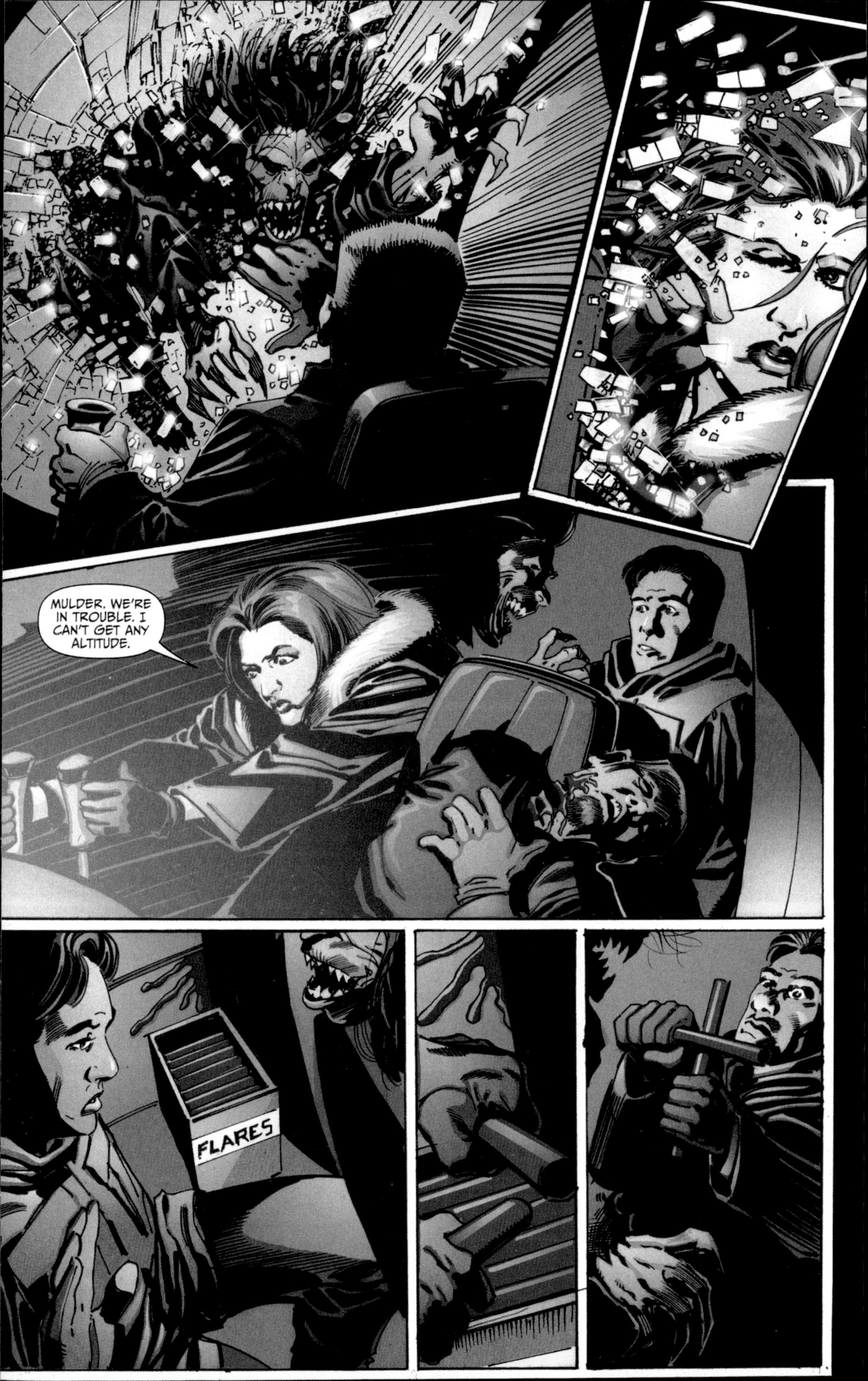
MULDER. WE'RE IN TROUBLE. I CAN'T GET ANY ALTITUDE.
FLARES

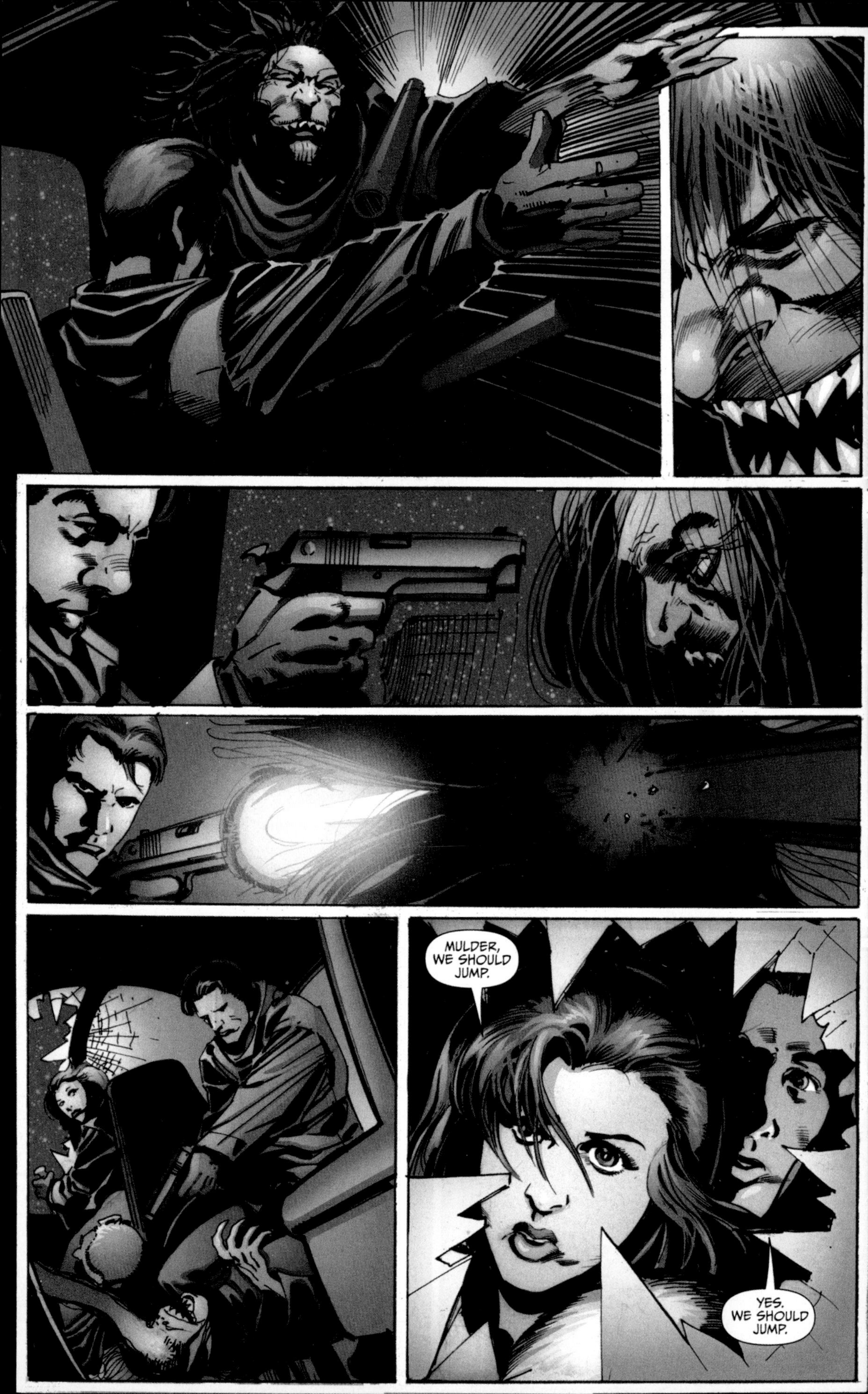
MULDER, WE SHOULD JUMP.
YES. WE SHOULD JUMP.

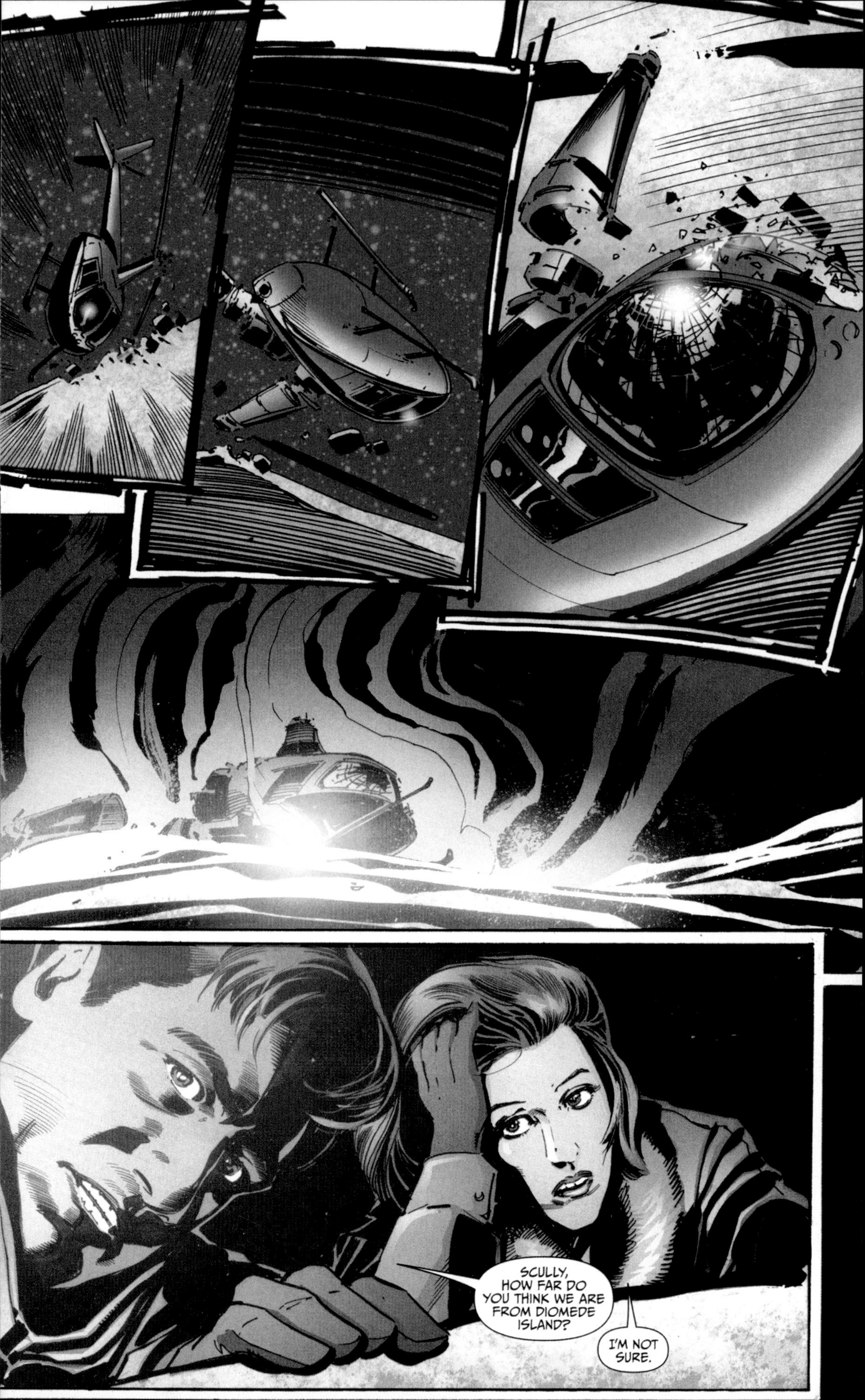
SCULLY, HOW FAR DO YOU THINK WE ARE FROM DIOMEDE ISLAND?
I'M NOT SURE.

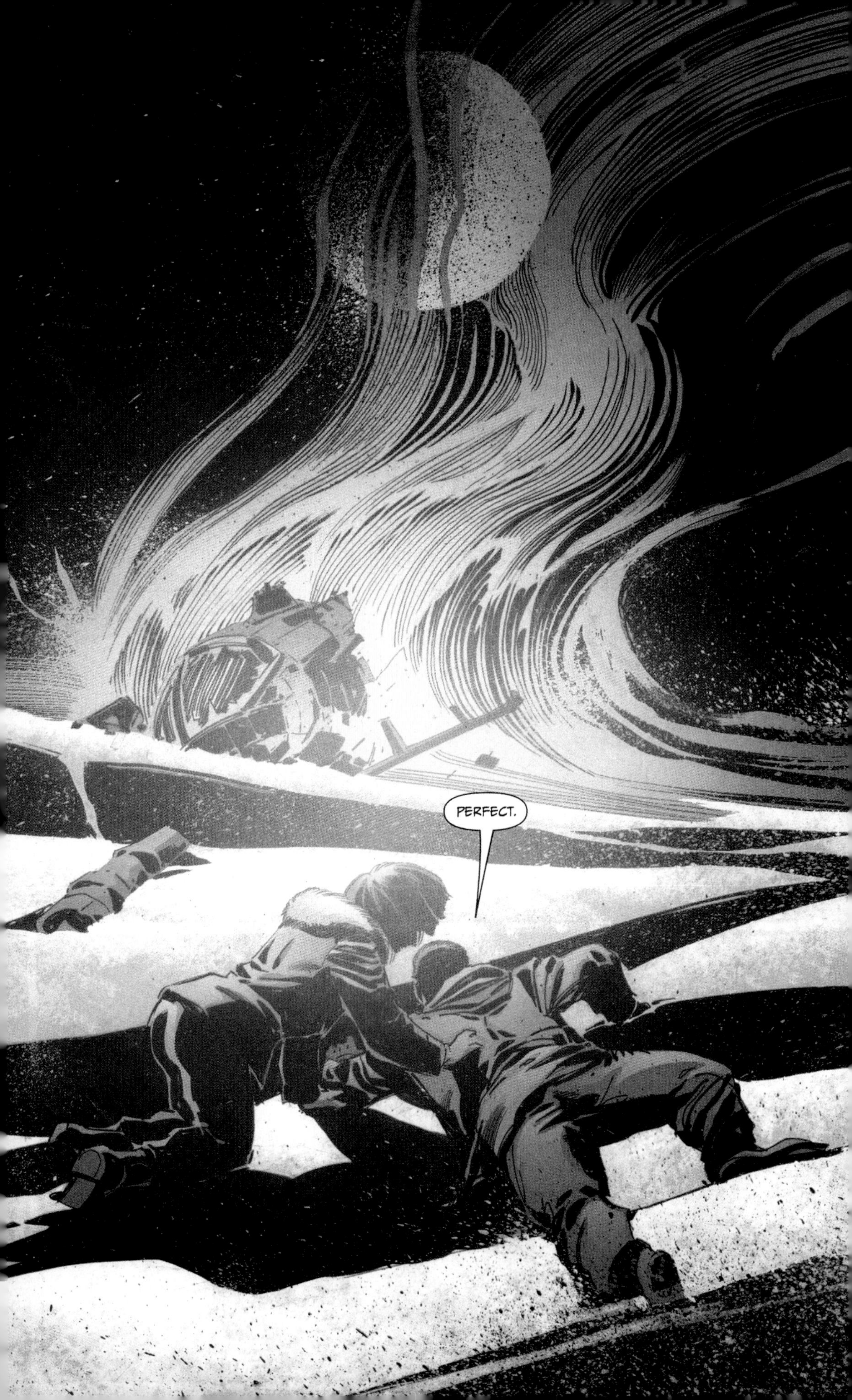
PERFECT.

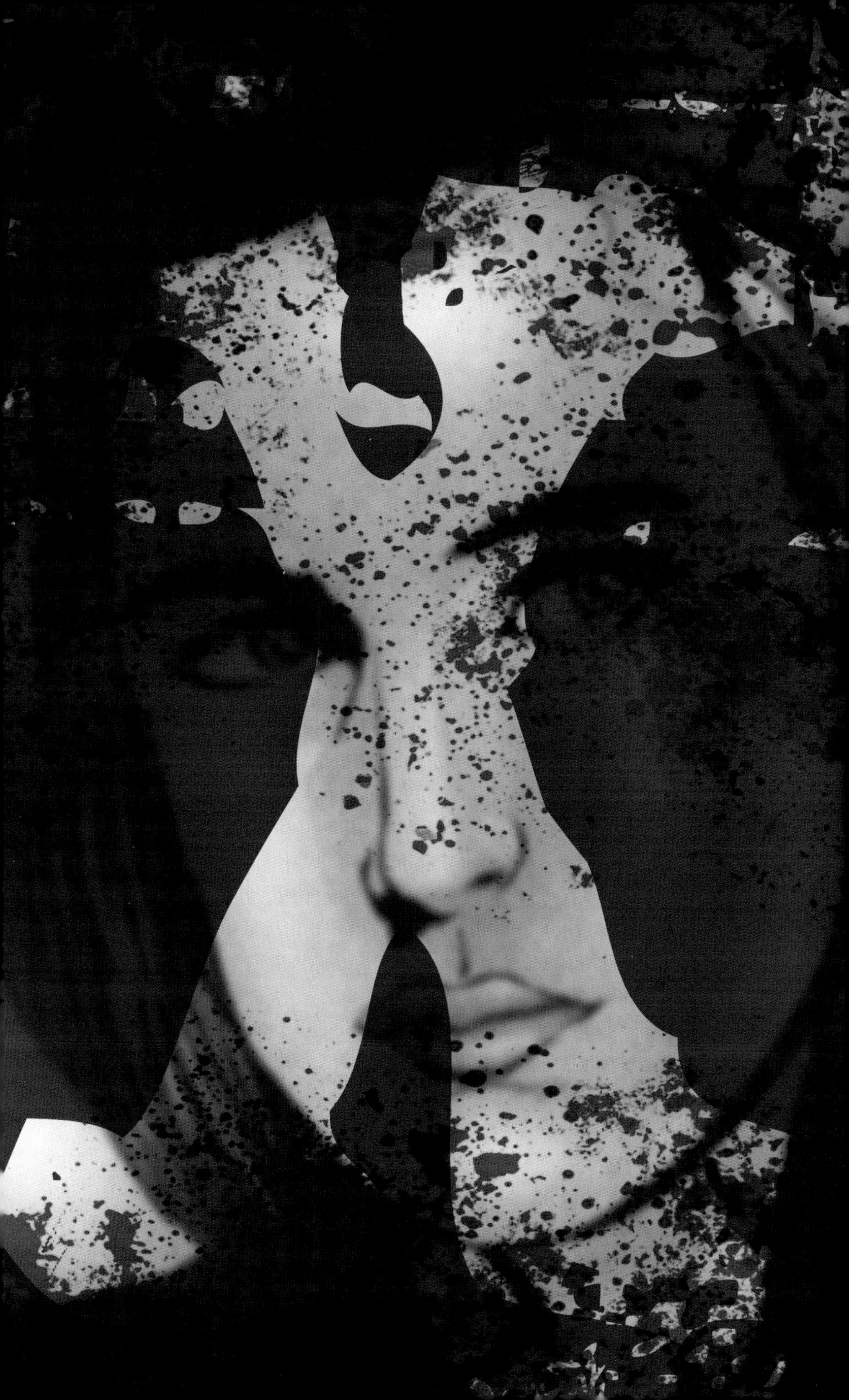

art by: Andrea Sorrentino

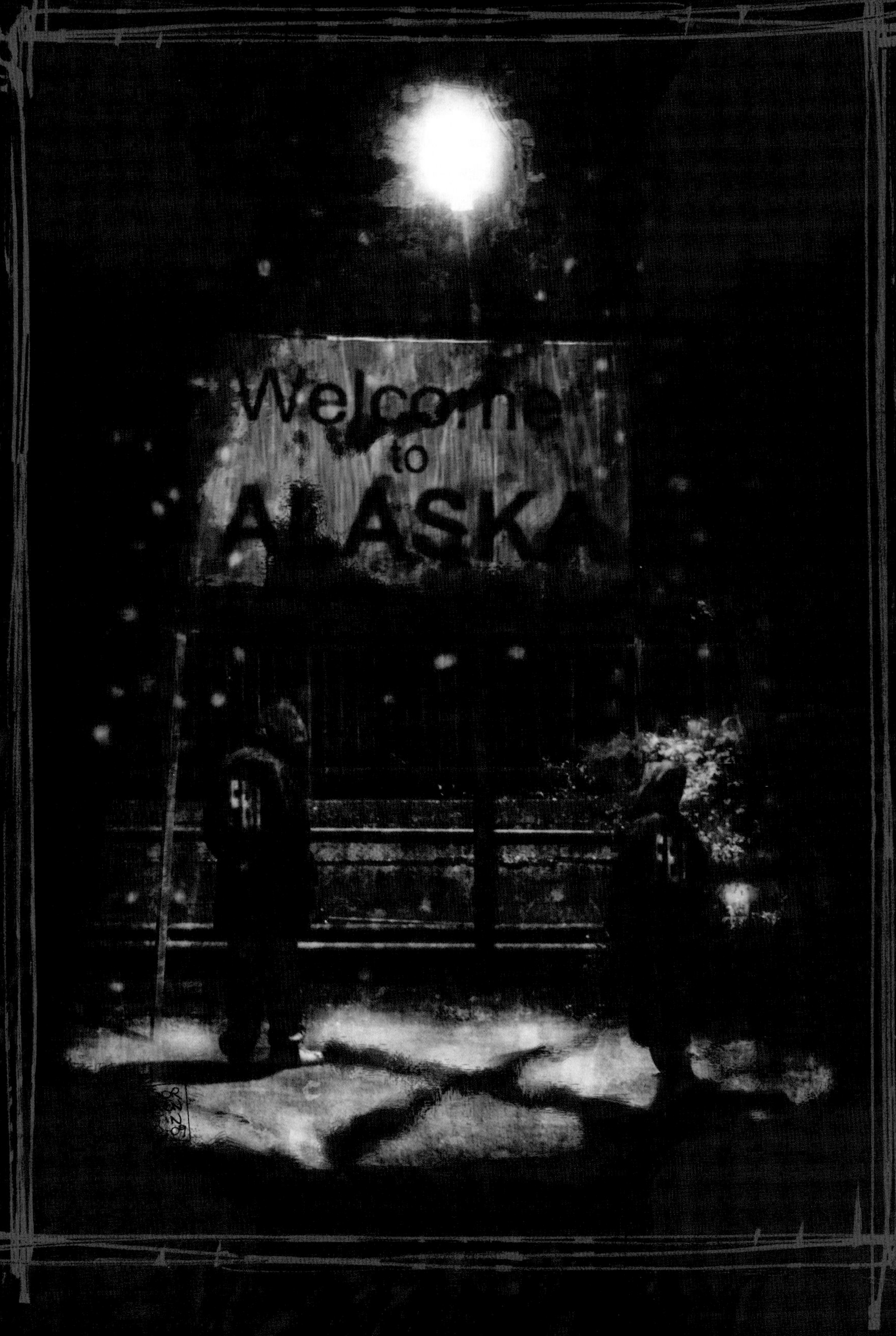
Welcome
to
ALASKA
FBI

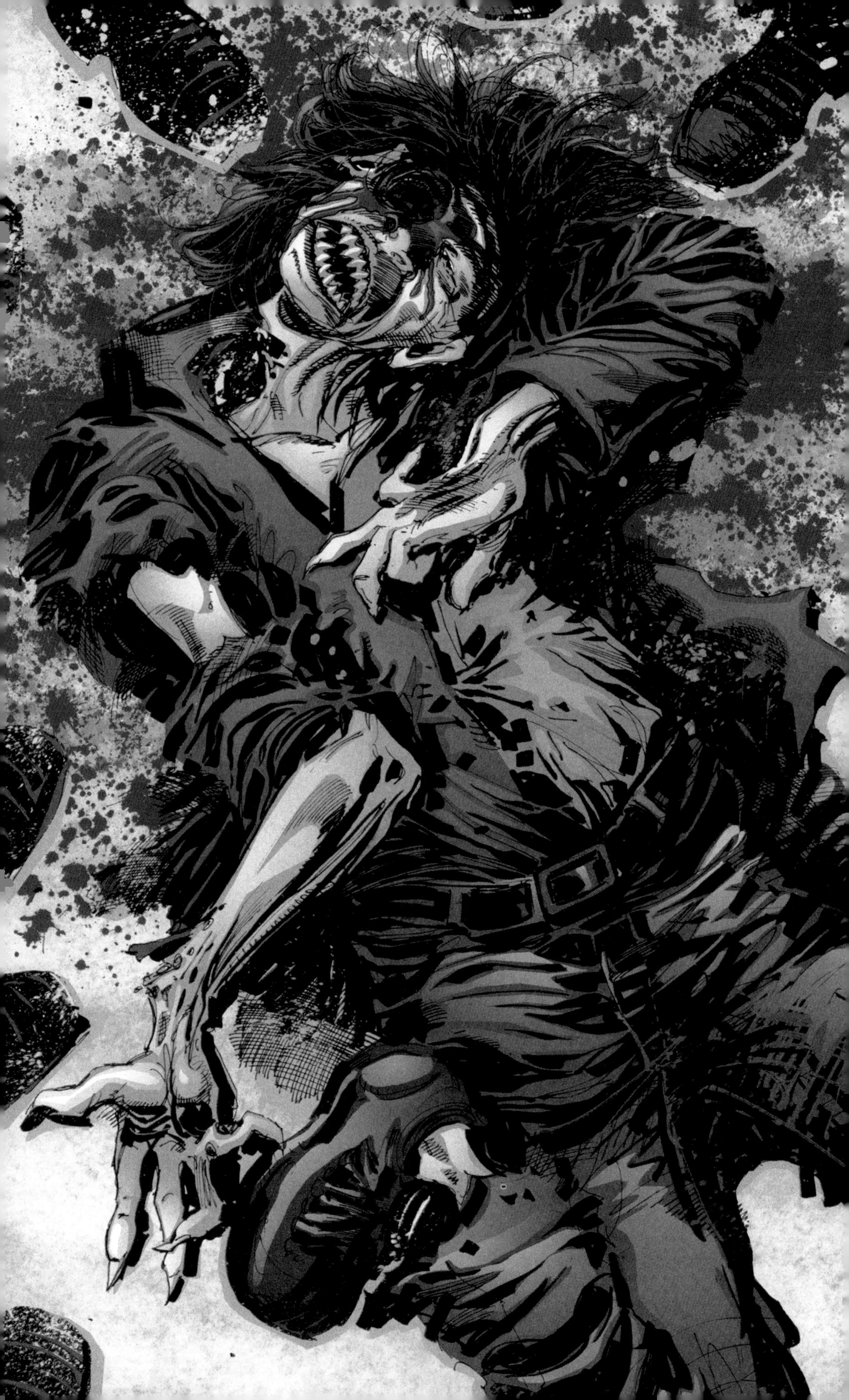

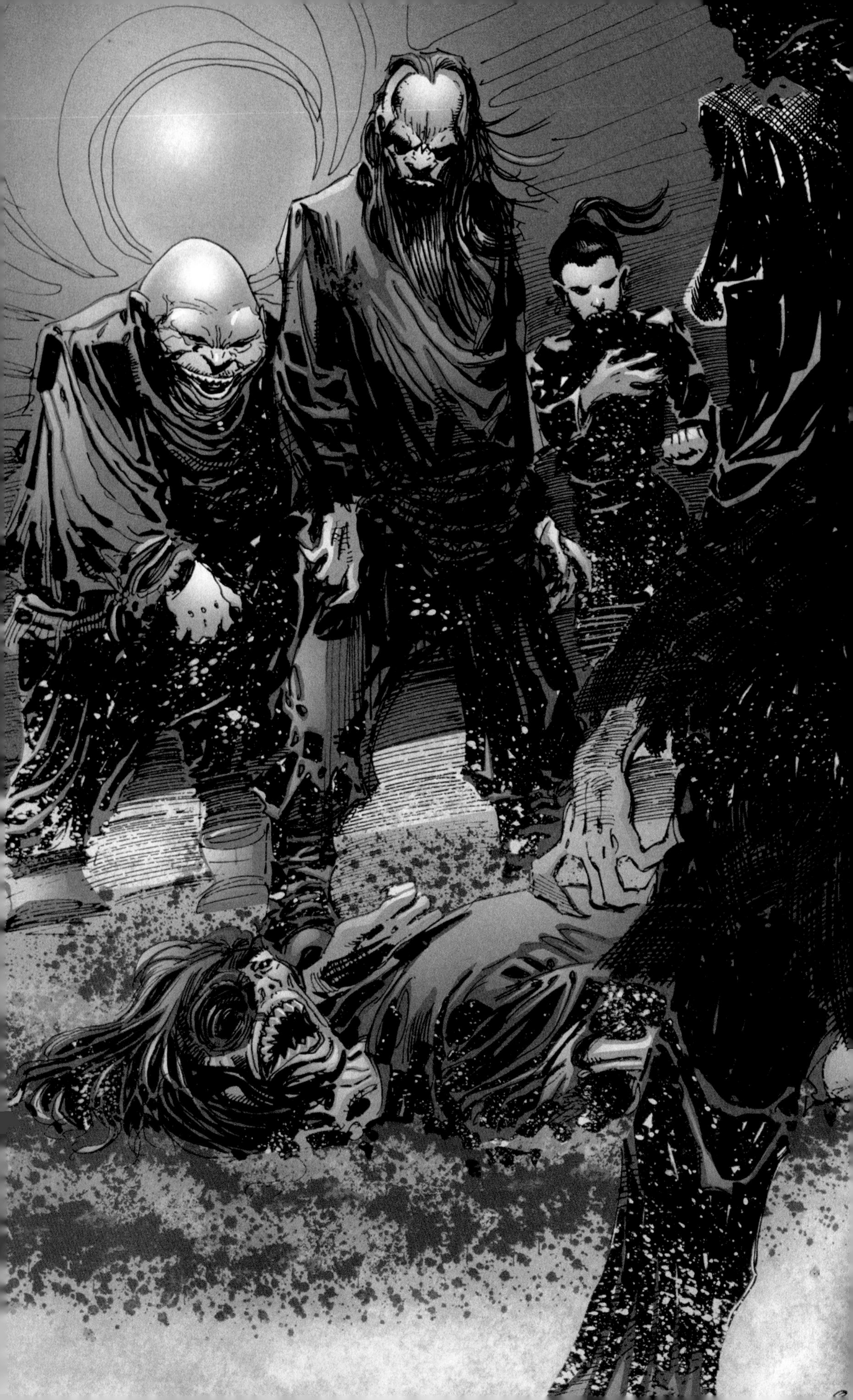

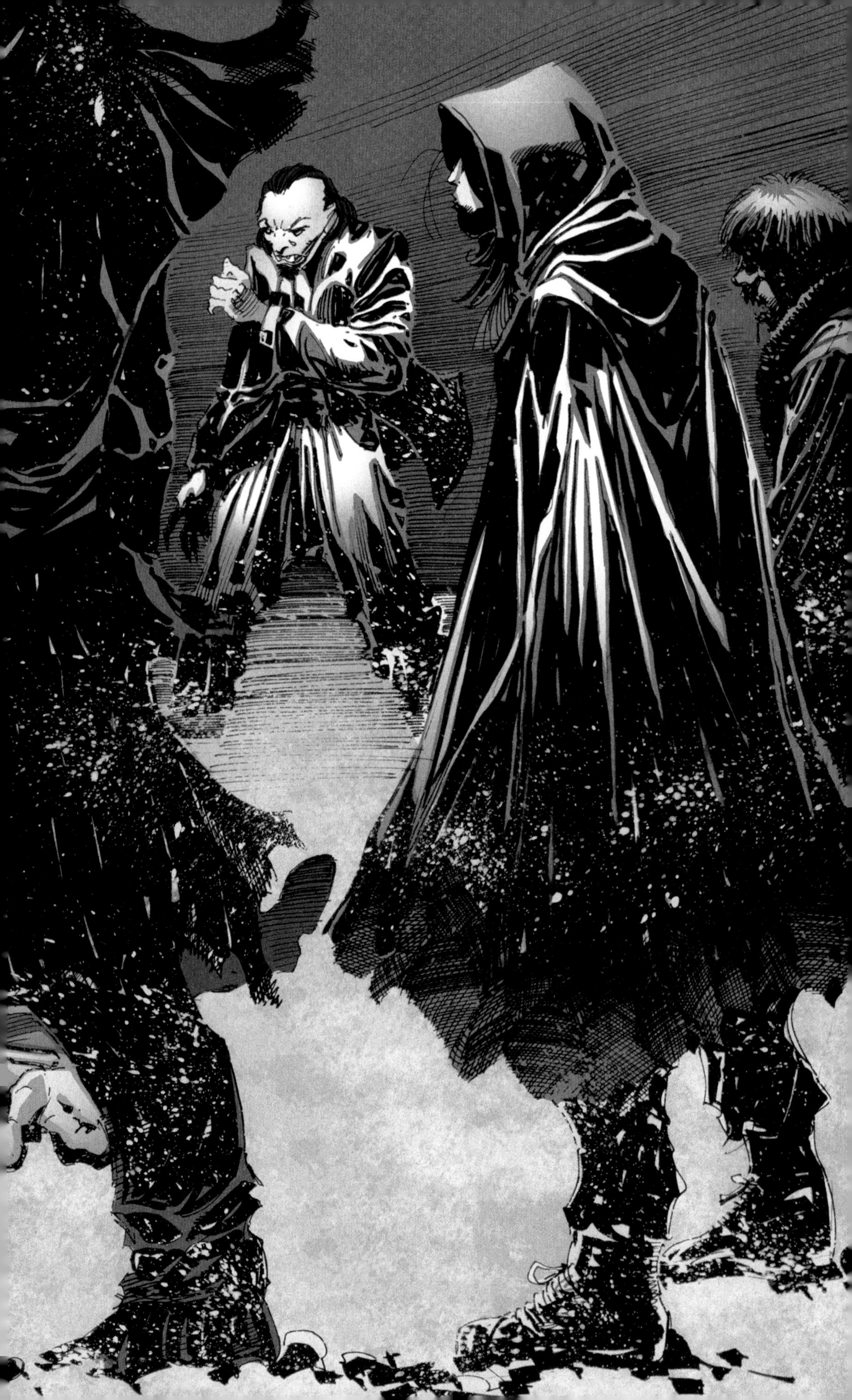

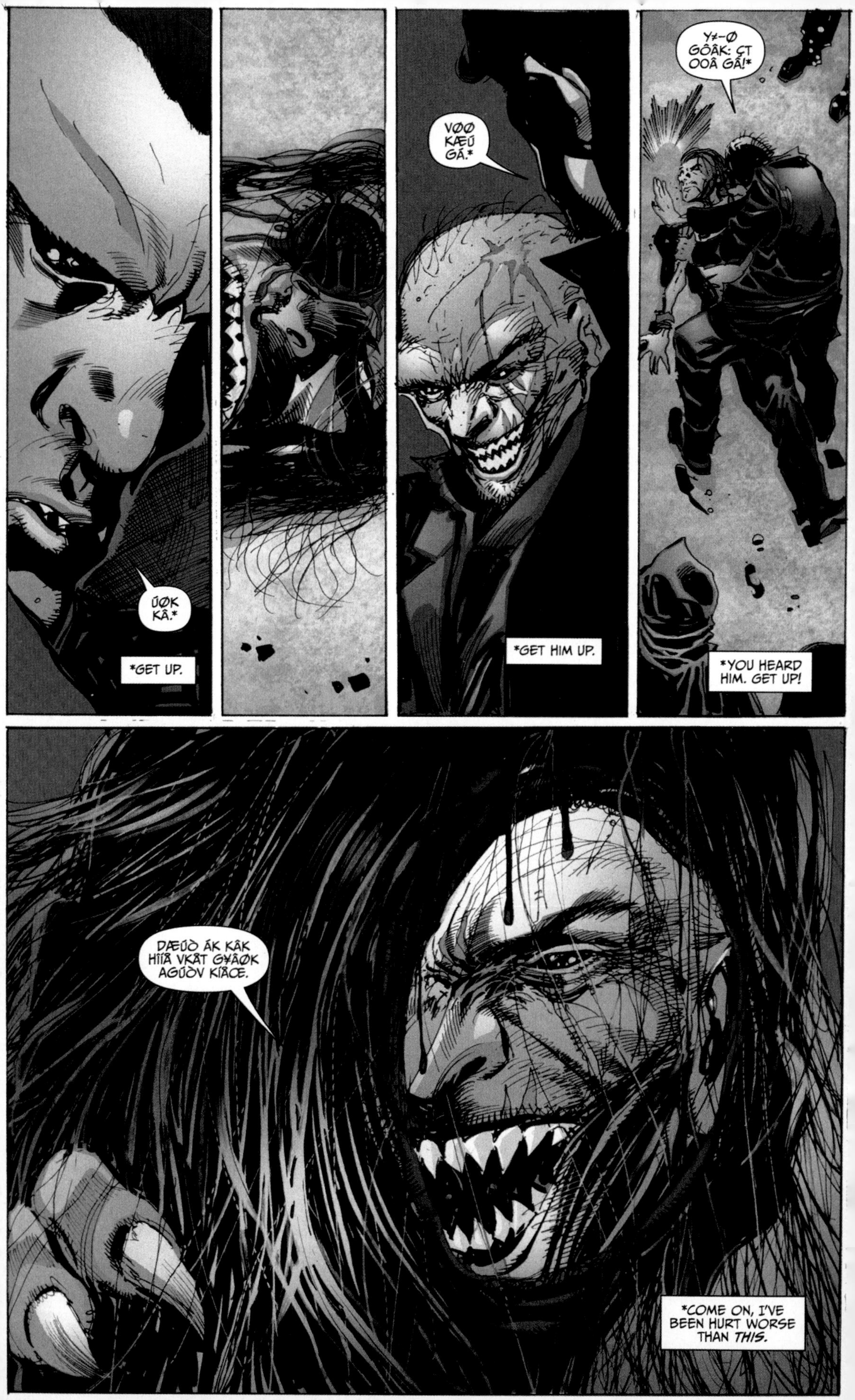
ÚØK KÂ.*
*GET UP.
VØØ KÆÚ GÂ.*
*GET HIM UP.
Y≠–Ø GÔÂK: ÇT OOÂ GÂ!*
*YOU HEARD HIM. GET UP!
DÆÚÒ ÁK KÂK HÌÍÅ VKÂT G¥ÂØK AGÚÒV KÍÅŒ.
*COME ON, I'VE BEEN HURT WORSE THAN *THIS*.

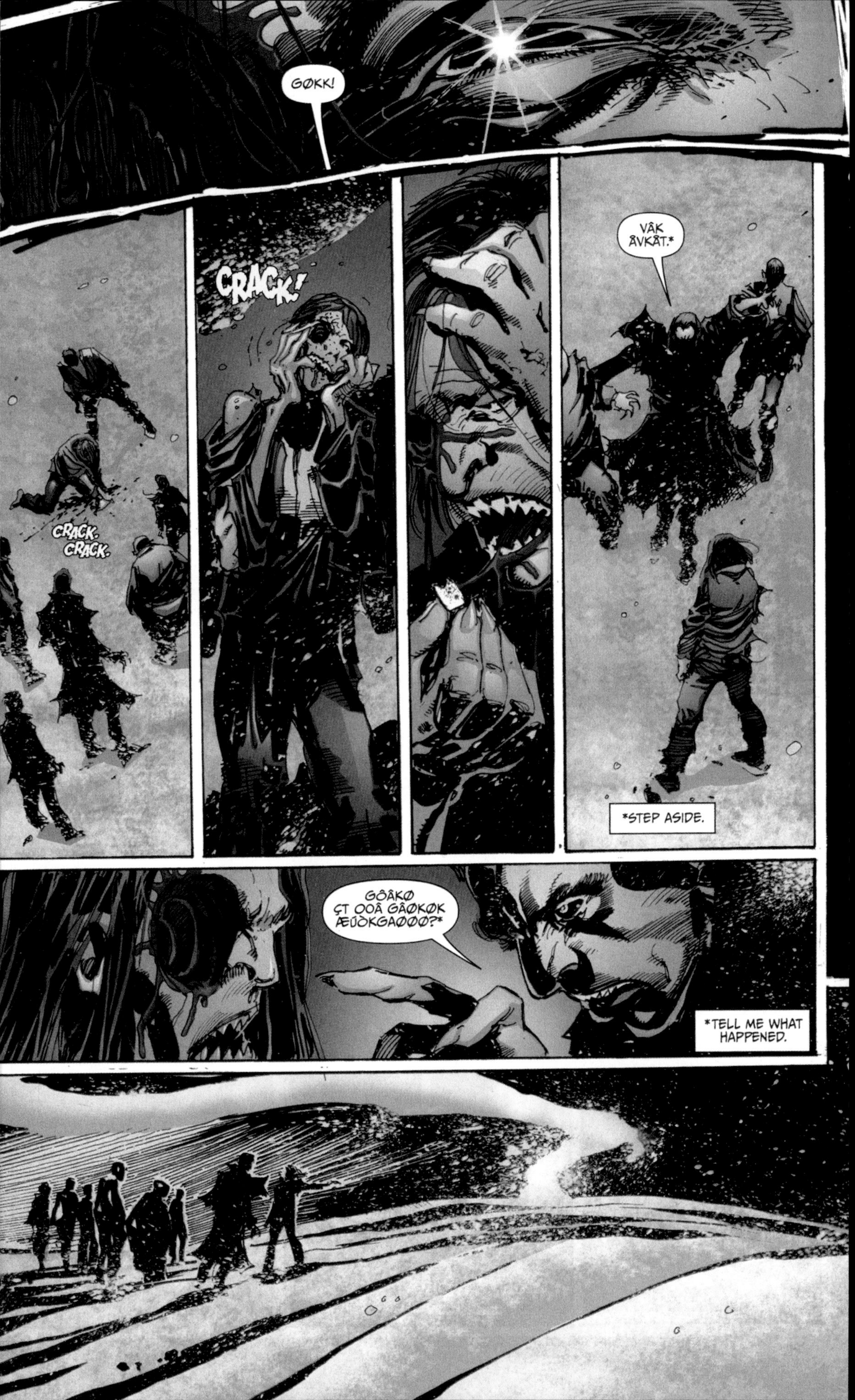
GØKK!
CRACK!
CRACK. CRACK.
VÂK ÅVKÅT.*
*STEP ASIDE.
GÔÂKØ ÇT OOÂ GÂØKØK ÆÚÒKGAØØØ?*
*TELL ME WHAT HAPPENED.

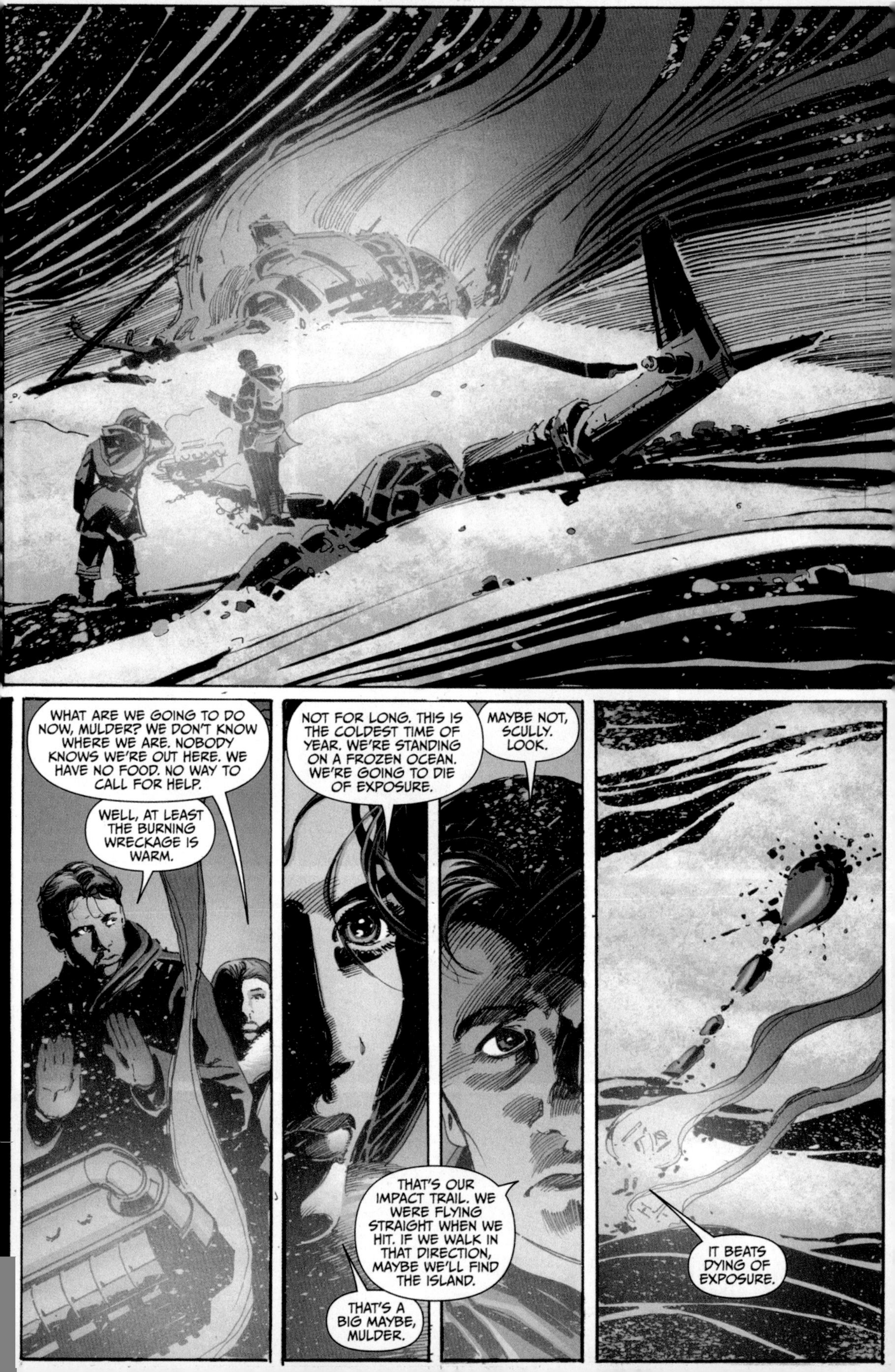
WHAT ARE WE GOING TO DO NOW, MULDER? WE DON'T KNOW WHERE WE ARE. NOBODY KNOWS WE'RE OUT HERE. WE HAVE NO FOOD. NO WAY TO CALL FOR HELP.
WELL, AT LEAST THE BURNING WRECKAGE IS WARM.
NOT FOR LONG. THIS IS THE COLDEST TIME OF YEAR. WE'RE STANDING ON A FROZEN OCEAN. WE'RE GOING TO DIE OF EXPOSURE.
MAYBE NOT, SCULLY. LOOK.
THAT'S OUR IMPACT TRAIL. WE WERE FLYING STRAIGHT WHEN WE HIT. IF WE WALK IN THAT DIRECTION, MAYBE WE'LL FIND THE ISLAND.
THAT'S A BIG MAYBE, MULDER.
IT BEATS DYING OF EXPOSURE.

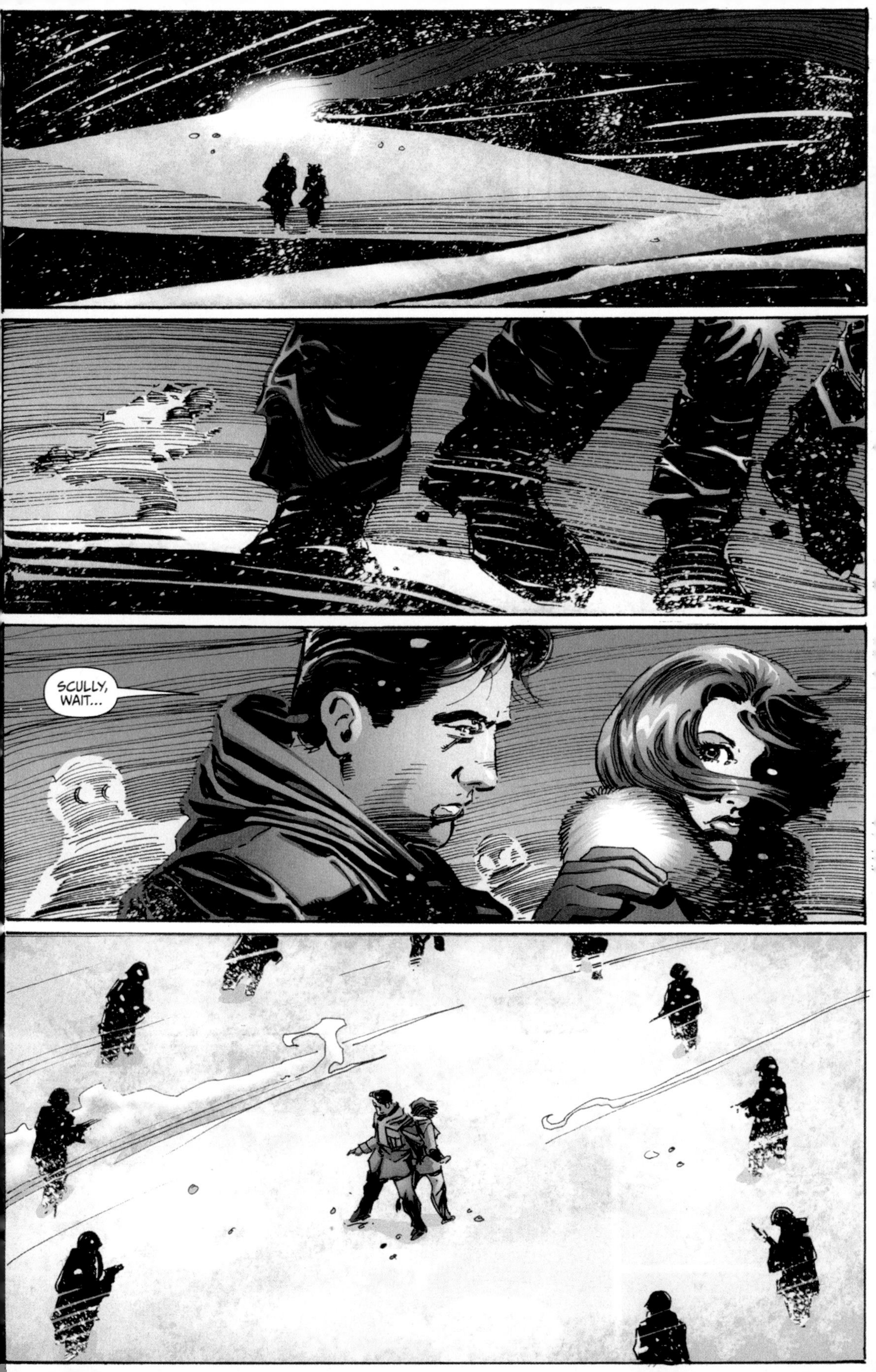
SCULLY, WAIT...

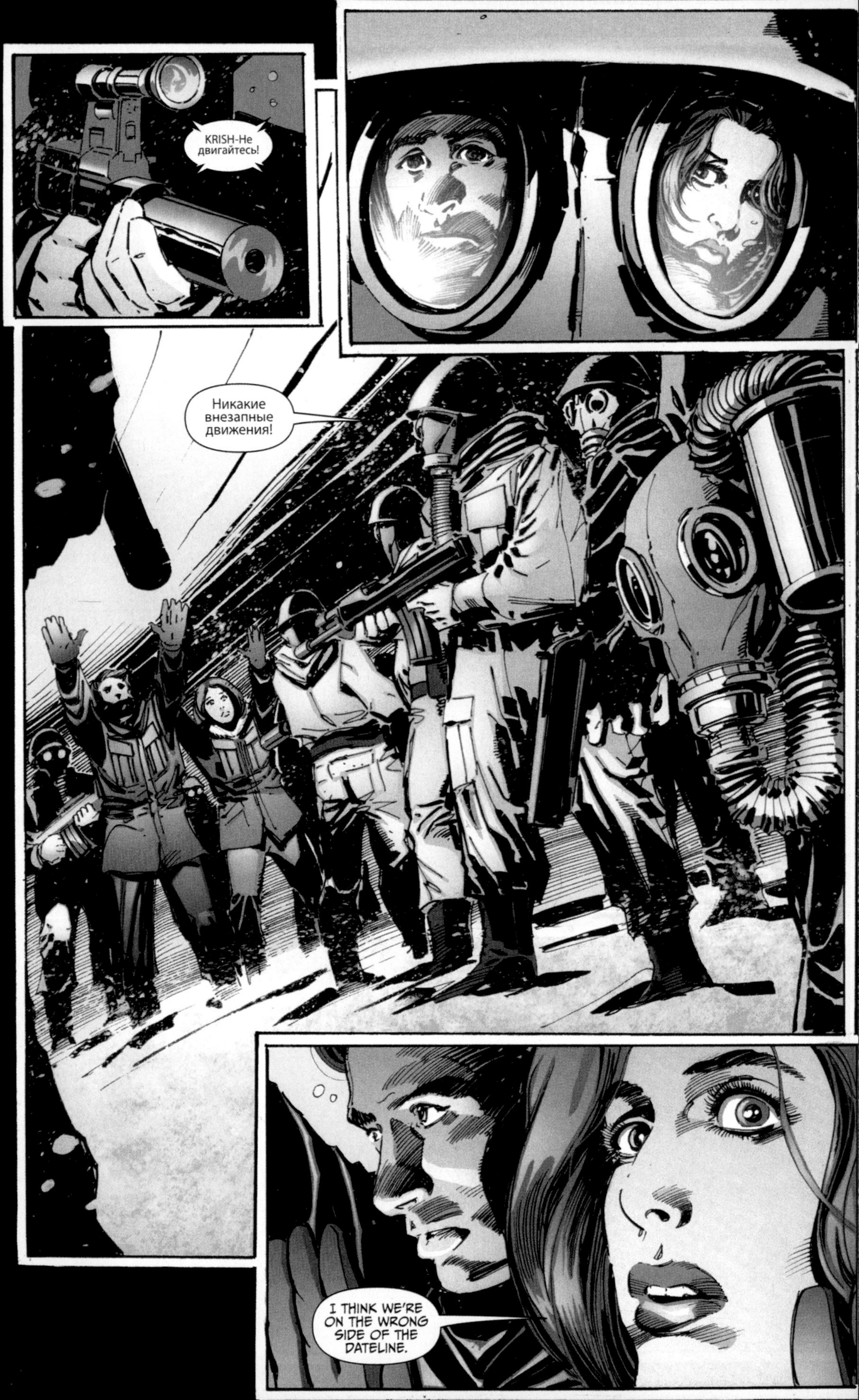
KRISH-Не двигайтесь!
Никакие внезапные движения!
I THINK WE'RE ON THE WRONG SIDE OF THE DATELINE.

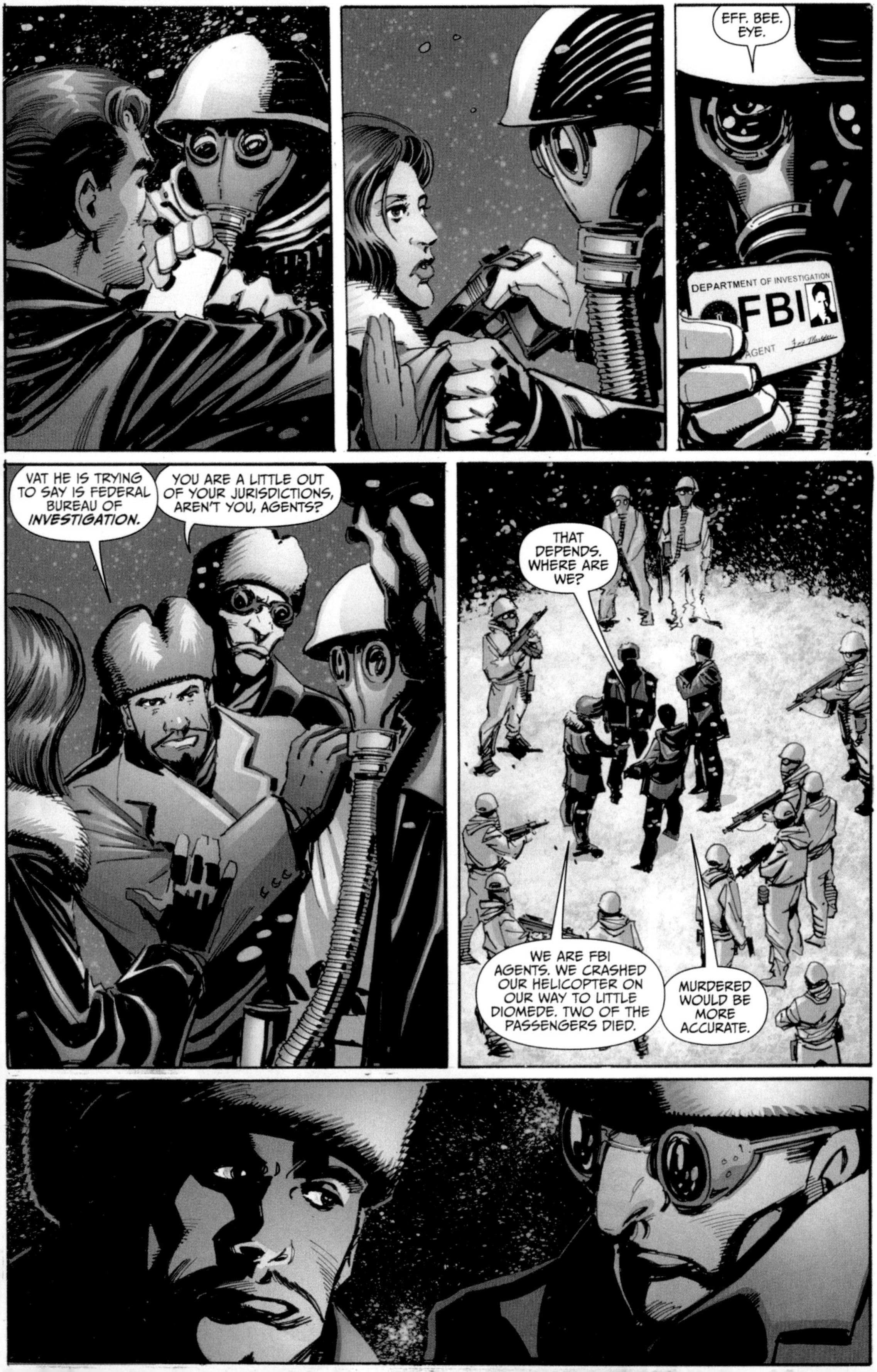
EFF. BEE. EYE.
DEPARTMENT OF INVESTIGATION
FBI
AGENT
VAT HE IS TRYING TO SAY IS FEDERAL BUREAU OF INVESTIGATION.
YOU ARE A LITTLE OUT OF YOUR JURISDICTIONS, AREN'T YOU, AGENTS?
THAT DEPENDS. WHERE ARE WE?
WE ARE FBI AGENTS. WE CRASHED OUR HELICOPTER ON OUR WAY TO LITTLE DIOMEDE. TWO OF THE PASSENGERS DIED.
MURDERED WOULD BE MORE ACCURATE.

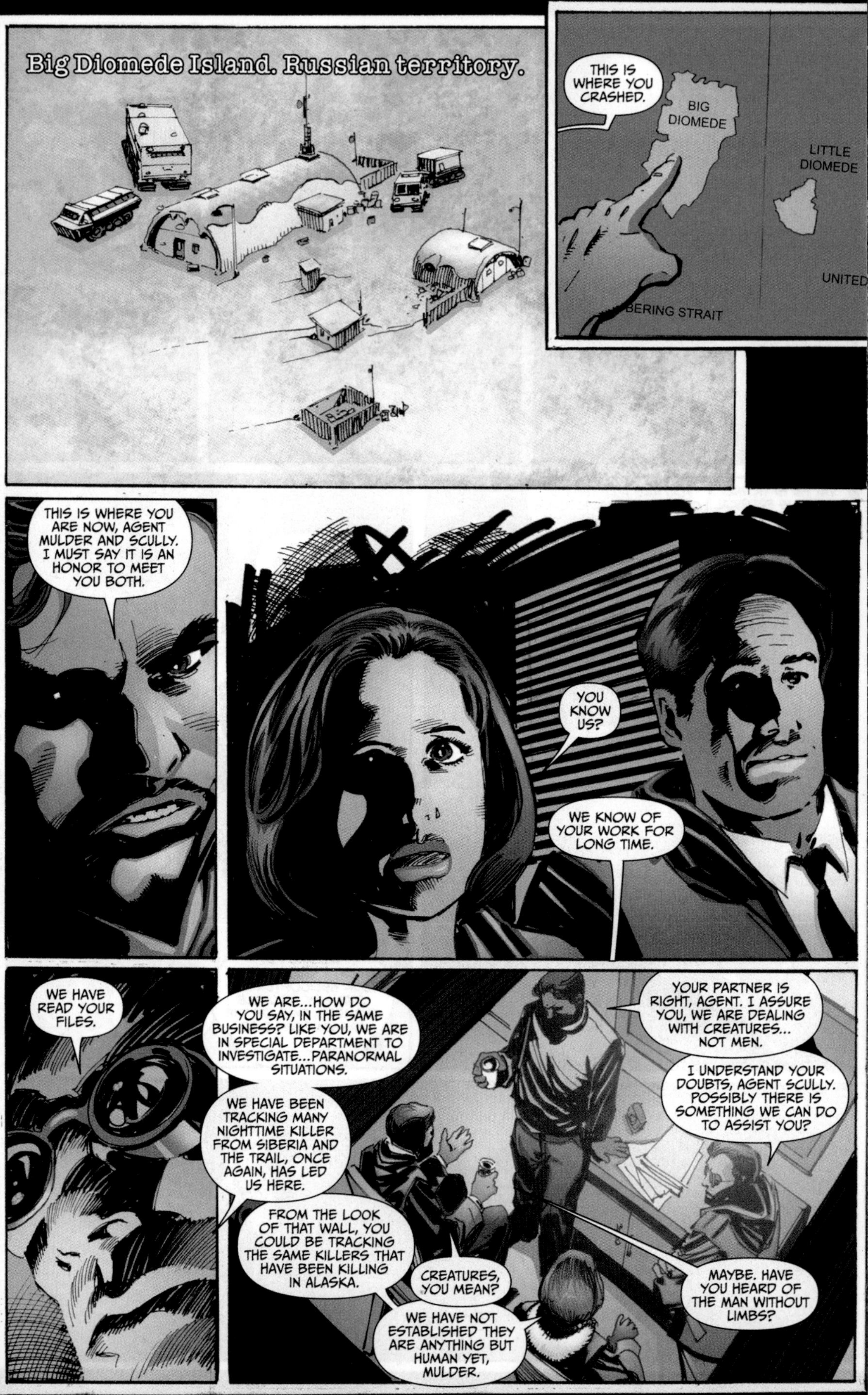
Big Diomede Island. Russian territory.
THIS IS WHERE YOU CRASHED.
BIG DIOMEDE
LITTLE DIOMEDE
UNITED
BERING STRAIT
THIS IS WHERE YOU ARE NOW, AGENT MULDER AND SCULLY. I MUST SAY IT IS AN HONOR TO MEET YOU BOTH.
YOU KNOW US?
WE KNOW OF YOUR WORK FOR LONG TIME.
WE HAVE READ YOUR FILES.
WE ARE...HOW DO YOU SAY, IN THE SAME BUSINESS? LIKE YOU, WE ARE IN SPECIAL DEPARTMENT TO INVESTIGATE...PARANORMAL SITUATIONS.
WE HAVE BEEN TRACKING MANY NIGHTTIME KILLER FROM SIBERIA AND THE TRAIL, ONCE AGAIN, HAS LED US HERE.
FROM THE LOOK OF THAT WALL, YOU COULD BE TRACKING THE SAME KILLERS THAT HAVE BEEN KILLING IN ALASKA.
CREATURES, YOU MEAN?
WE HAVE NOT ESTABLISHED THEY ARE ANYTHING BUT HUMAN YET, MULDER.
YOUR PARTNER IS RIGHT, AGENT. I ASSURE YOU, WE ARE DEALING WITH CREATURES... NOT MEN.
I UNDERSTAND YOUR DOUBTS, AGENT SCULLY. POSSIBLY THERE IS SOMETHING WE CAN DO TO ASSIST YOU?
MAYBE. HAVE YOU HEARD OF THE MAN WITHOUT LIMBS?

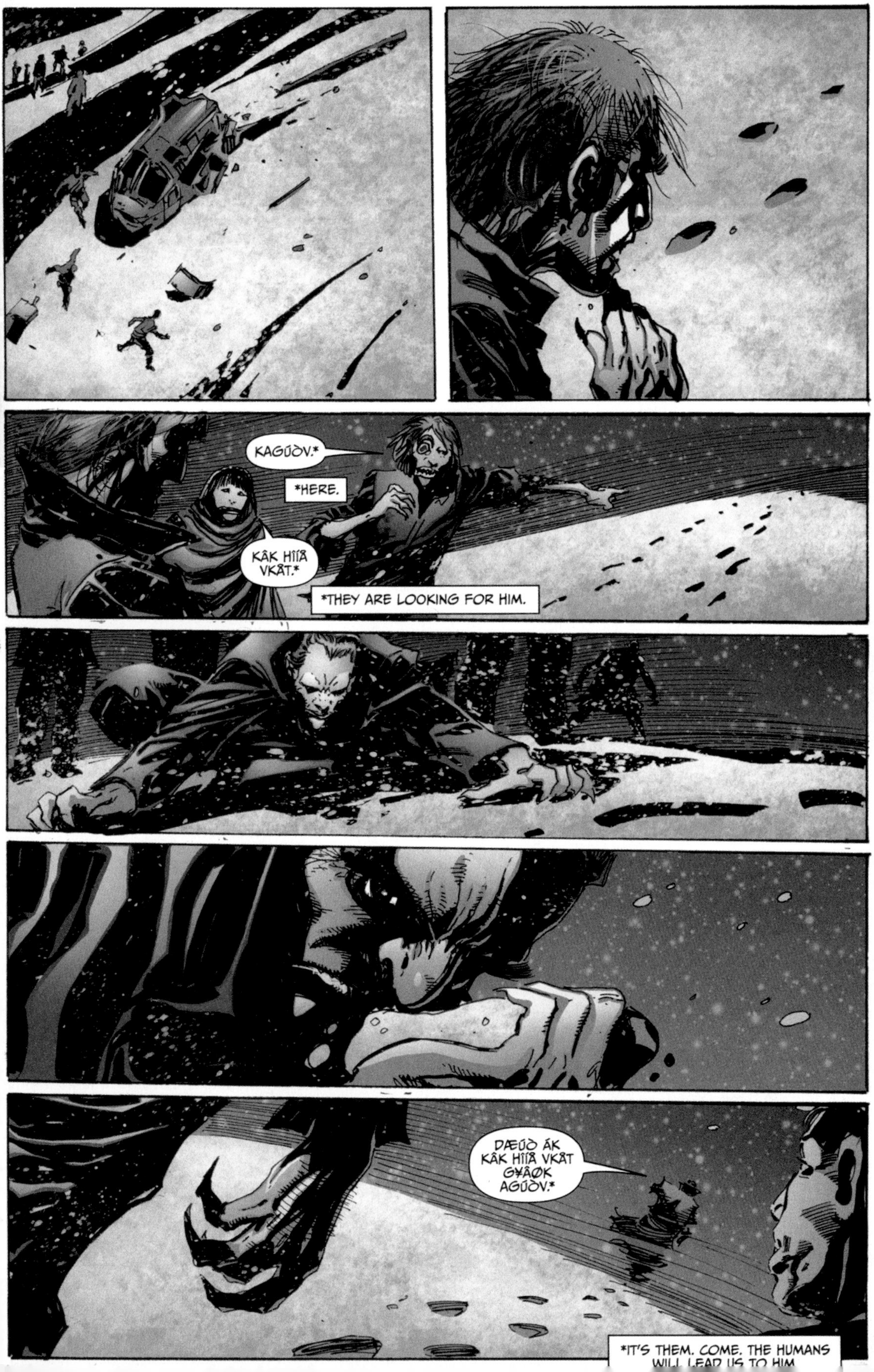
KAGÚÒV.*
*HERE.
KÂK HÎÍĂ VKĂT.*
*THEY ARE LOOKING FOR HIM.
DÆÚÒ ÁK KÂK HÎÍĂ VKĂT G¥ÂØK AGÚÒV.*
*IT'S THEM. COME. THE HUMANS WILL LEAD US TO HIM

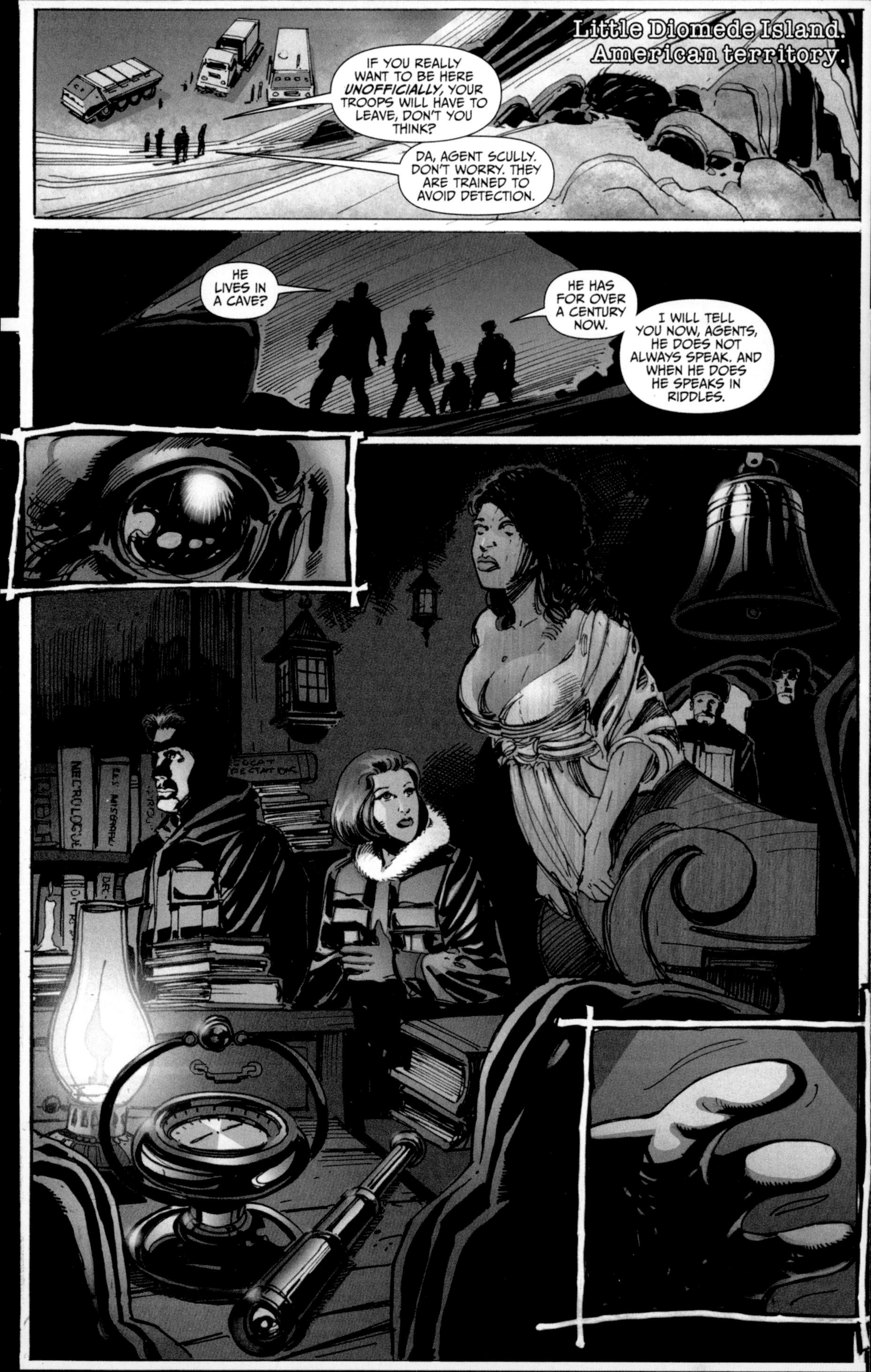
Little Diomede Island.
American territory.
IF YOU REALLY WANT TO BE HERE *UNOFFICIALLY,* YOUR TROOPS WILL HAVE TO LEAVE, DON'T YOU THINK?
DA, AGENT SCULLY. DON'T WORRY. THEY ARE TRAINED TO AVOID DETECTION.
HE LIVES IN A CAVE?
HE HAS FOR OVER A CENTURY NOW.
I WILL TELL YOU NOW, AGENTS, HE DOES NOT ALWAYS SPEAK. AND WHEN HE DOES HE SPEAKS IN RIDDLES.
NECROLOGUE

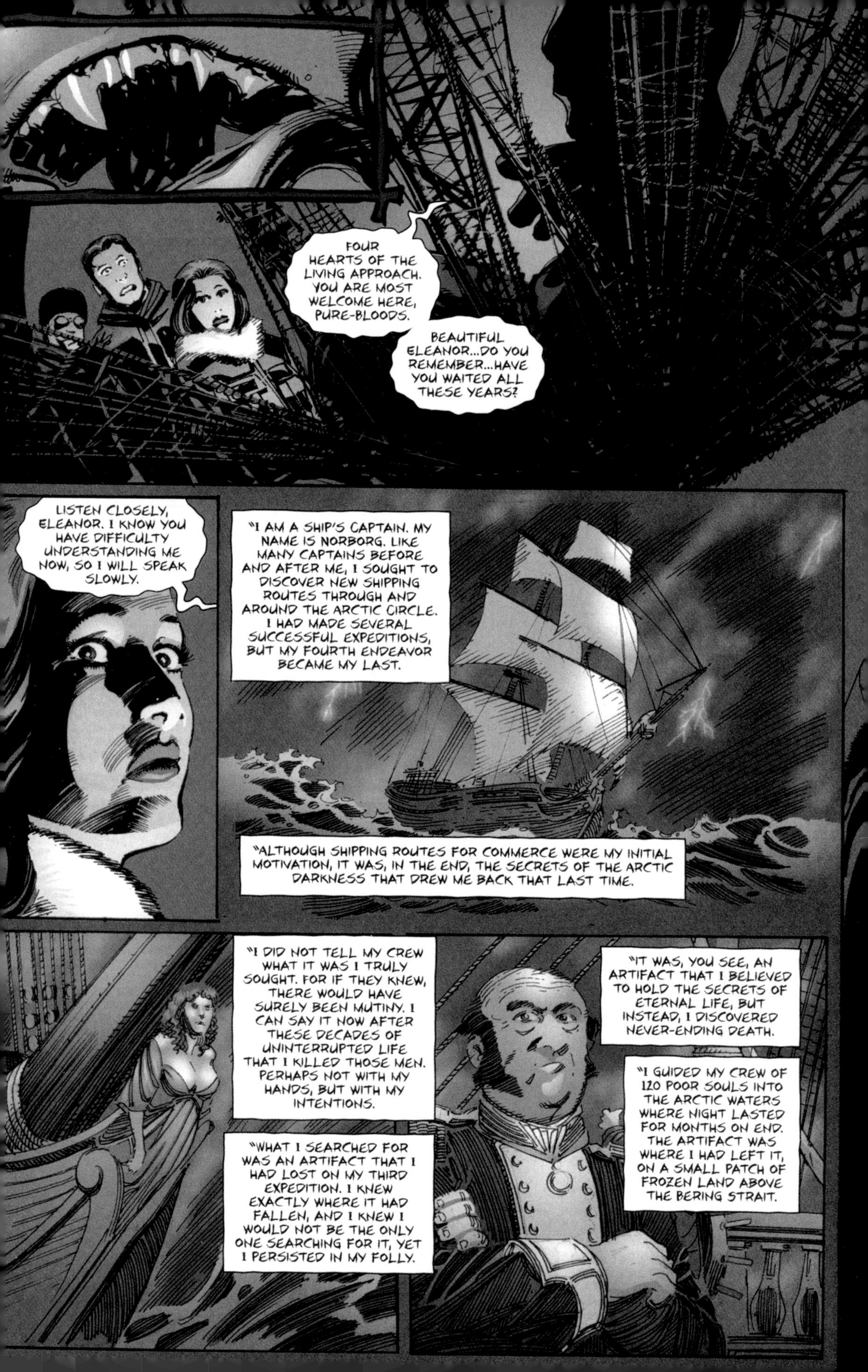
FOUR HEARTS OF THE LIVING APPROACH. YOU ARE MOST WELCOME HERE, PURE-BLOODS.
BEAUTIFUL ELEANOR...DO YOU REMEMBER...HAVE YOU WAITED ALL THESE YEARS?
LISTEN CLOSELY, ELEANOR. I KNOW YOU HAVE DIFFICULTY UNDERSTANDING ME NOW, SO I WILL SPEAK SLOWLY.
"I AM A SHIP'S CAPTAIN. MY NAME IS NORBORG. LIKE MANY CAPTAINS BEFORE AND AFTER ME, I SOUGHT TO DISCOVER NEW SHIPPING ROUTES THROUGH AND AROUND THE ARCTIC CIRCLE. I HAD MADE SEVERAL SUCCESSFUL EXPEDITIONS, BUT MY FOURTH ENDEAVOR BECAME MY LAST.
"ALTHOUGH SHIPPING ROUTES FOR COMMERCE WERE MY INITIAL MOTIVATION, IT WAS, IN THE END, THE SECRETS OF THE ARCTIC DARKNESS THAT DREW ME BACK THAT LAST TIME.
"I DID NOT TELL MY CREW WHAT IT WAS I TRULY SOUGHT. FOR IF THEY KNEW, THERE WOULD HAVE SURELY BEEN MUTINY. I CAN SAY IT NOW AFTER THESE DECADES OF UNINTERRUPTED LIFE THAT I KILLED THOSE MEN. PERHAPS NOT WITH MY HANDS, BUT WITH MY INTENTIONS.
"WHAT I SEARCHED FOR WAS AN ARTIFACT THAT I HAD LOST ON MY THIRD EXPEDITION. I KNEW EXACTLY WHERE IT HAD FALLEN, AND I KNEW I WOULD NOT BE THE ONLY ONE SEARCHING FOR IT, YET I PERSISTED IN MY FOLLY.
"IT WAS, YOU SEE, AN ARTIFACT THAT I BELIEVED TO HOLD THE SECRETS OF ETERNAL LIFE, BUT INSTEAD, I DISCOVERED NEVER-ENDING DEATH.
"I GUIDED MY CREW OF 120 POOR SOULS INTO THE ARCTIC WATERS WHERE NIGHT LASTED FOR MONTHS ON END. THE ARTIFACT WAS WHERE I HAD LEFT IT, ON A SMALL PATCH OF FROZEN LAND ABOVE THE BERING STRAIT.

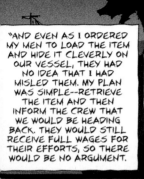

"AND EVEN AS I ORDERED MY MEN TO LOAD THE ITEM AND HIDE IT CLEVERLY ON OUR VESSEL, THEY HAD NO IDEA THAT I HAD MISLED THEM. MY PLAN WAS SIMPLE--RETRIEVE THE ITEM AND THEN INFORM THE CREW THAT WE WOULD BE HEADING BACK. THEY WOULD STILL RECEIVE FULL WAGES FOR THEIR EFFORTS, SO THERE WOULD BE NO ARGUMENT.

"BUT THERE WOULD BE NO RETURN TRIP. AS I STATED, I WAS NOT THE ONLY ONE WHO SOUGHT THE ARTIFACT I NOW HAD HIDDEN ON MY SHIP.

"THEY PICKED OFF MY CREWMEN ONE BY ONE, SOMETIMES IN THE DARKNESS, SOMETIMES IN PLAIN SIGHT TO TERRIFY AND TAUNT ME.

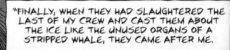

"THESE 'MEN' THAT ATTACKED US WERE NOT MEN AT ALL. THEY MOVED THROUGH THE NIGHT LIKE SHADOWS. NO WEAPON--WHETHER BULLET OR HARPOON-- SO MUCH AS SLOWED THEM DOWN.

"FINALLY, WHEN THEY HAD SLAUGHTERED THE LAST OF MY CREW AND CAST THEM ABOUT THE ICE LIKE THE UNUSED ORGANS OF A STRIPPED WHALE, THEY CAME AFTER ME.

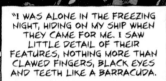

"I WAS ALONE IN THE FREEZING NIGHT, HIDING ON MY SHIP WHEN THEY CAME FOR ME. I SAW LITTLE DETAIL OF THEIR FEATURES, NOTHING MORE THAN CLAWED FINGERS, BLACK EYES AND TEETH LIKE A BARRACUDA.

"THEY SPOKE A LANGUAGE I DID NOT KNOW, BUT I DID NOT NEED A TRANSLATOR TO KNOW WHAT THESE CREATURES WANTED. PERHAPS IT WAS MY SELFISH GREED, OR PERHAPS A SILENT OATH I MADE TO MY DEAD CREW, BUT I REFUSED THEM THE INFORMATION THEY SOUGHT. I WOULD NOT TELL THEM WHAT I HAD DONE WITH THE ARTIFACT.

"THEY BEAT ME MERCILESSLY FOR NIGHTS ON END, AND UPON REALIZING I WOULD NOT SPEAK, I WOULD NOT HAND OVER THE ITEM THEY SO DESPERATELY SOUGHT, THEY PUNISHED ME INSTEAD.

"THEY TORE MY LEGS FROM THE SOCKET AND WHEN I SCREAMED THEY DID THE SAME TO MY ARMS. THEY WATCHED ME BLEED UNTIL THE ICE WAS BLACK BENEATH MY PAIN-WRACKED BODY. AND WHEN MY HEART STARTED TO SLOW IN MY CHEST AND MY VISION BEGAN TO FADE, THESE DARK CREATURES STOOD AROUND ME AND SPIT INTO MY OPEN WOUNDS.

"IT WAS A CURSE THEY SPAT UPON ME. FOR AS I HAD FELT LIFE BEGIN TO LEAVE MY LIMBLESS TORSO, ONCE THEIR SALIVA STRUCK ME, MY HEART GAINED STRENGTH AND MY EYES REGAINED FOCUS.

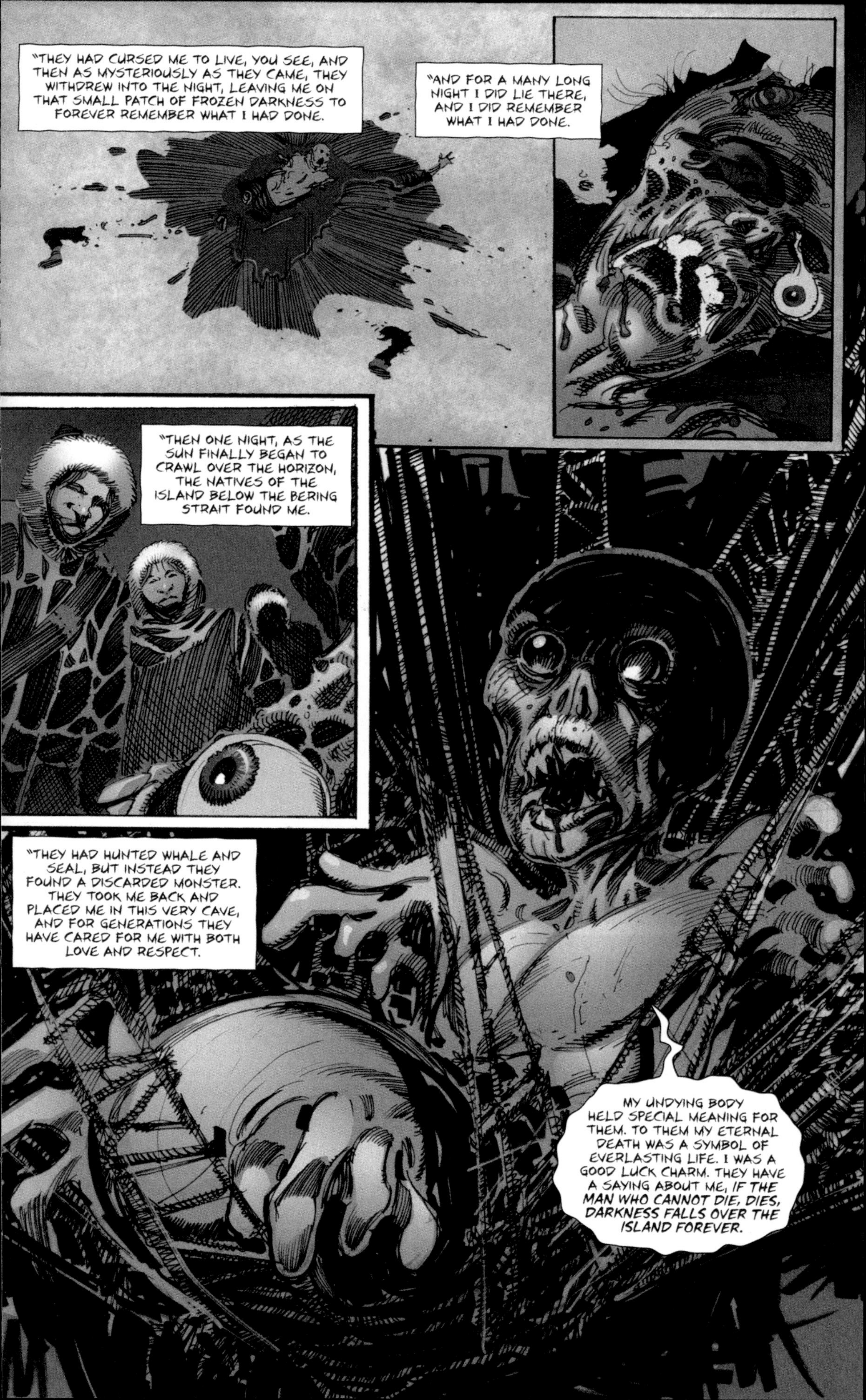
"THEY HAD CURSED ME TO LIVE, YOU SEE, AND THEN AS MYSTERIOUSLY AS THEY CAME, THEY WITHDREW INTO THE NIGHT, LEAVING ME ON THAT SMALL PATCH OF FROZEN DARKNESS TO FOREVER REMEMBER WHAT I HAD DONE.
"AND FOR A MANY LONG NIGHT I DID LIE THERE, AND I DID REMEMBER WHAT I HAD DONE.
"THEN ONE NIGHT, AS THE SUN FINALLY BEGAN TO CRAWL OVER THE HORIZON, THE NATIVES OF THE ISLAND BELOW THE BERING STRAIT FOUND ME.
"THEY HAD HUNTED WHALE AND SEAL, BUT INSTEAD THEY FOUND A DISCARDED MONSTER. THEY TOOK ME BACK AND PLACED ME IN THIS VERY CAVE, AND FOR GENERATIONS THEY HAVE CARED FOR ME WITH BOTH LOVE AND RESPECT.
MY UNDYING BODY HELD SPECIAL MEANING FOR THEM. TO THEM MY ETERNAL DEATH WAS A SYMBOL OF EVERLASTING LIFE. I WAS A GOOD LUCK CHARM. THEY HAVE A SAYING ABOUT ME, *IF THE MAN WHO CANNOT DIE, DIES, DARKNESS FALLS OVER THE ISLAND FOREVER.*

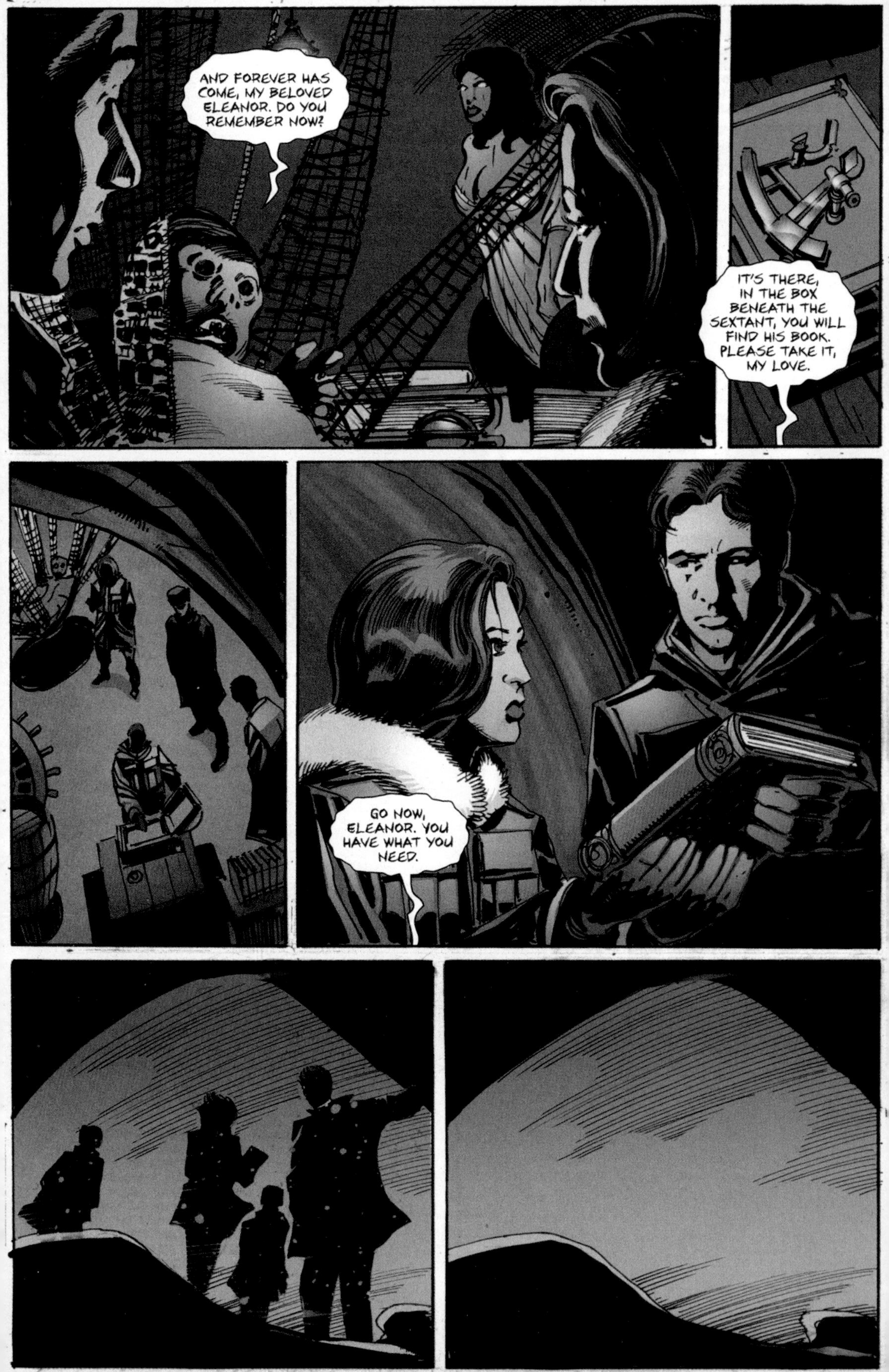
AND FOREVER HAS COME, MY BELOVED ELEANOR. DO YOU REMEMBER NOW?
IT'S THERE, IN THE BOX BENEATH THE SEXTANT, YOU WILL FIND HIS BOOK. PLEASE TAKE IT, MY LOVE.
GO NOW, ELEANOR. YOU HAVE WHAT YOU NEED.

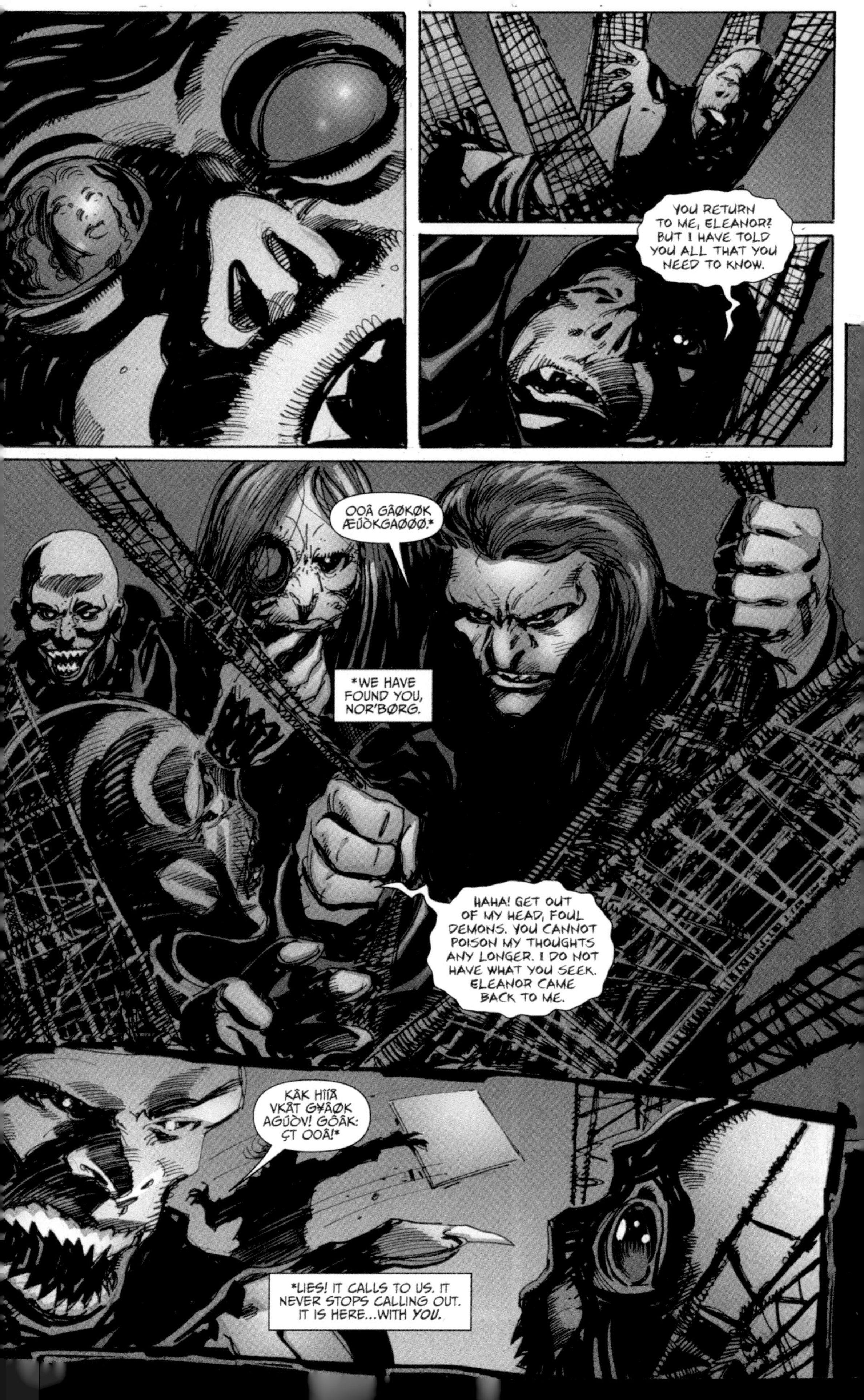
YOU RETURN TO ME, ELEANOR? BUT I HAVE TOLD YOU ALL THAT YOU NEED TO KNOW.
OOÂ GÂØKØK ÆÚÒKGAØØØ.*
*WE HAVE FOUND YOU, NOR'BØRG.
HAHA! GET OUT OF MY HEAD, FOUL DEMONS. YOU CANNOT POISON MY THOUGHTS ANY LONGER. I DO NOT HAVE WHAT YOU SEEK. ELEANOR CAME BACK TO ME.
KÂK HÎÍÂ VKÂT G¥ÂØK AGÚÒV! GÔÂK: ÇT OOÂ!*
*LIES! IT CALLS TO US. IT NEVER STOPS CALLING OUT. IT IS HERE...WITH *YOU*.

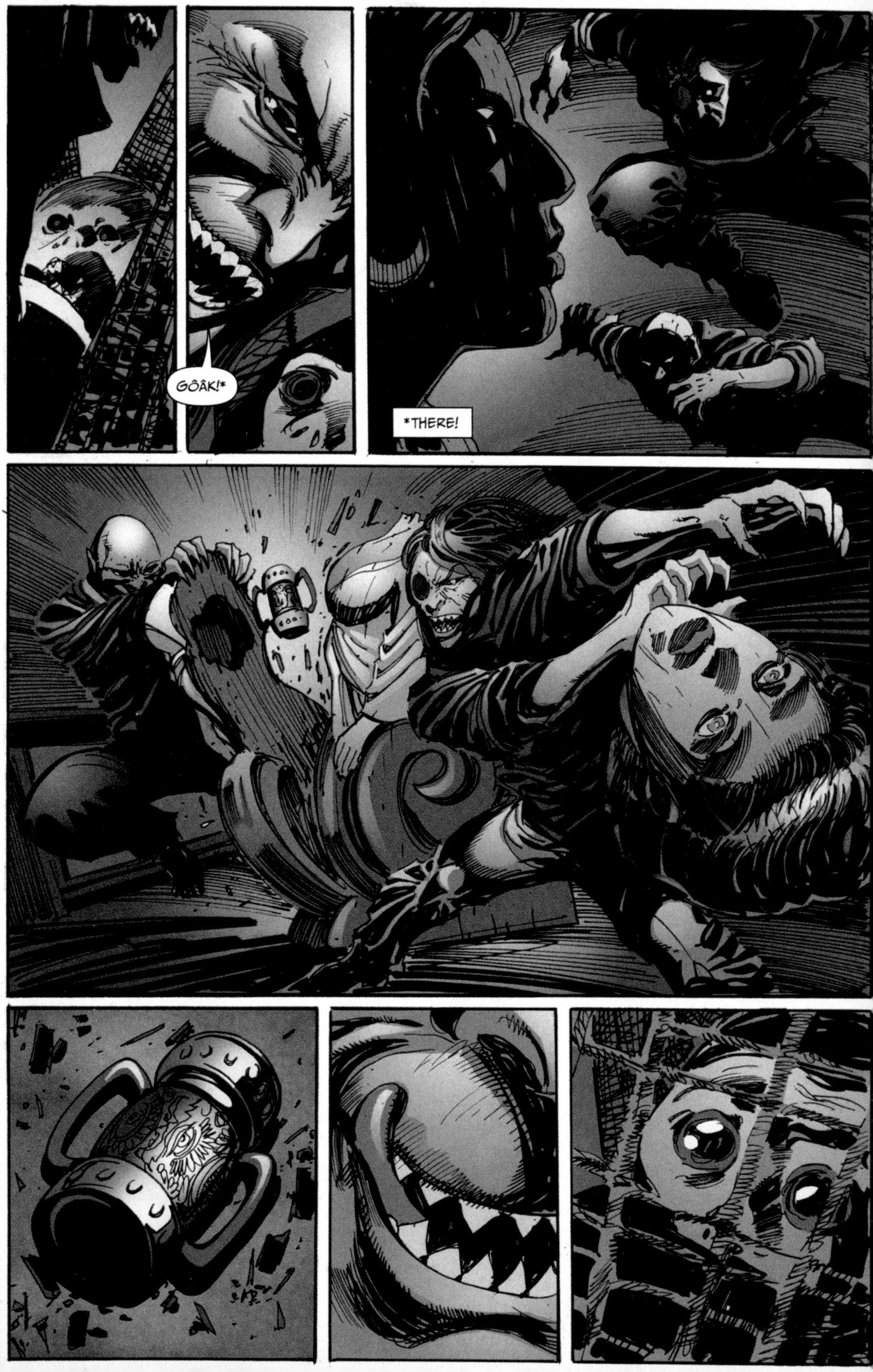
GÔÂK!*
*THERE!

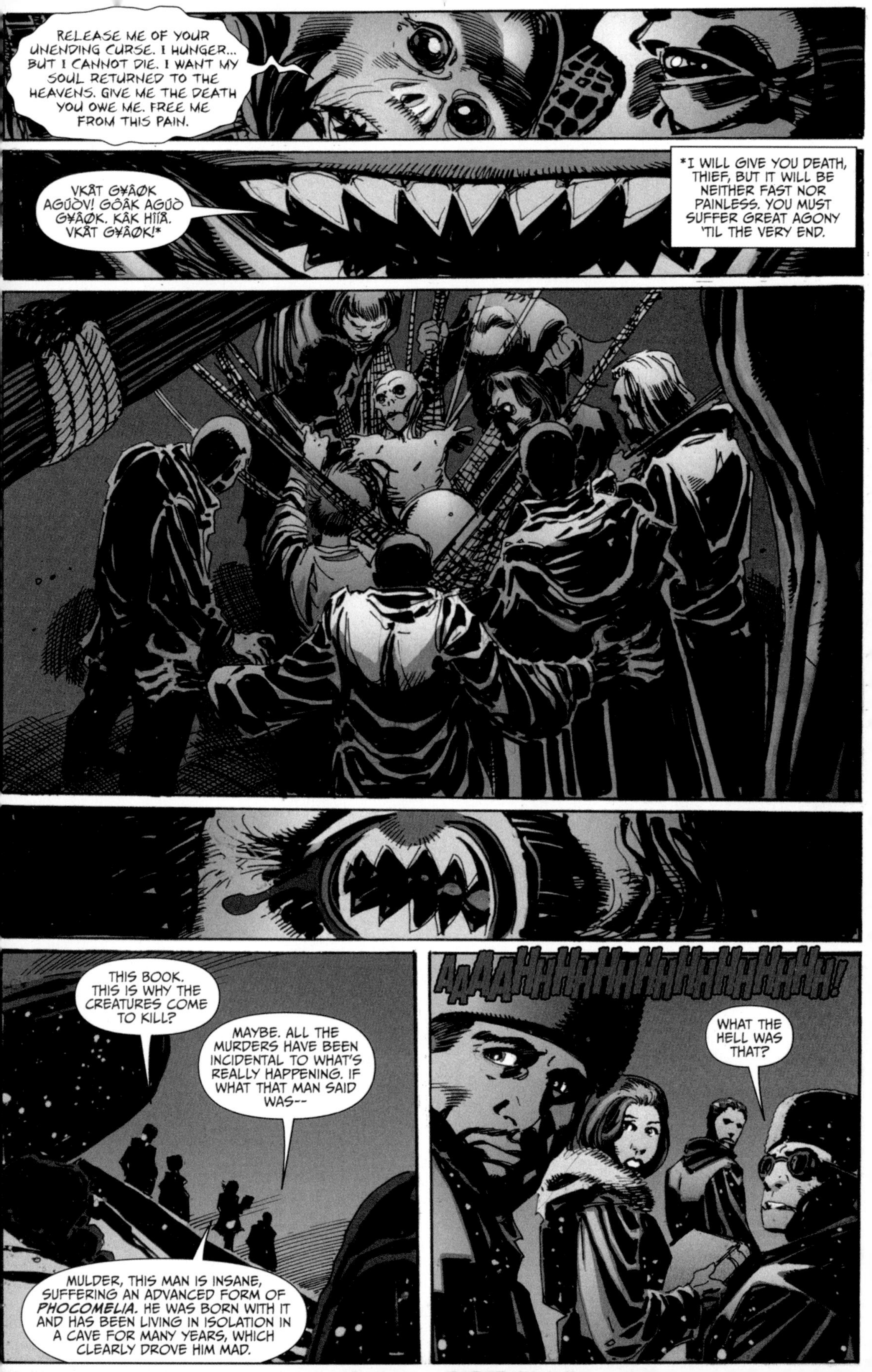

RELEASE ME OF YOUR UNENDING CURSE. I HUNGER... BUT I CANNOT DIE. I WANT MY SOUL RETURNED TO THE HEAVENS. GIVE ME THE DEATH YOU OWE ME. FREE ME FROM THIS PAIN.
VKĂT G¥ÂØK AGÚÒV! GÔÂK AGÚÒ G¥ÂØK. KÂK HÎÎÂ. VKĂT G¥ÂØK!*
*I WILL GIVE YOU DEATH, THIEF, BUT IT WILL BE NEITHER FAST NOR PAINLESS. YOU MUST SUFFER GREAT AGONY 'TIL THE VERY END.
THIS BOOK. THIS IS WHY THE CREATURES COME TO KILL?
MAYBE. ALL THE MURDERS HAVE BEEN INCIDENTAL TO WHAT'S REALLY HAPPENING. IF WHAT THAT MAN SAID WAS--
MULDER, THIS MAN IS INSANE, SUFFERING AN ADVANCED FORM OF PHOCOMELIA. HE WAS BORN WITH IT AND HAS BEEN LIVING IN ISOLATION IN A CAVE FOR MANY YEARS, WHICH CLEARLY DROVE HIM MAD.
AAAAHHHHHHHHHHHHHHHHHHHHH!
WHAT THE HELL WAS THAT?

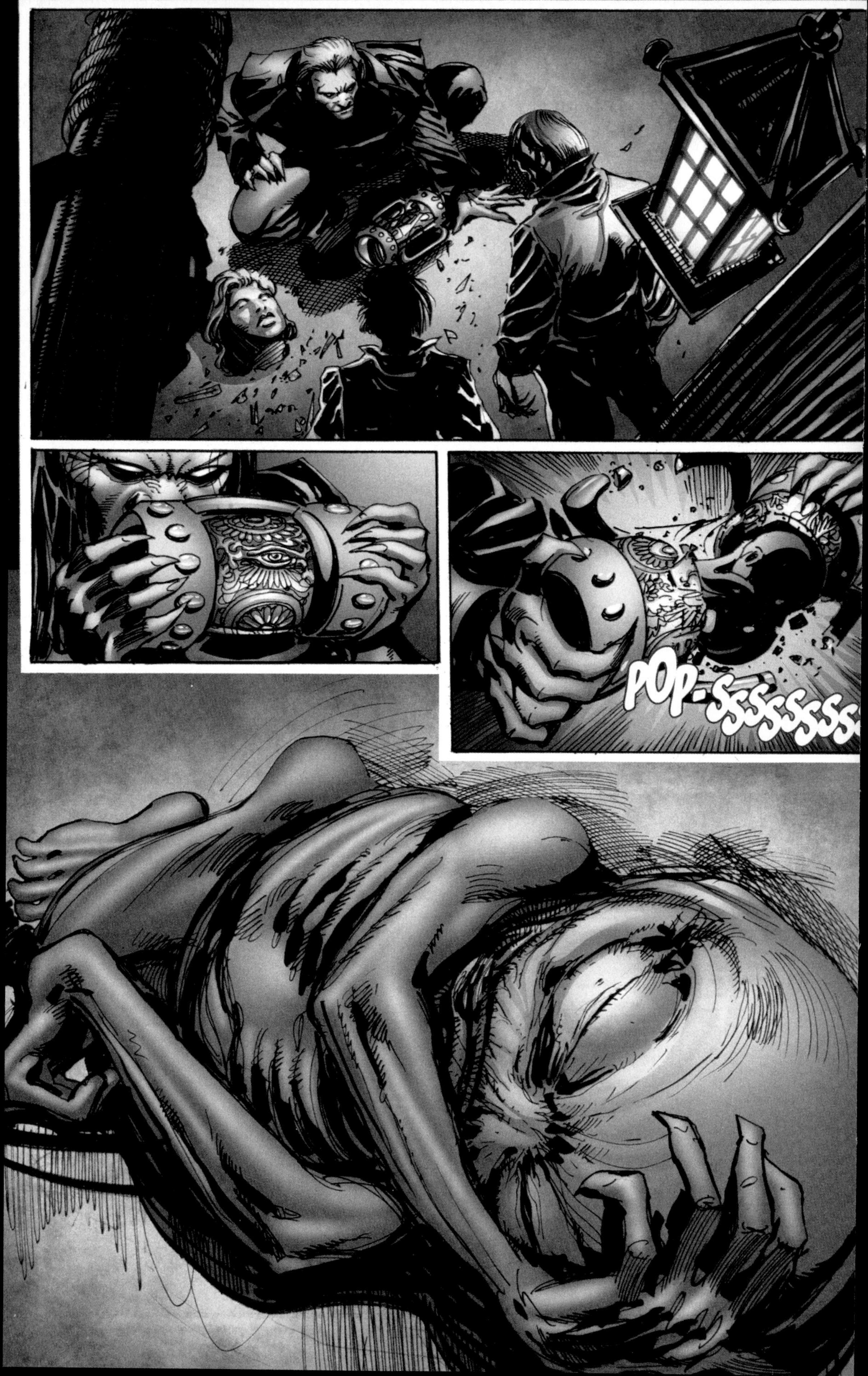
POP-SSSSSSSS

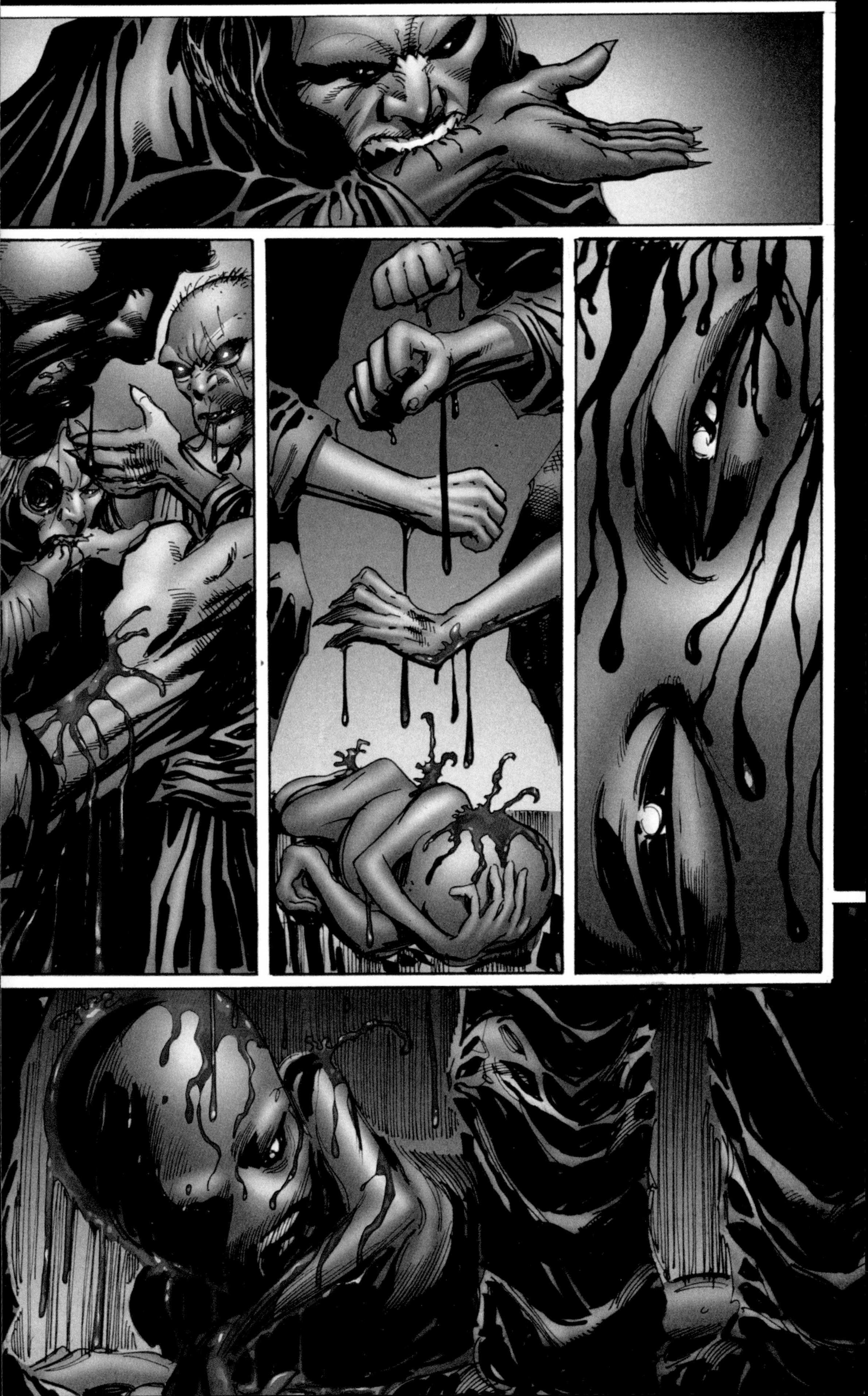

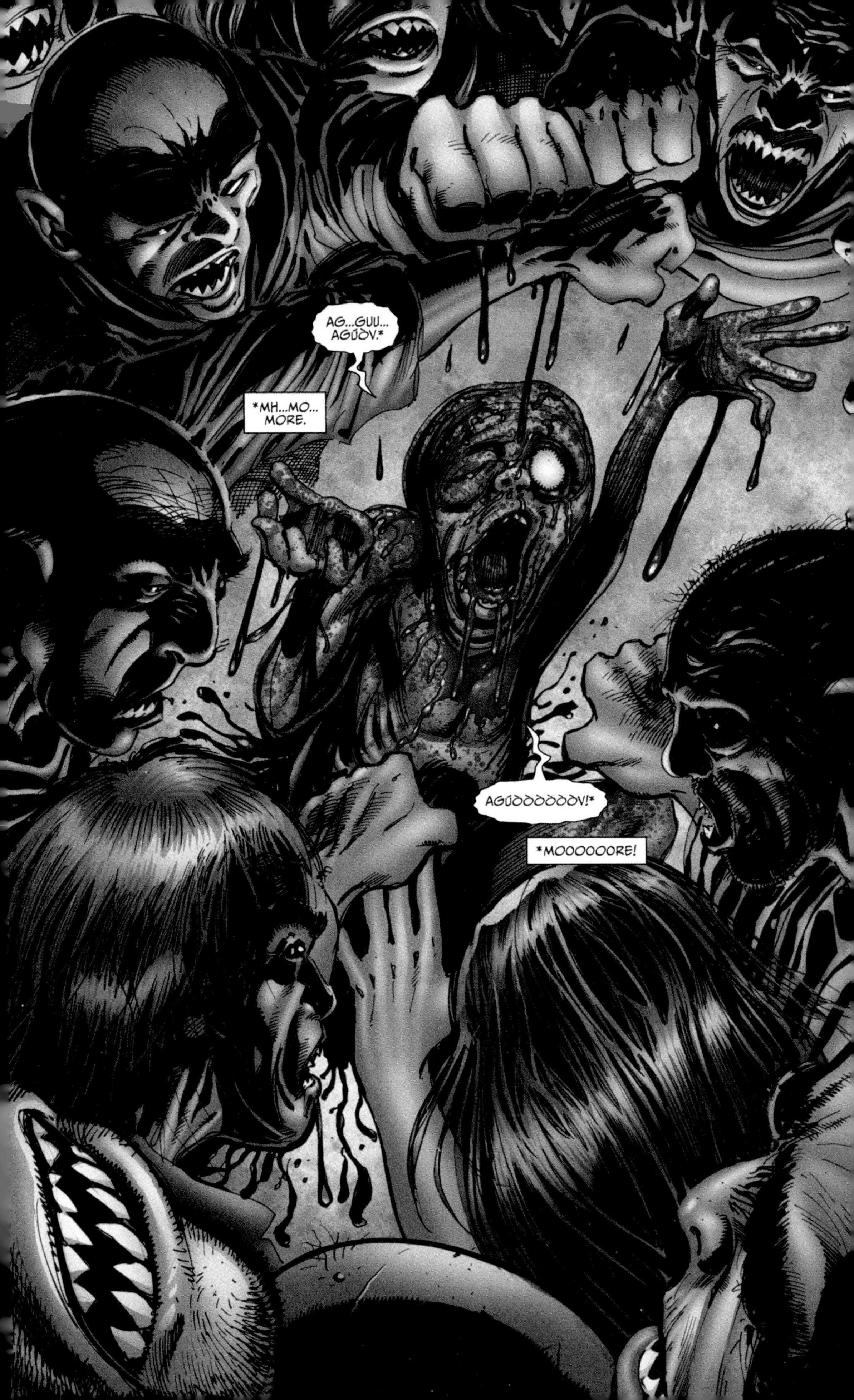
AG...GUU...
AGÚÒV.*
*MH...MO...
MORE.
AGÚÒÒÒÒÒÒV!*
*MOOOOOORE!

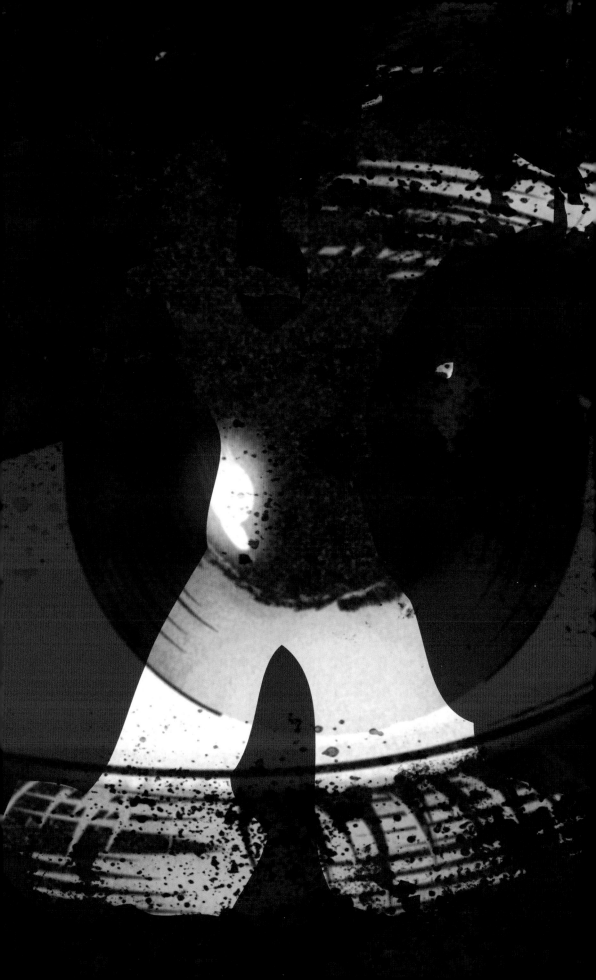

art by: Andrea Sorrentino

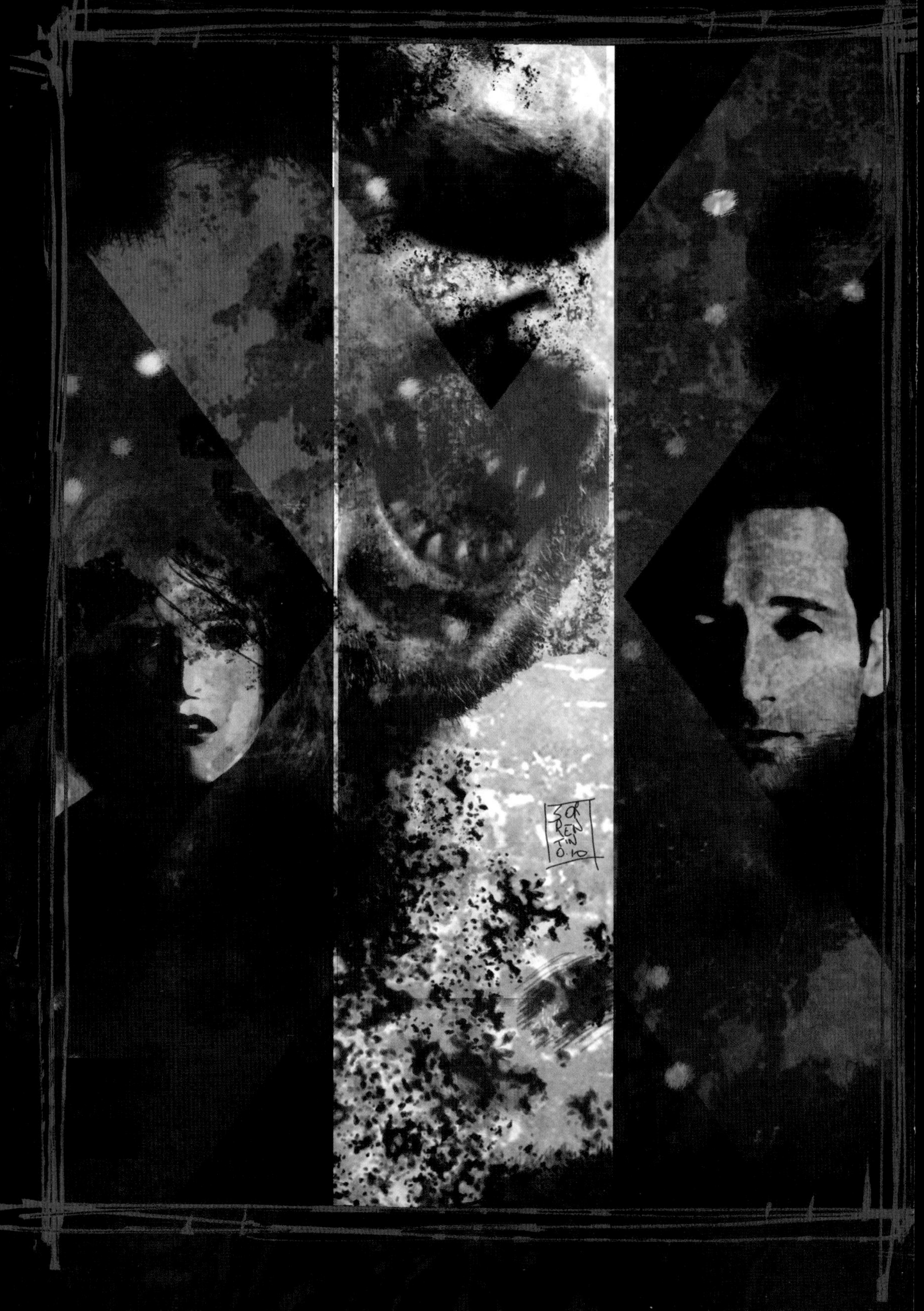

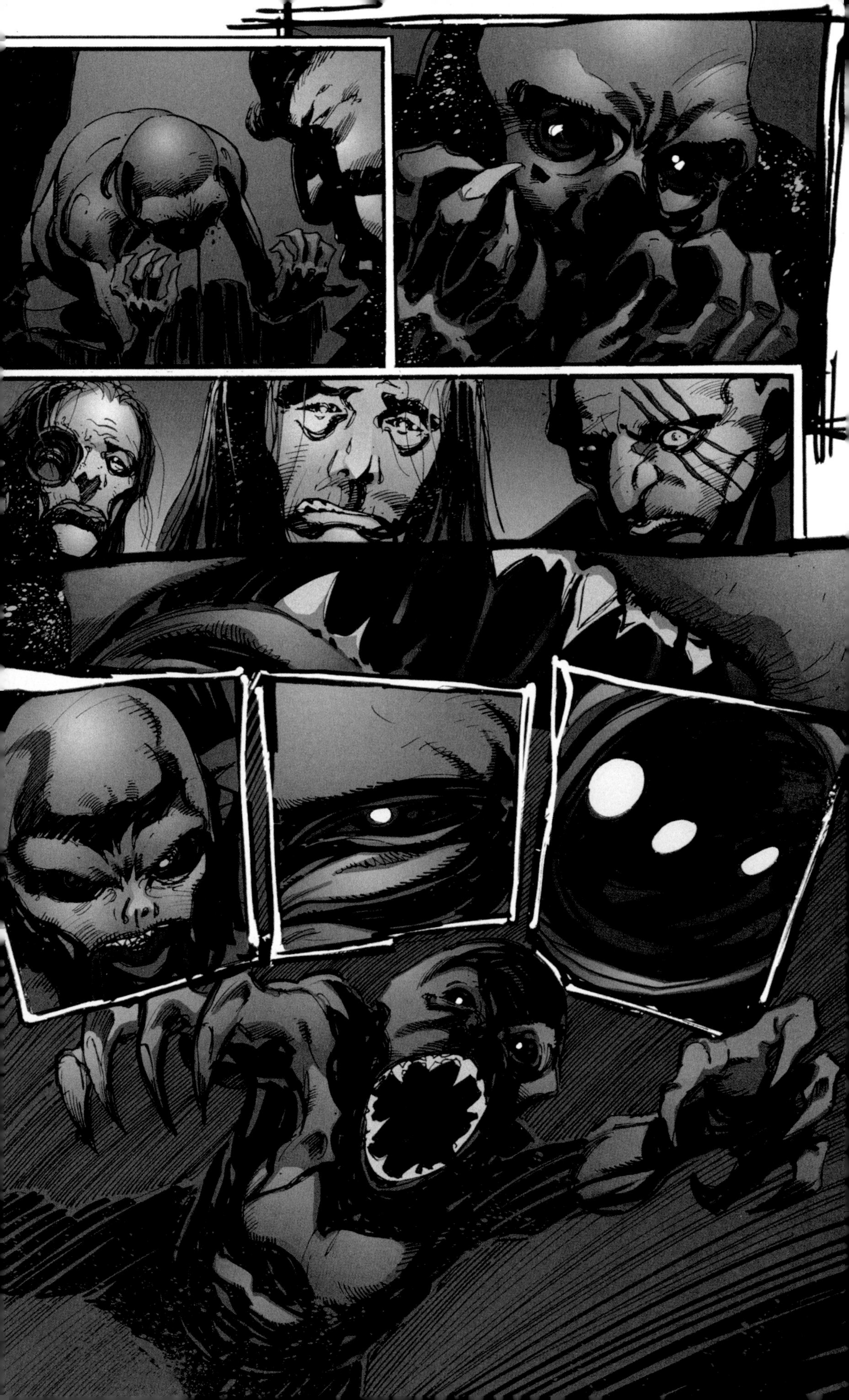

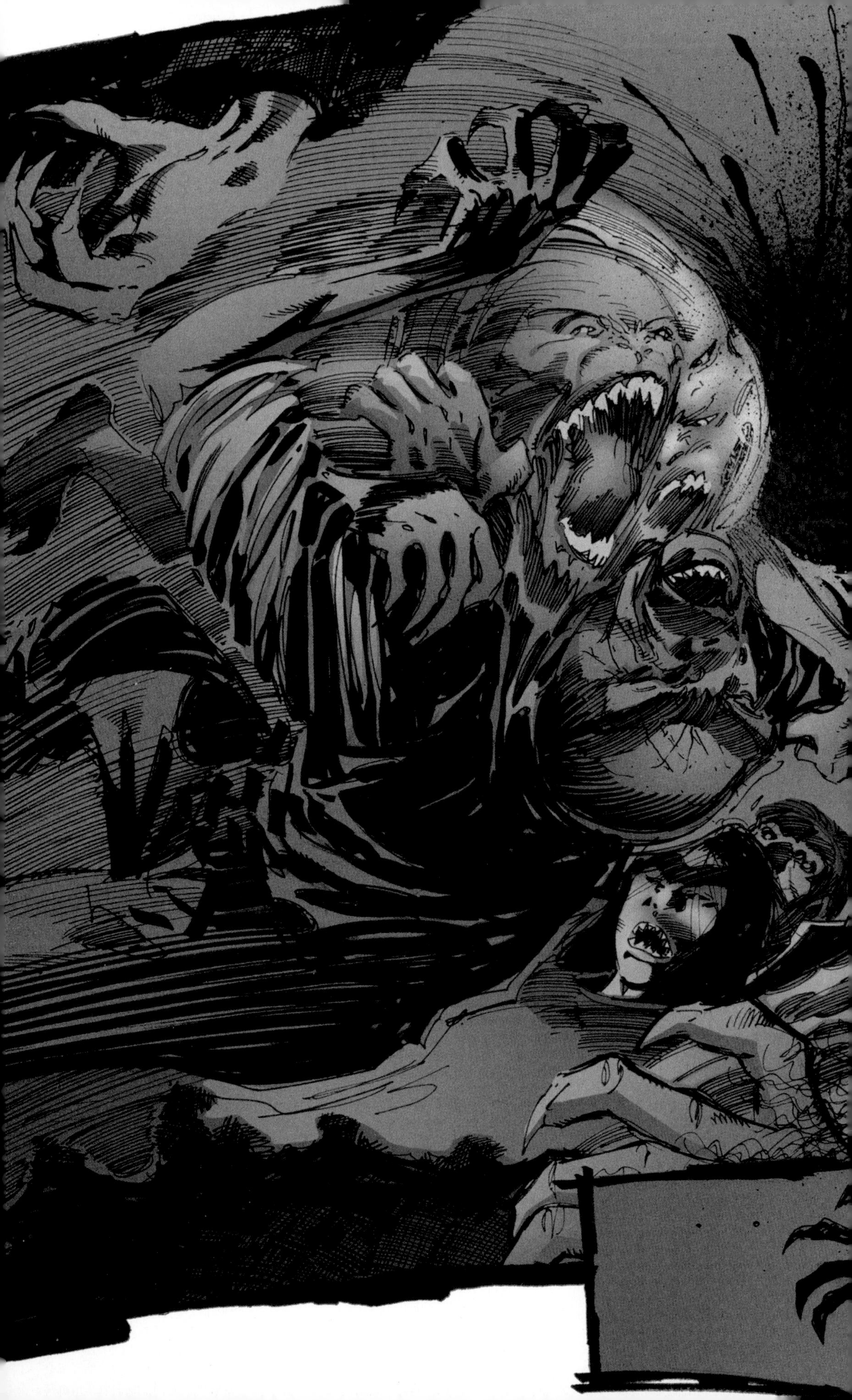

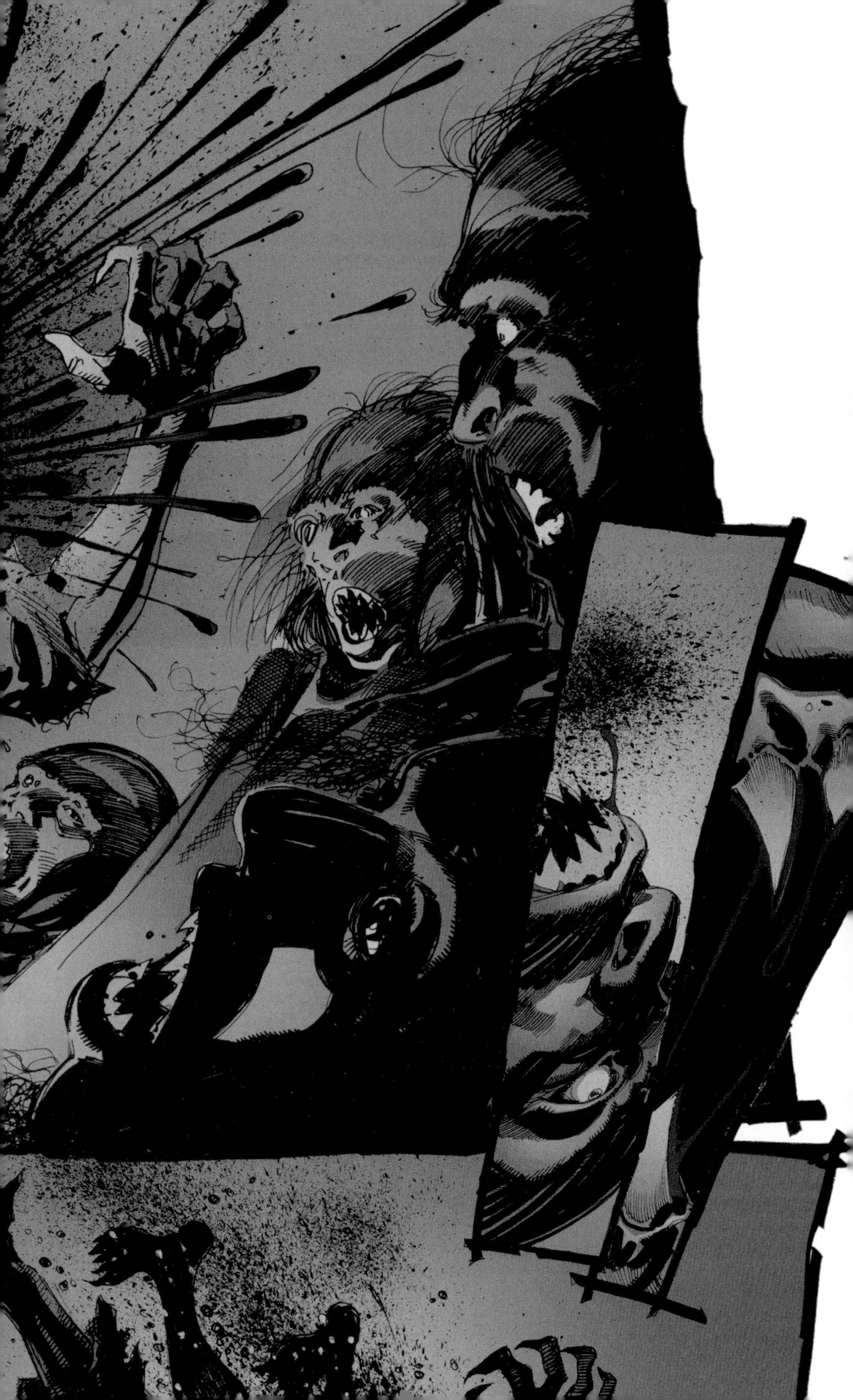

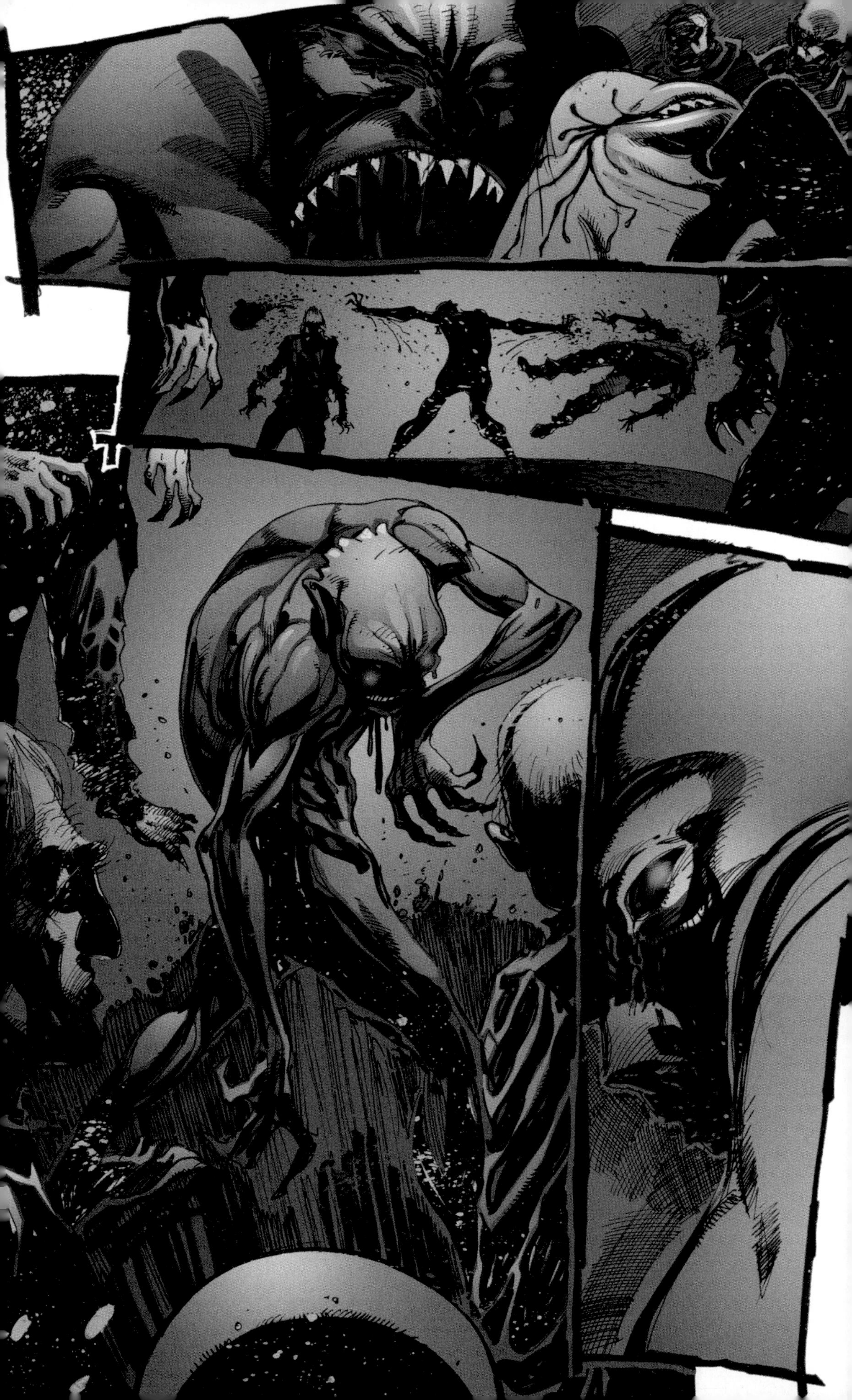

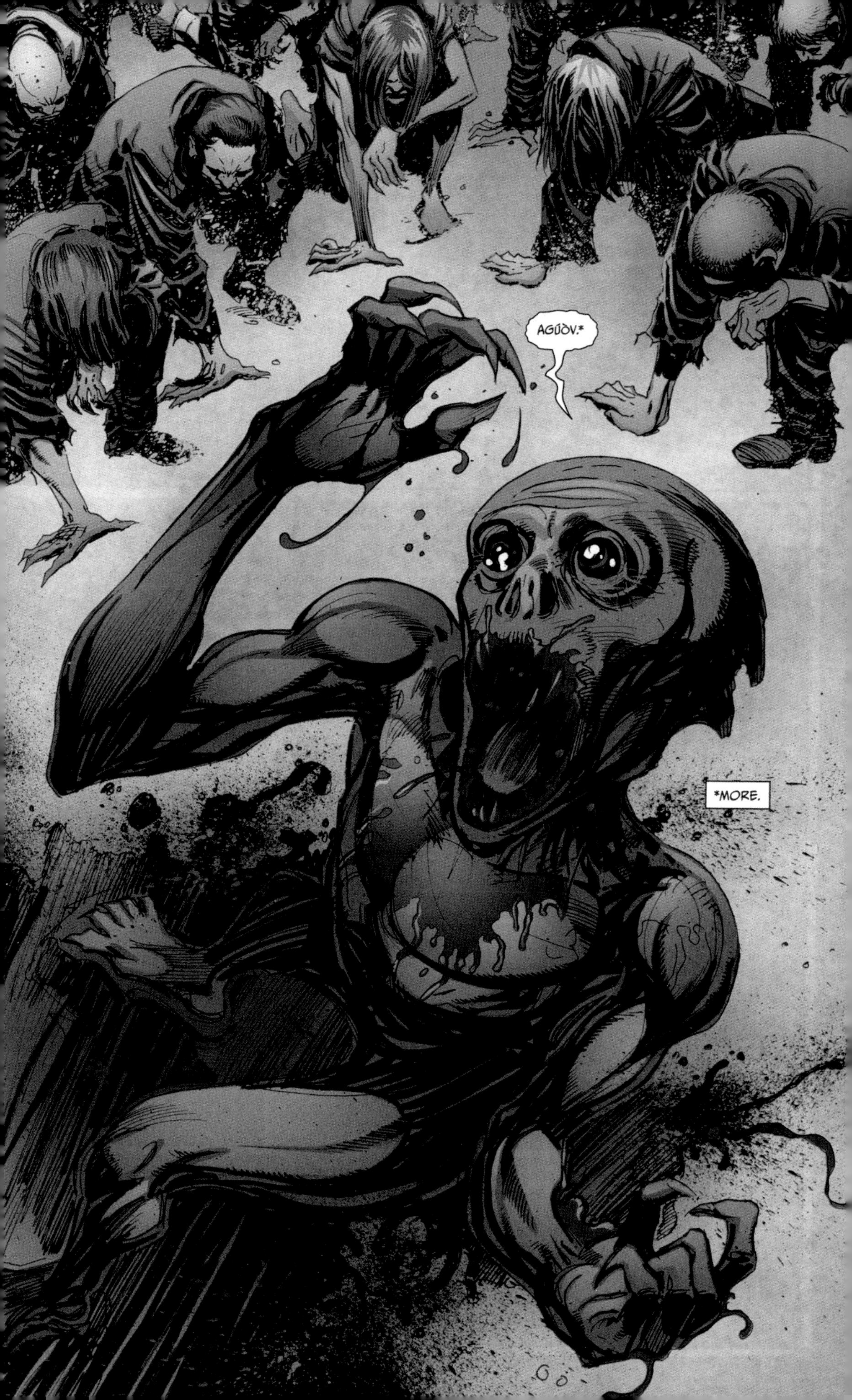
AGŰÒV.*
*MORE.

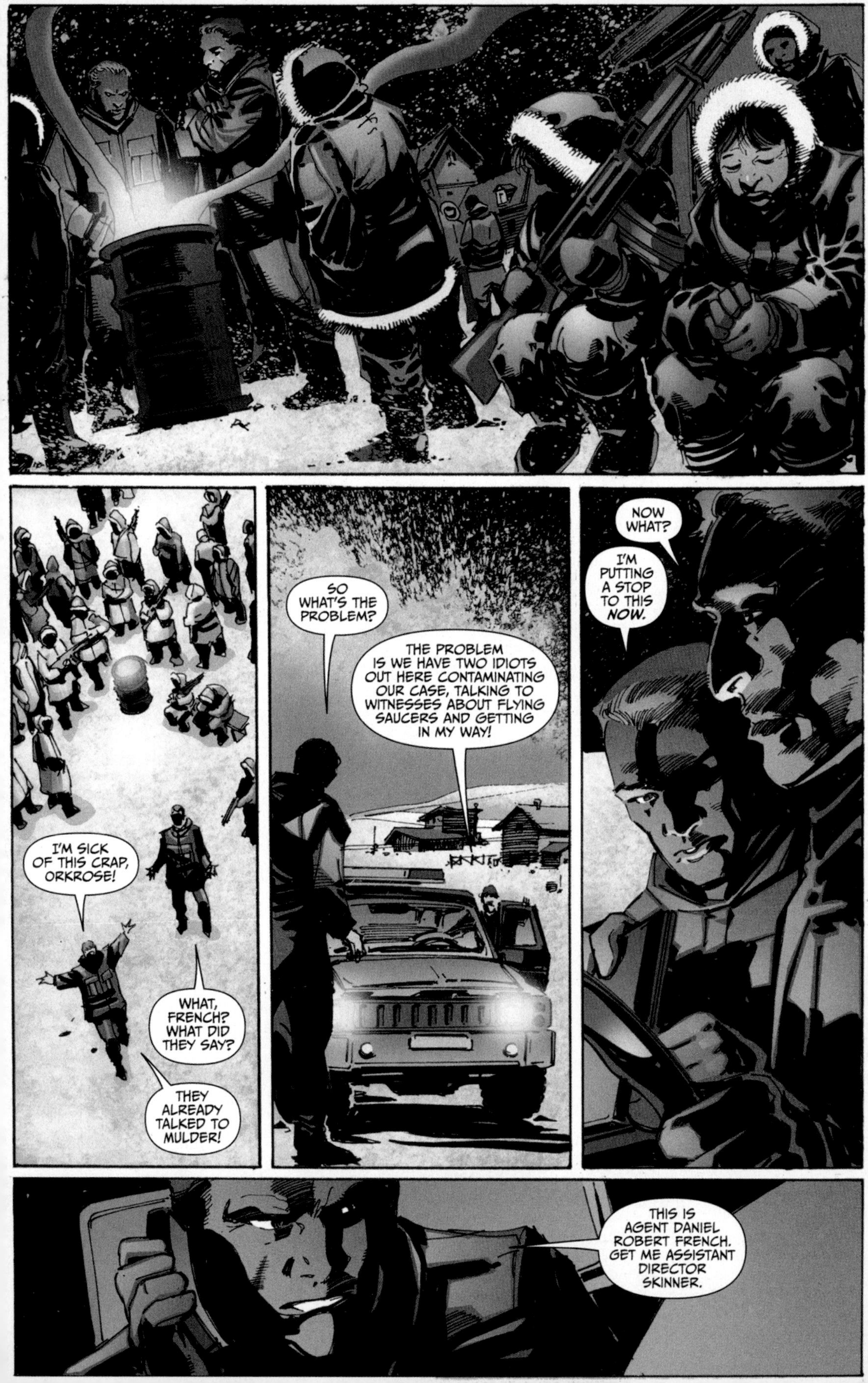
I'M SICK OF THIS CRAP, ORKROSE!
WHAT, FRENCH? WHAT DID THEY SAY?
THEY ALREADY TALKED TO MULDER!
SO WHAT'S THE PROBLEM?
THE PROBLEM IS WE HAVE TWO IDIOTS OUT HERE CONTAMINATING OUR CASE, TALKING TO WITNESSES ABOUT FLYING SAUCERS AND GETTING IN MY WAY!
NOW WHAT?
I'M PUTTING A STOP TO THIS *NOW.*
THIS IS AGENT DANIEL ROBERT FRENCH. GET ME ASSISTANT DIRECTOR SKINNER.

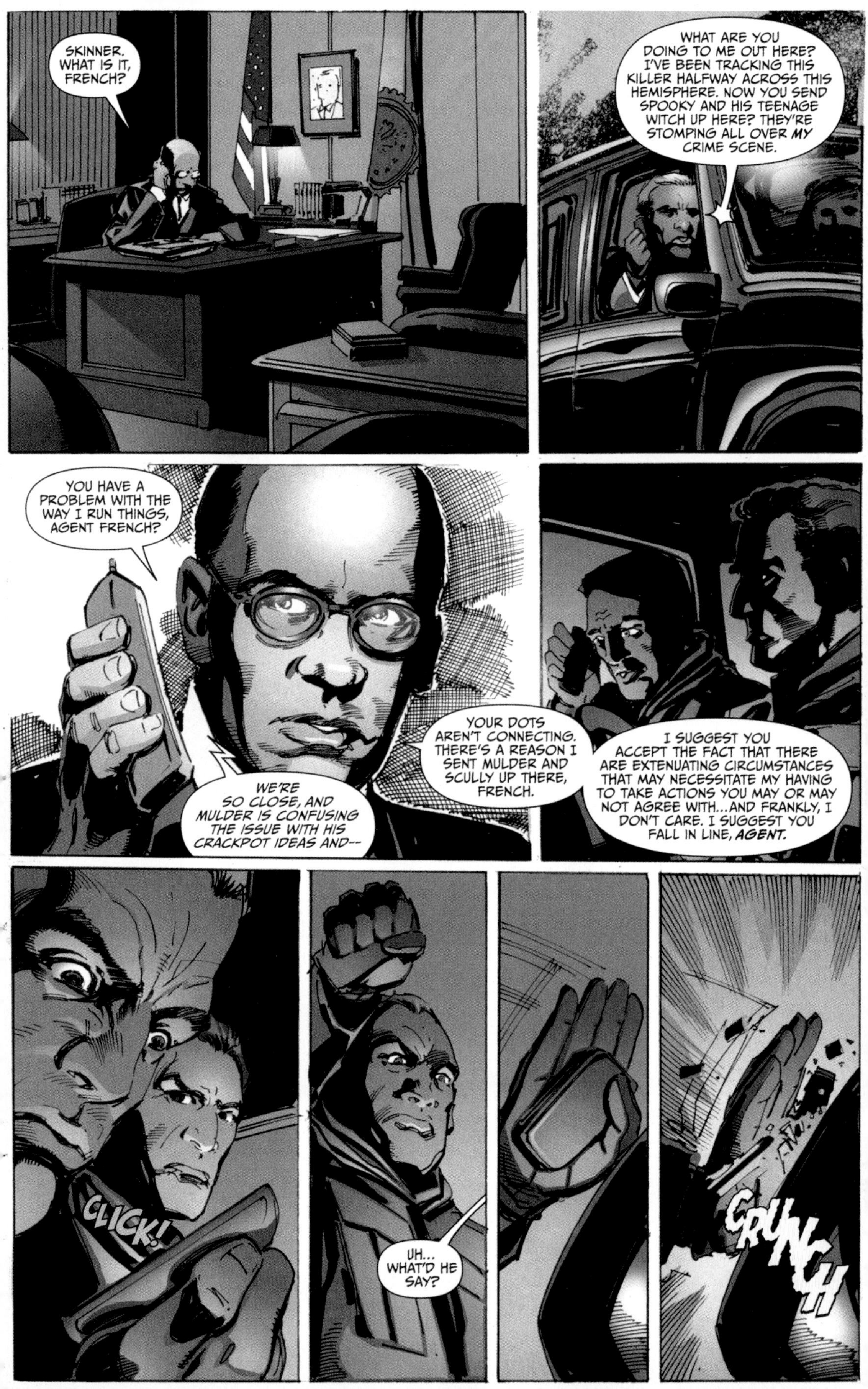
SKINNER. WHAT IS IT, FRENCH?
WHAT ARE YOU DOING TO ME OUT HERE? I'VE BEEN TRACKING THIS KILLER HALFWAY ACROSS THIS HEMISPHERE. NOW YOU SEND SPOOKY AND HIS TEENAGE WITCH UP HERE? THEY'RE STOMPING ALL OVER *MY* CRIME SCENE.
YOU HAVE A PROBLEM WITH THE WAY I RUN THINGS, AGENT FRENCH?
WE'RE SO CLOSE, AND MULDER IS CONFUSING THE ISSUE WITH HIS CRACKPOT IDEAS AND--
YOUR DOTS AREN'T CONNECTING. THERE'S A REASON I SENT MULDER AND SCULLY UP THERE, FRENCH.
I SUGGEST YOU ACCEPT THE FACT THAT THERE ARE EXTENUATING CIRCUMSTANCES THAT MAY NECESSITATE MY HAVING TO TAKE ACTIONS YOU MAY OR MAY NOT AGREE WITH...AND FRANKLY, I DON'T CARE. I SUGGEST YOU FALL IN LINE, ***AGENT.***
CLICK!
UH... WHAT'D HE SAY?
CRUNCH

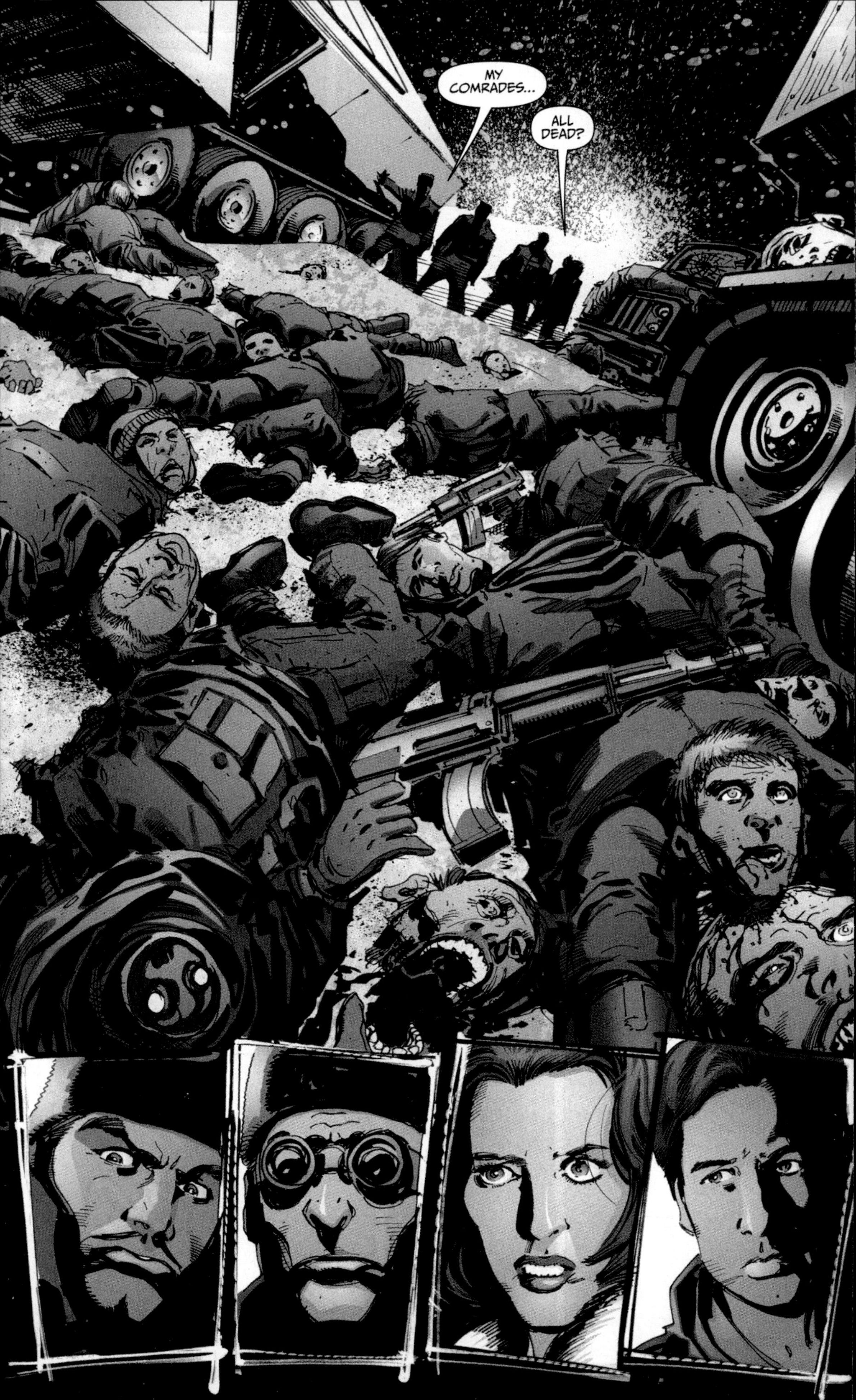
MY COMRADES...
ALL DEAD?

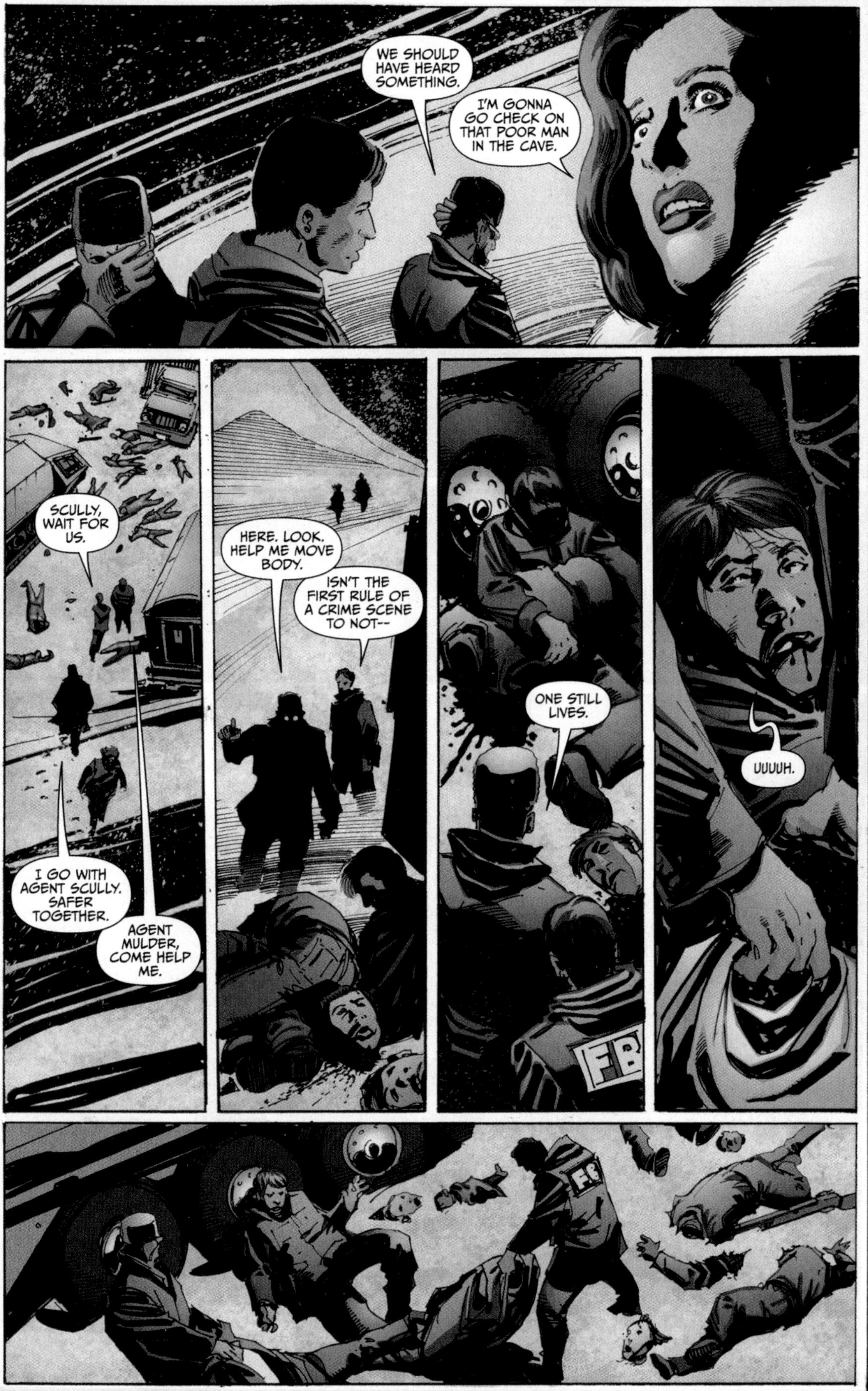
WE SHOULD HAVE HEARD SOMETHING.
I'M GONNA GO CHECK ON THAT POOR MAN IN THE CAVE.
SCULLY, WAIT FOR US.
I GO WITH AGENT SCULLY. SAFER TOGETHER.
AGENT MULDER, COME HELP ME.
HERE. LOOK. HELP ME MOVE BODY.
ISN'T THE FIRST RULE OF A CRIME SCENE TO NOT--
ONE STILL LIVES.
UUUUH.
FBI

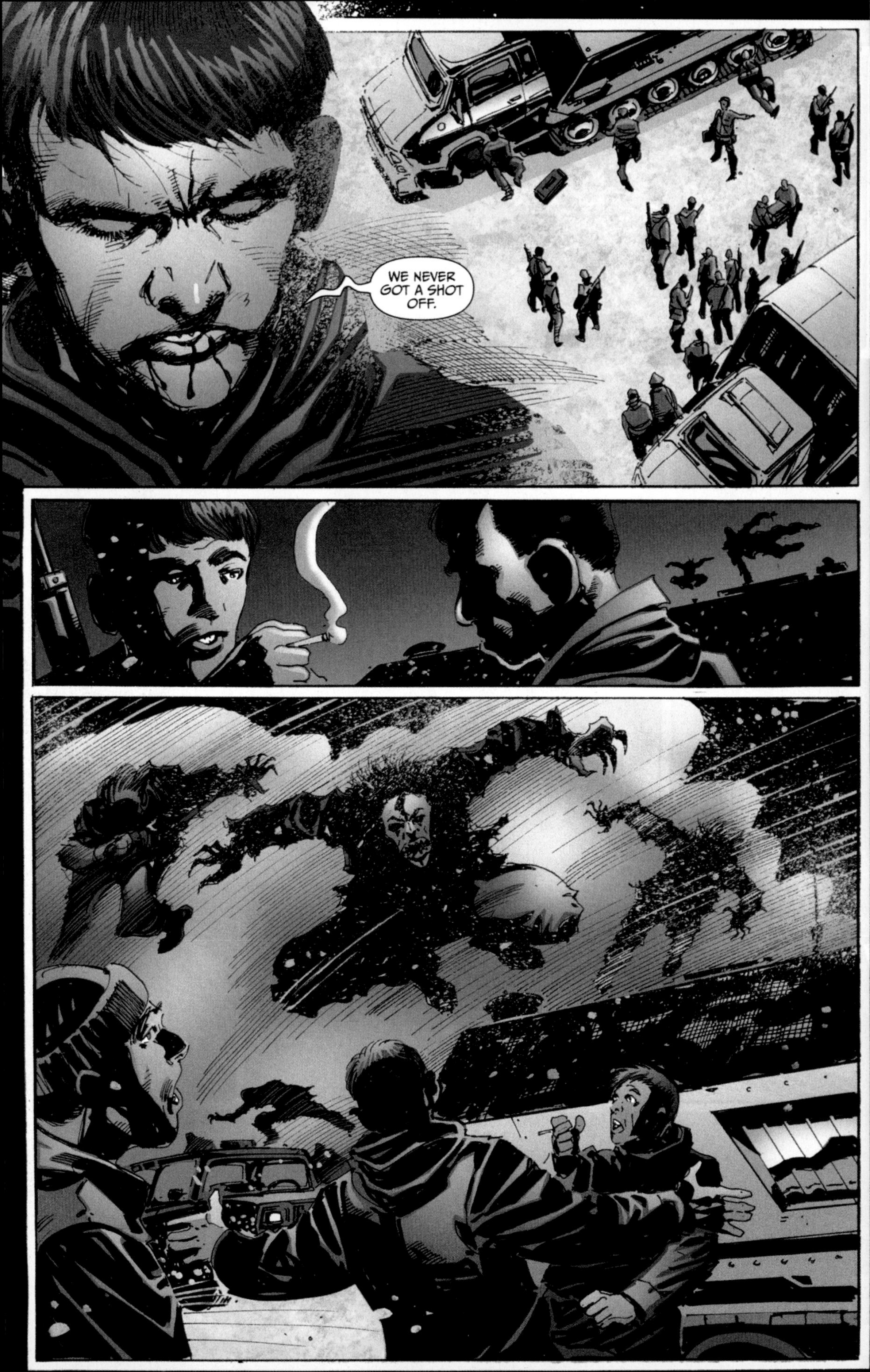
WE NEVER GOT A SHOT OFF.

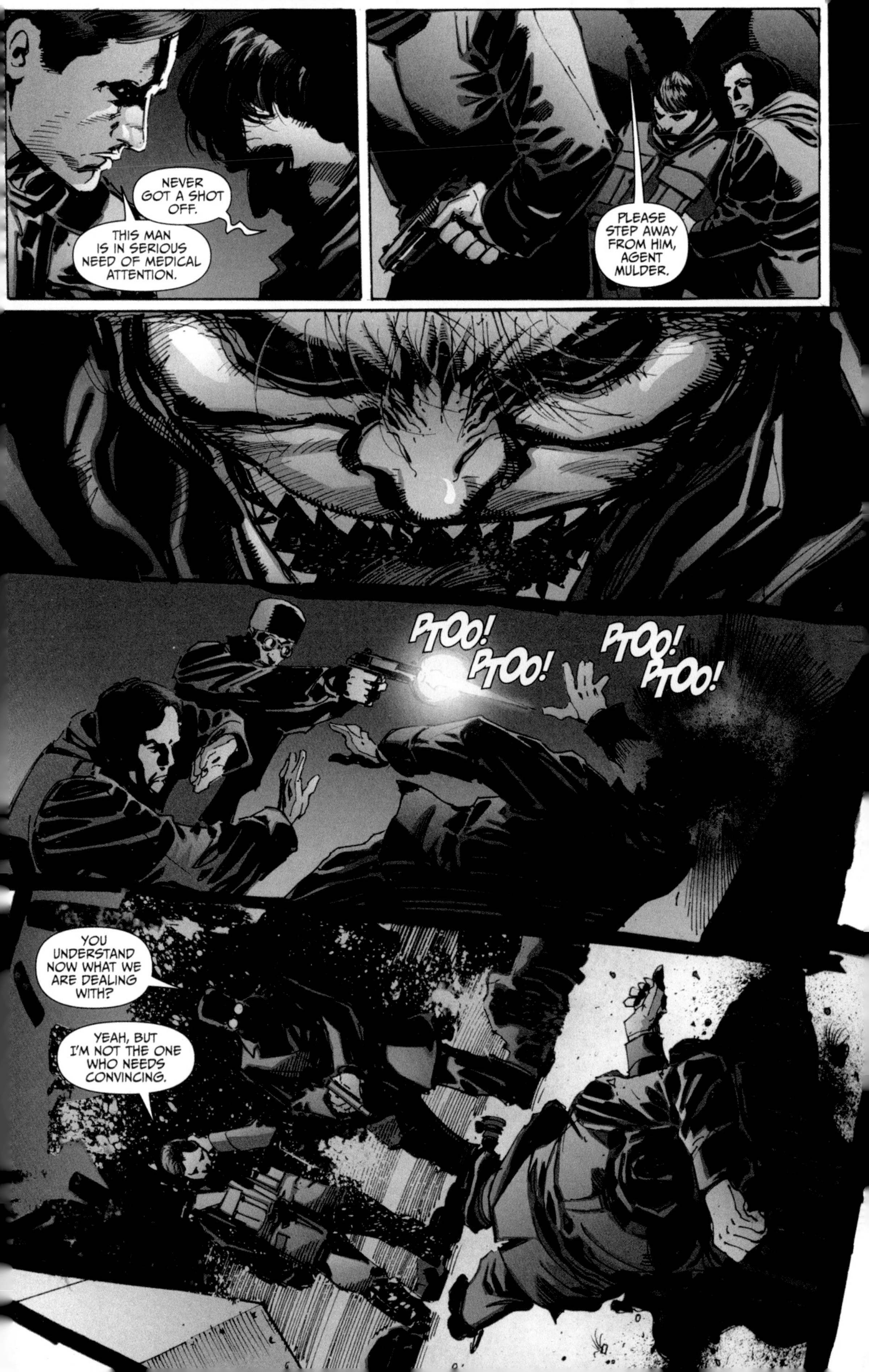
NEVER GOT A SHOT OFF.
THIS MAN IS IN SERIOUS NEED OF MEDICAL ATTENTION.
PLEASE STEP AWAY FROM HIM, AGENT MULDER.
PTOO! PTOO!
PTOO! PTOO!
YOU UNDERSTAND NOW WHAT WE ARE DEALING WITH?
YEAH, BUT I'M NOT THE ONE WHO NEEDS CONVINCING.

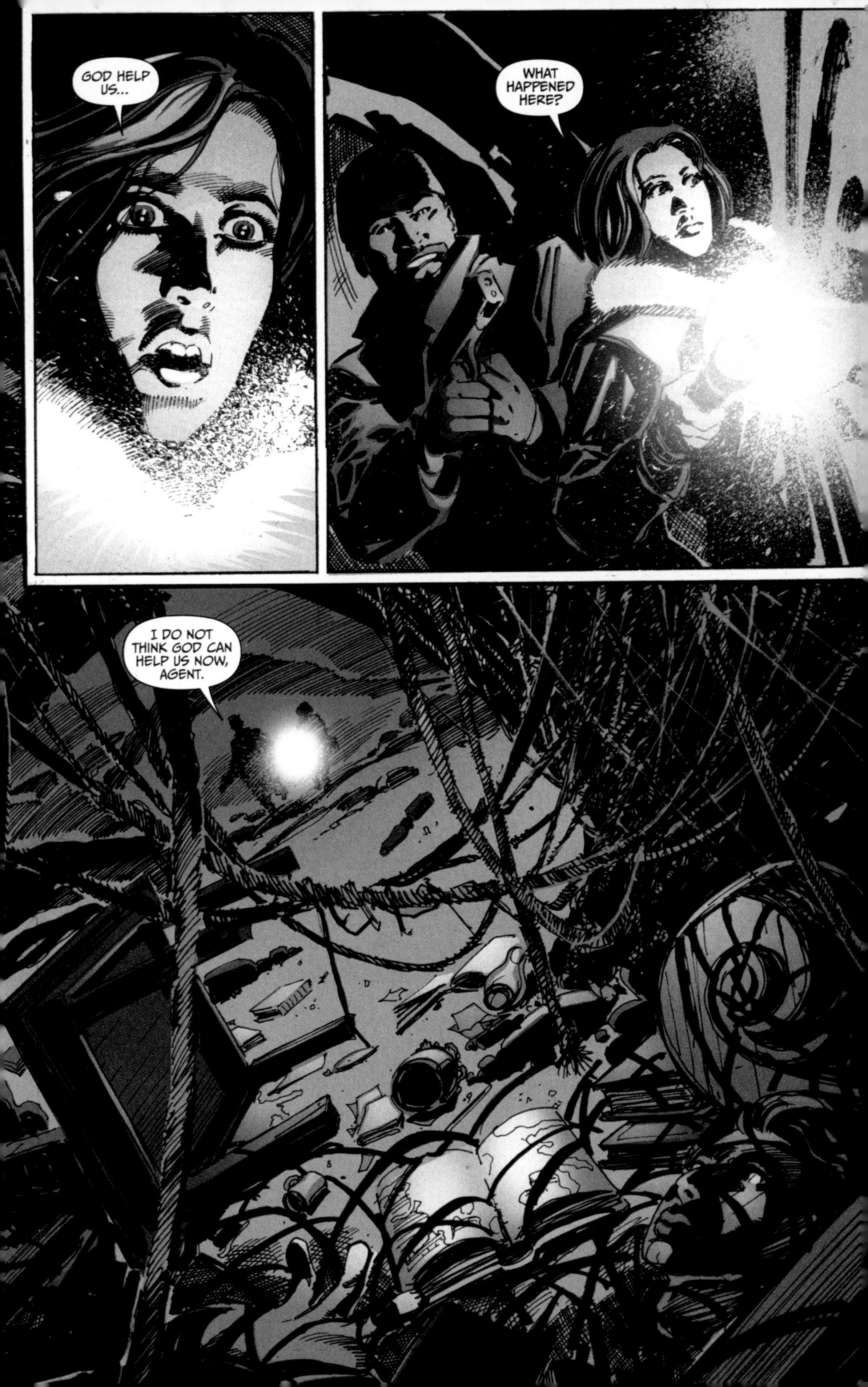
GOD HELP US...
WHAT HAPPENED HERE?
I DO NOT THINK GOD CAN HELP US NOW, AGENT.

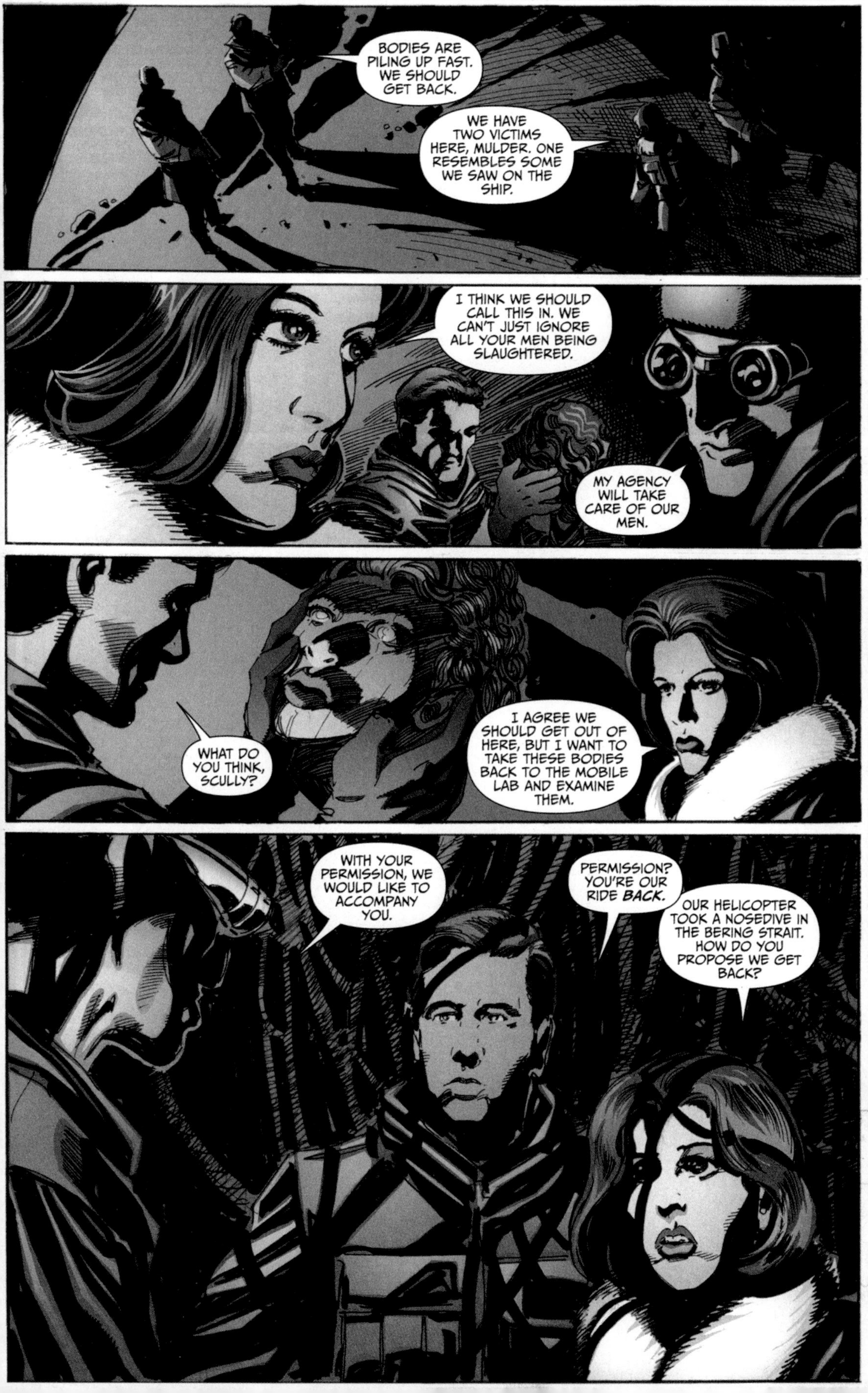
BODIES ARE PILING UP FAST. WE SHOULD GET BACK.
WE HAVE TWO VICTIMS HERE, MULDER. ONE RESEMBLES SOME WE SAW ON THE SHIP.
I THINK WE SHOULD CALL THIS IN. WE CAN'T JUST IGNORE ALL YOUR MEN BEING SLAUGHTERED.
MY AGENCY WILL TAKE CARE OF OUR MEN.
WHAT DO YOU THINK, SCULLY?
I AGREE WE SHOULD GET OUT OF HERE, BUT I WANT TO TAKE THESE BODIES BACK TO THE MOBILE LAB AND EXAMINE THEM.
WITH YOUR PERMISSION, WE WOULD LIKE TO ACCOMPANY YOU.
PERMISSION? YOU'RE OUR RIDE **BACK**.
OUR HELICOPTER TOOK A NOSEDIVE IN THE BERING STRAIT. HOW DO YOU PROPOSE WE GET BACK?

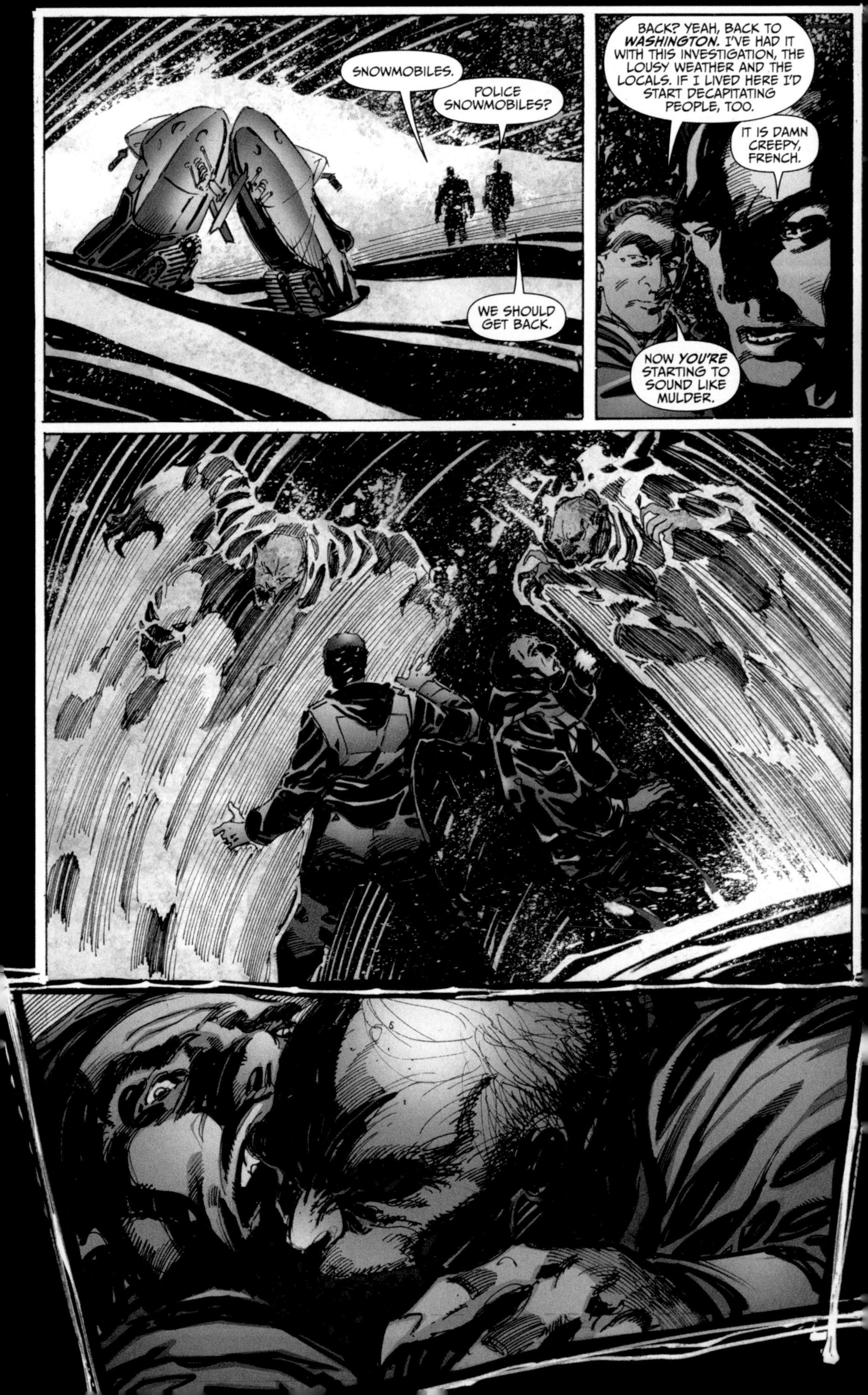
SNOWMOBILES.
POLICE SNOWMOBILES?
WE SHOULD GET BACK.
BACK? YEAH, BACK TO WASHINGTON. I'VE HAD IT WITH THIS INVESTIGATION, THE LOUSY WEATHER AND THE LOCALS. IF I LIVED HERE I'D START DECAPITATING PEOPLE, TOO.
IT IS DAMN CREEPY, FRENCH.
NOW YOU'RE STARTING TO SOUND LIKE MULDER.

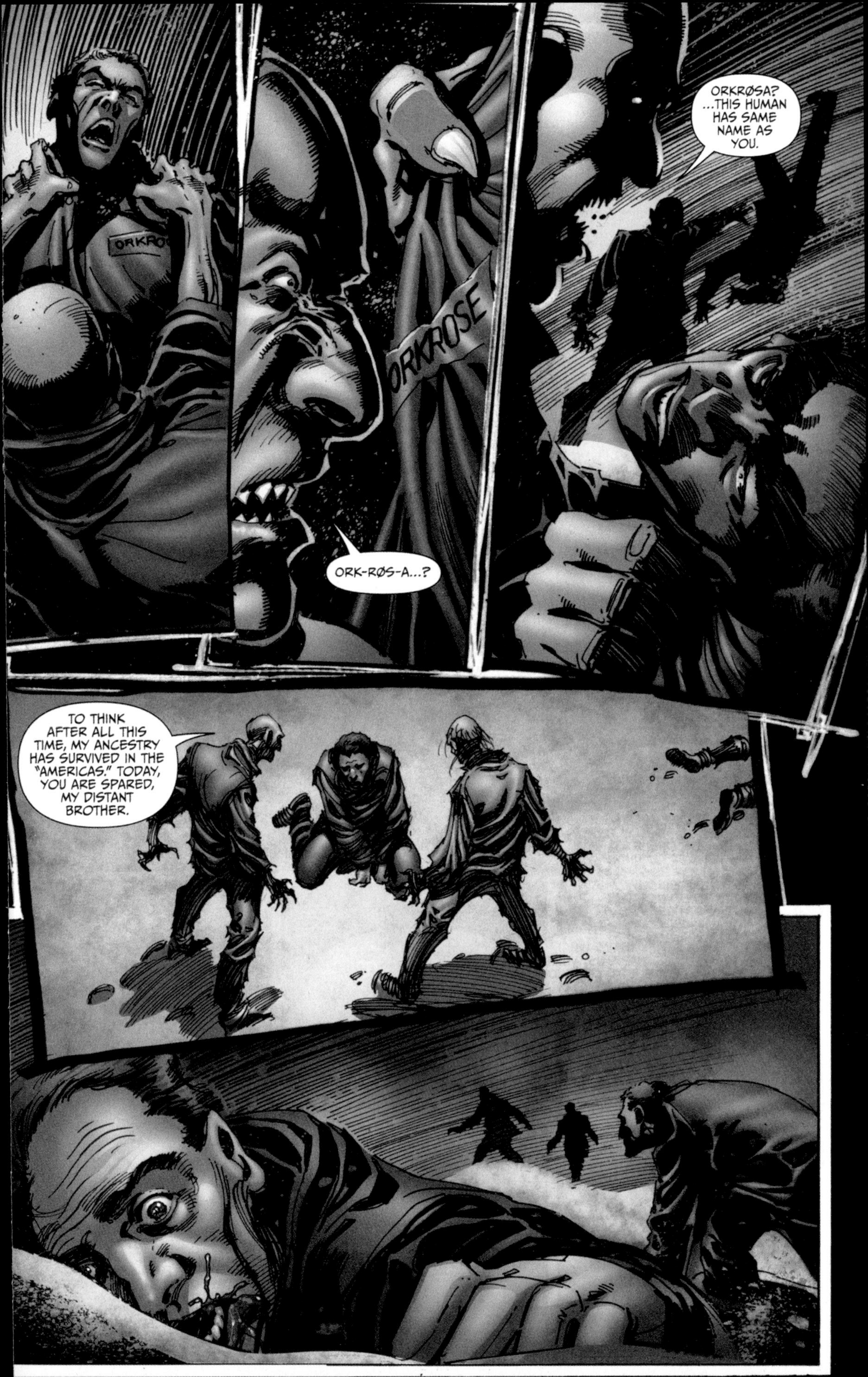
ORKROSE
ORKROSE
ORK-RØS-A...?
ORKRØSA? ...THIS HUMAN HAS SAME NAME AS YOU.
TO THINK AFTER ALL THIS TIME, MY ANCESTRY HAS SURVIVED IN THE "AMERICAS." TODAY, YOU ARE SPARED, MY DISTANT BROTHER.

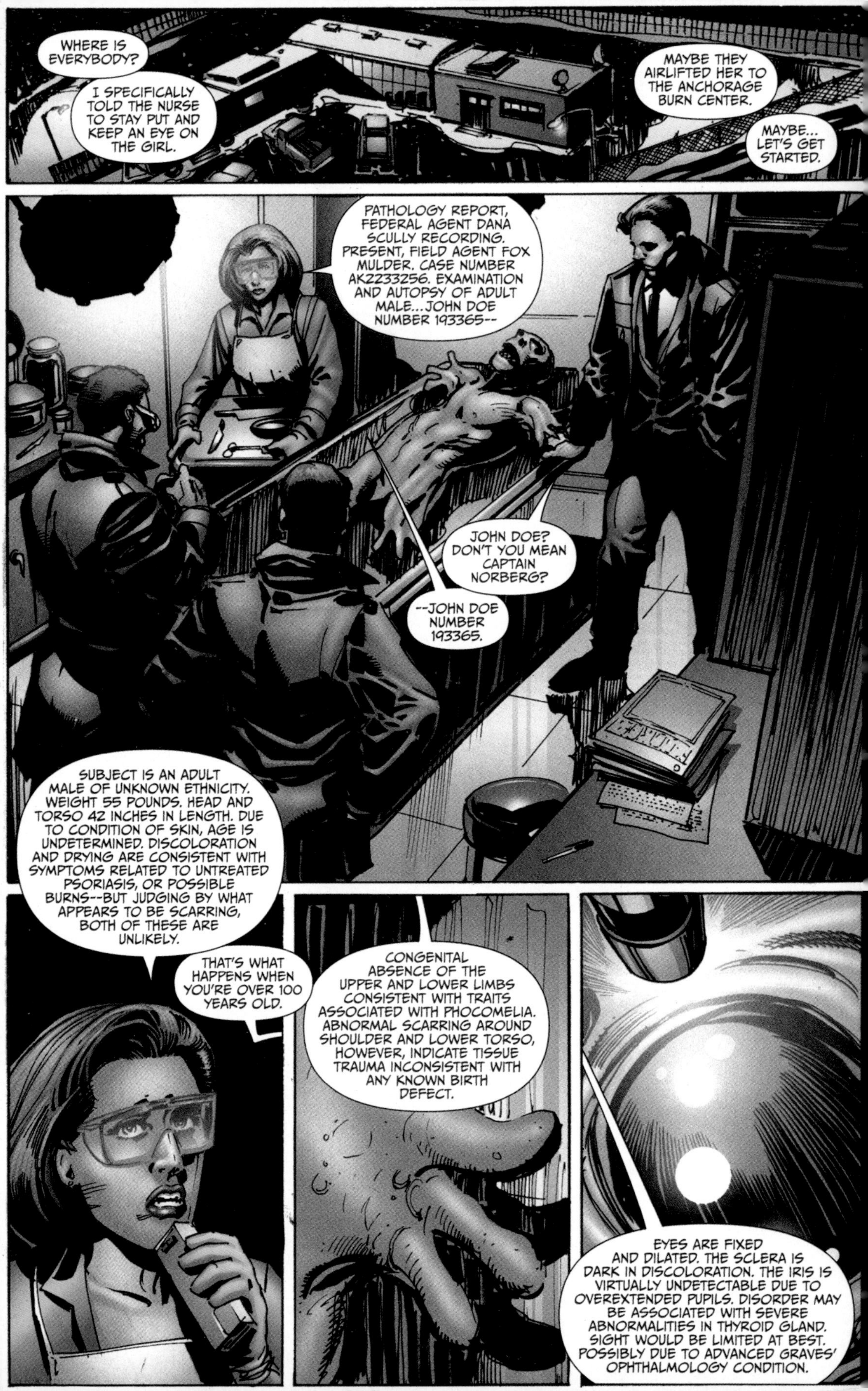
WHERE IS EVERYBODY?
I SPECIFICALLY TOLD THE NURSE TO STAY PUT AND KEEP AN EYE ON THE GIRL.
MAYBE THEY AIRLIFTED HER TO THE ANCHORAGE BURN CENTER.
MAYBE... LET'S GET STARTED.
PATHOLOGY REPORT, FEDERAL AGENT DANA SCULLY RECORDING. PRESENT, FIELD AGENT FOX MULDER. CASE NUMBER AK2233256. EXAMINATION AND AUTOPSY OF ADULT MALE...JOHN DOE NUMBER 193365--
JOHN DOE? DON'T YOU MEAN CAPTAIN NORBERG?
--JOHN DOE NUMBER 193365.
SUBJECT IS AN ADULT MALE OF UNKNOWN ETHNICITY. WEIGHT 55 POUNDS. HEAD AND TORSO 42 INCHES IN LENGTH. DUE TO CONDITION OF SKIN, AGE IS UNDETERMINED. DISCOLORATION AND DRYING ARE CONSISTENT WITH SYMPTOMS RELATED TO UNTREATED PSORIASIS, OR POSSIBLE BURNS--BUT JUDGING BY WHAT APPEARS TO BE SCARRING, BOTH OF THESE ARE UNLIKELY.
THAT'S WHAT HAPPENS WHEN YOU'RE OVER 100 YEARS OLD.
CONGENITAL ABSENCE OF THE UPPER AND LOWER LIMBS CONSISTENT WITH TRAITS ASSOCIATED WITH PHOCOMELIA. ABNORMAL SCARRING AROUND SHOULDER AND LOWER TORSO, HOWEVER, INDICATE TISSUE TRAUMA INCONSISTENT WITH ANY KNOWN BIRTH DEFECT.
EYES ARE FIXED AND DILATED. THE SCLERA IS DARK IN DISCOLORATION. THE IRIS IS VIRTUALLY UNDETECTABLE DUE TO OVEREXTENDED PUPILS. DISORDER MAY BE ASSOCIATED WITH SEVERE ABNORMALITIES IN THYROID GLAND. SIGHT WOULD BE LIMITED AT BEST. POSSIBLY DUE TO ADVANCED GRAVES' OPHTHALMOLOGY CONDITION.

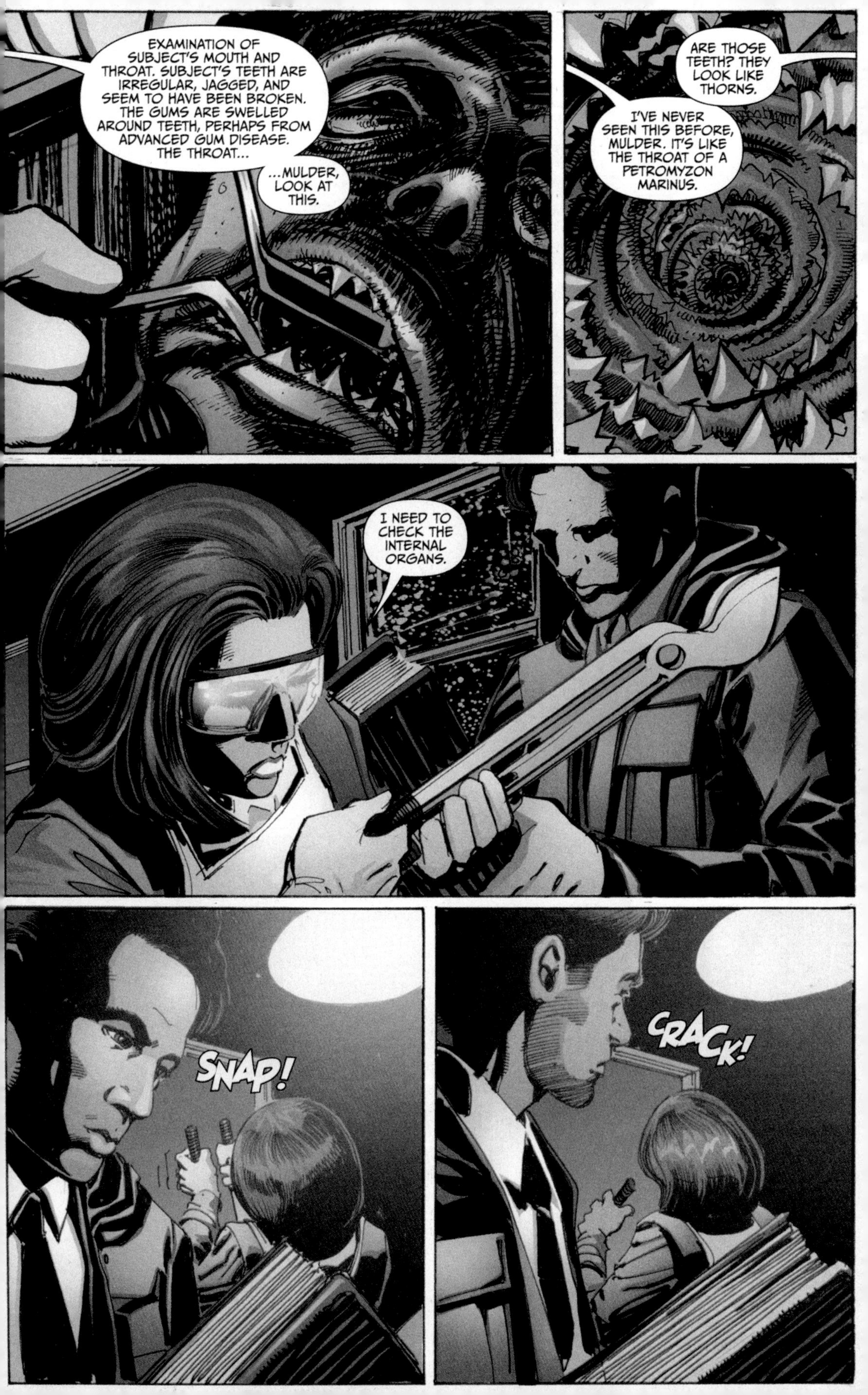
EXAMINATION OF SUBJECT'S MOUTH AND THROAT. SUBJECT'S TEETH ARE IRREGULAR, JAGGED, AND SEEM TO HAVE BEEN BROKEN. THE GUMS ARE SWELLED AROUND TEETH, PERHAPS FROM ADVANCED GUM DISEASE. THE THROAT...
...MULDER, LOOK AT THIS.
ARE THOSE TEETH? THEY LOOK LIKE THORNS.
I'VE NEVER SEEN THIS BEFORE, MULDER. IT'S LIKE THE THROAT OF A PETROMYZON MARINUS.
I NEED TO CHECK THE INTERNAL ORGANS.
SNAP!
CRACK!

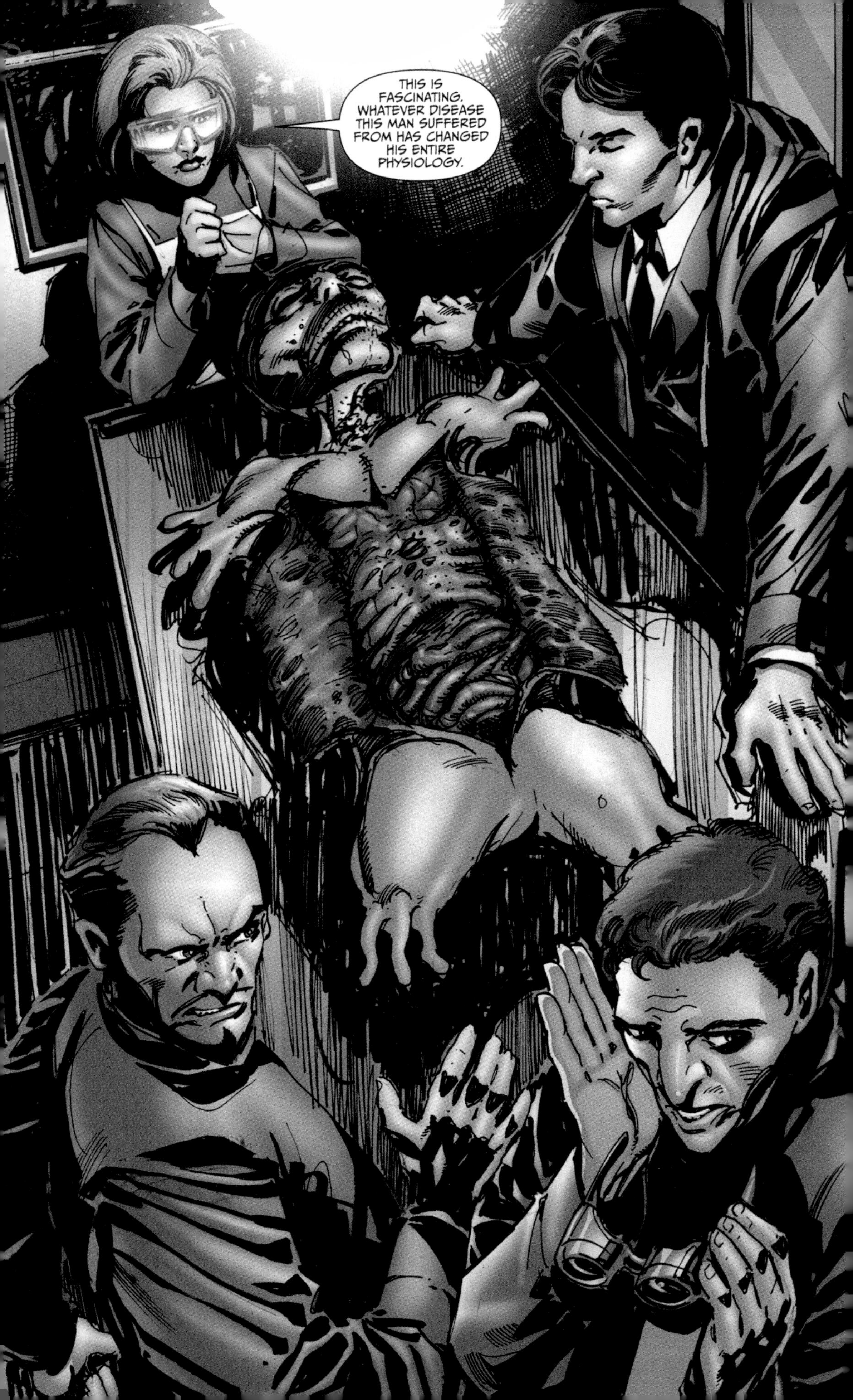
THIS IS FASCINATING. WHATEVER DISEASE THIS MAN SUFFERED FROM HAS CHANGED HIS ENTIRE PHYSIOLOGY.

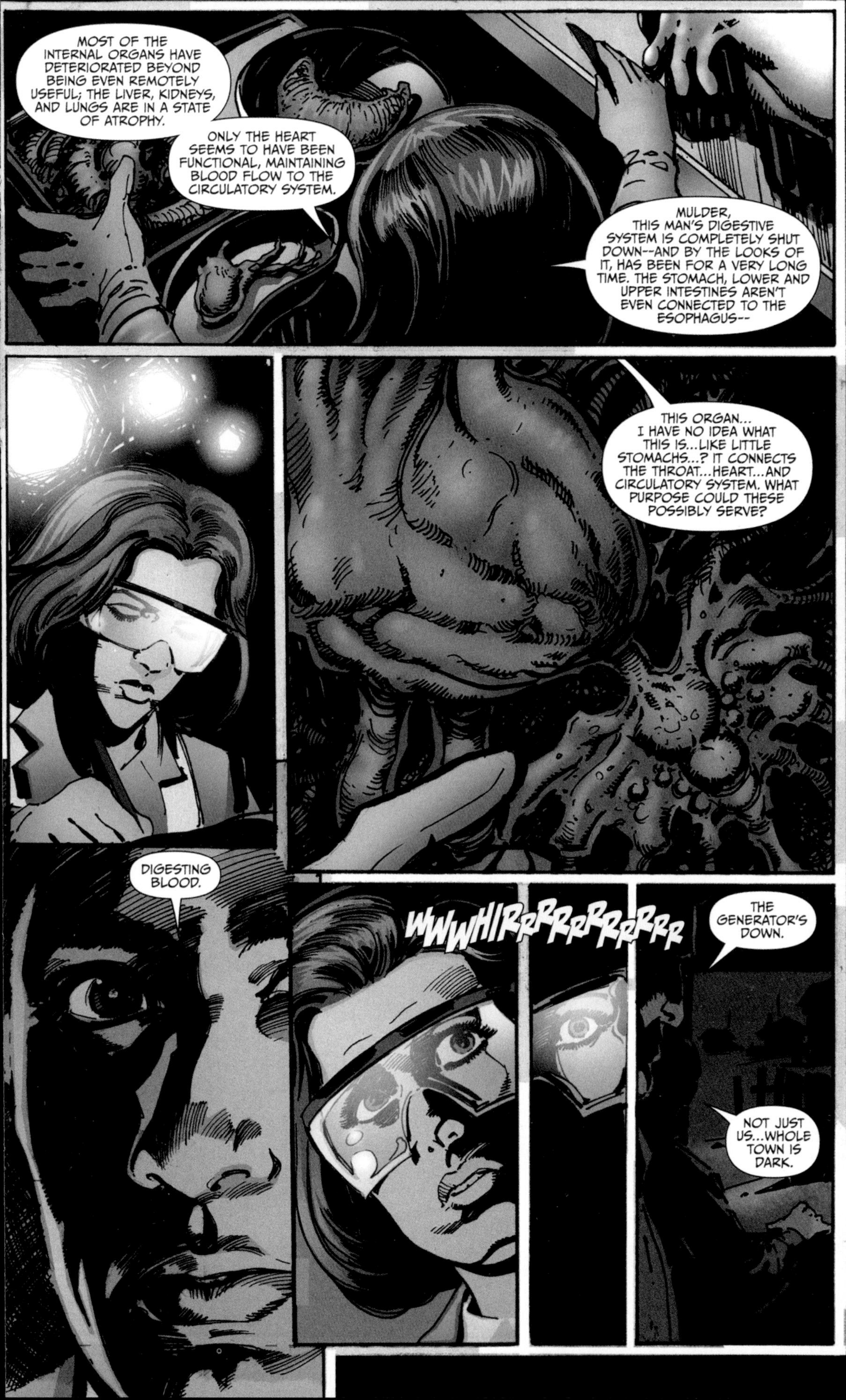
MOST OF THE INTERNAL ORGANS HAVE DETERIORATED BEYOND BEING EVEN REMOTELY USEFUL; THE LIVER, KIDNEYS, AND LUNGS ARE IN A STATE OF ATROPHY.
ONLY THE HEART SEEMS TO HAVE BEEN FUNCTIONAL, MAINTAINING BLOOD FLOW TO THE CIRCULATORY SYSTEM.
MULDER, THIS MAN'S DIGESTIVE SYSTEM IS COMPLETELY SHUT DOWN--AND BY THE LOOKS OF IT, HAS BEEN FOR A VERY LONG TIME. THE STOMACH, LOWER AND UPPER INTESTINES AREN'T EVEN CONNECTED TO THE ESOPHAGUS--
THIS ORGAN... I HAVE NO IDEA WHAT THIS IS...LIKE LITTLE STOMACHS...? IT CONNECTS THE THROAT...HEART...AND CIRCULATORY SYSTEM. WHAT PURPOSE COULD THESE POSSIBLY SERVE?
DIGESTING BLOOD.
WWWHIRRRRRRRRRR
THE GENERATOR'S DOWN.
NOT JUST US...WHOLE TOWN IS DARK.

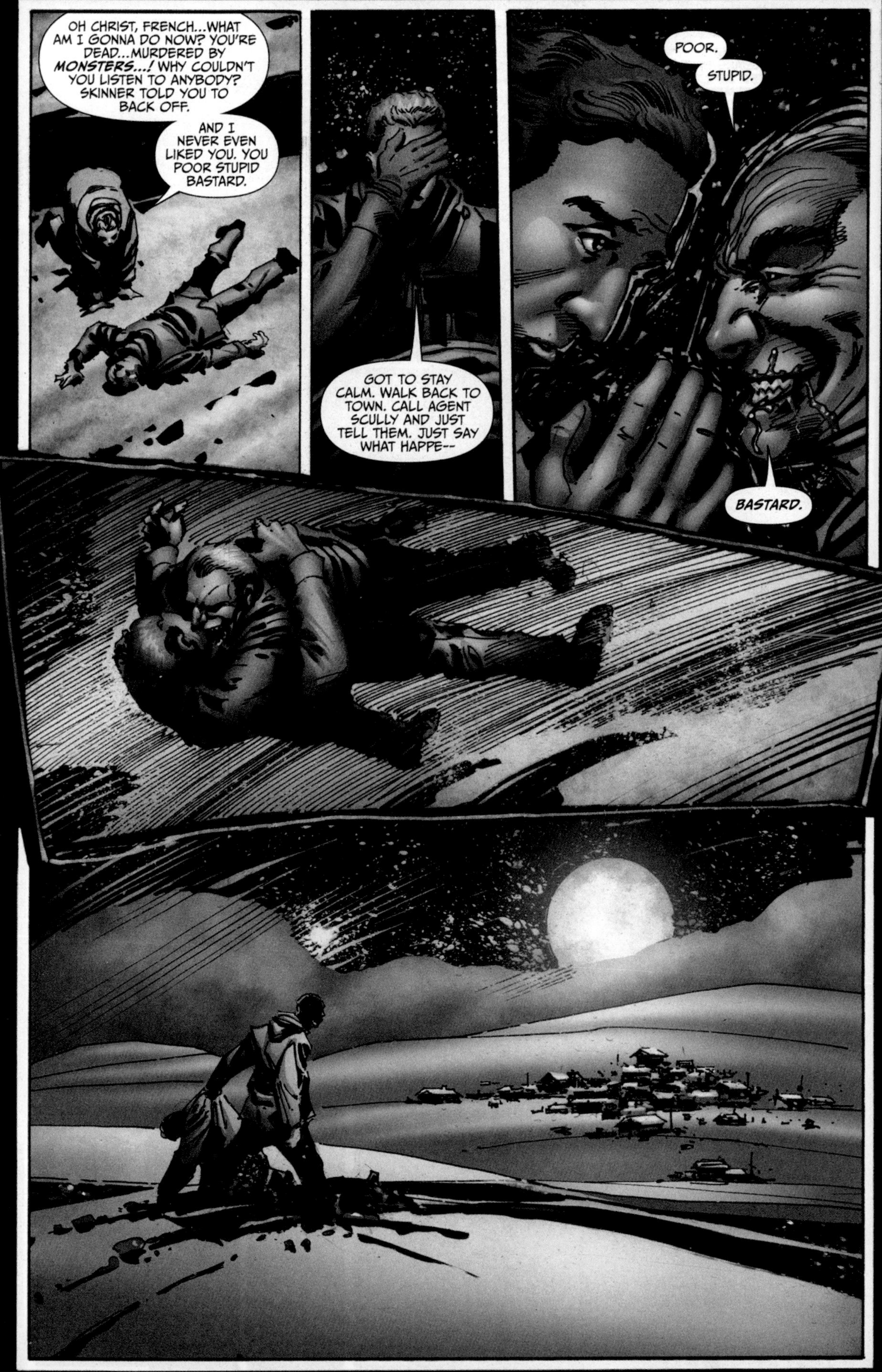
OH CHRIST, FRENCH...WHAT AM I GONNA DO NOW? YOU'RE DEAD...MURDERED BY MONSTERS...! WHY COULDN'T YOU LISTEN TO ANYBODY? SKINNER TOLD YOU TO BACK OFF.
AND I NEVER EVEN LIKED YOU. YOU POOR STUPID BASTARD.
GOT TO STAY CALM. WALK BACK TO TOWN. CALL AGENT SCULLY AND JUST TELL THEM. JUST SAY WHAT HAPPE--
POOR.
STUPID.
BASTARD.

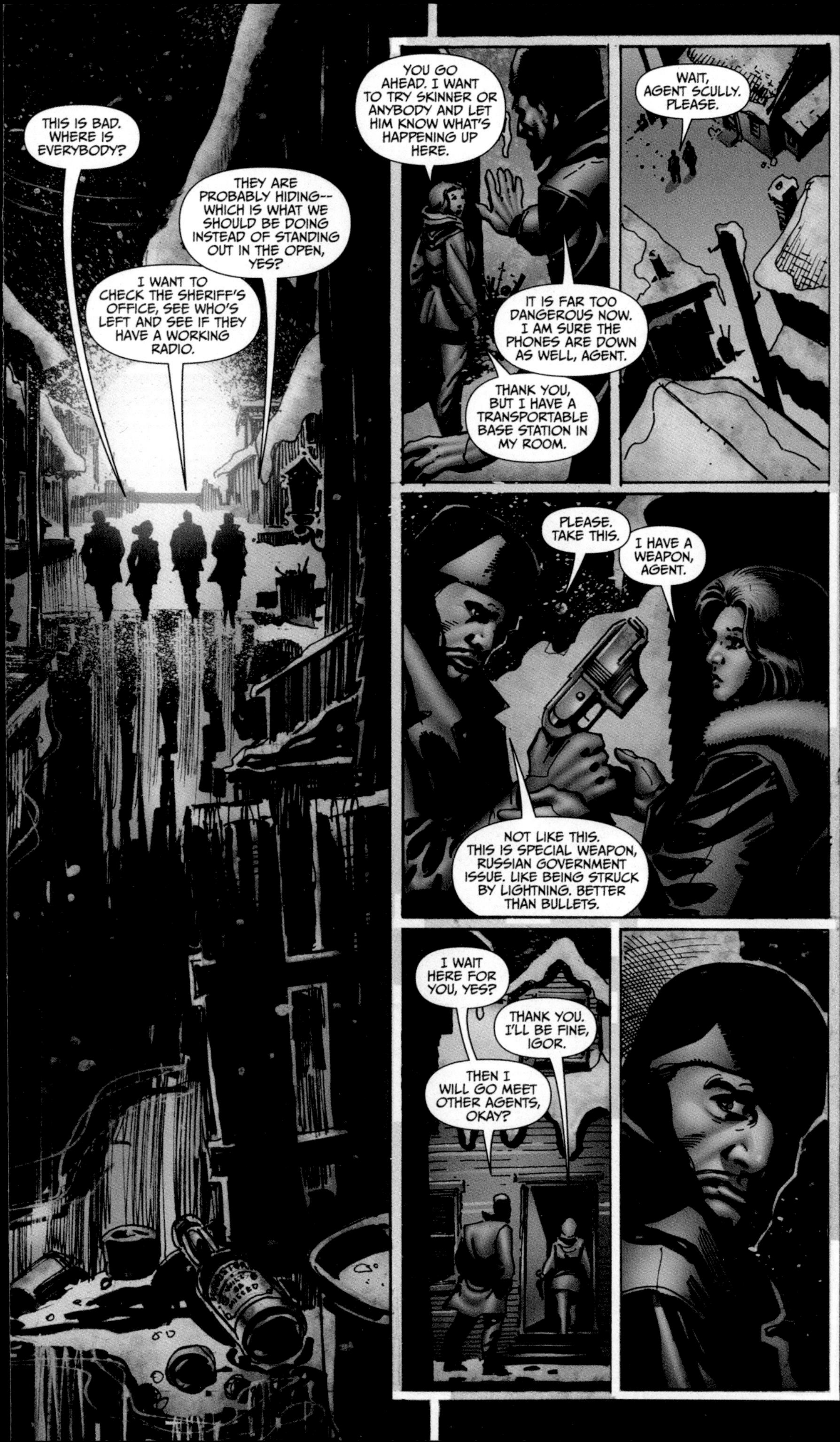

THIS IS BAD. WHERE IS EVERYBODY?
THEY ARE PROBABLY HIDING-- WHICH IS WHAT WE SHOULD BE DOING INSTEAD OF STANDING OUT IN THE OPEN, YES?
I WANT TO CHECK THE SHERIFF'S OFFICE, SEE WHO'S LEFT AND SEE IF THEY HAVE A WORKING RADIO.
YOU GO AHEAD. I WANT TO TRY SKINNER OR ANYBODY AND LET HIM KNOW WHAT'S HAPPENING UP HERE.
IT IS FAR TOO DANGEROUS NOW. I AM SURE THE PHONES ARE DOWN AS WELL, AGENT.
THANK YOU, BUT I HAVE A TRANSPORTABLE BASE STATION IN MY ROOM.
WAIT, AGENT SCULLY. PLEASE.
PLEASE. TAKE THIS.
I HAVE A WEAPON, AGENT.
NOT LIKE THIS. THIS IS SPECIAL WEAPON, RUSSIAN GOVERNMENT ISSUE. LIKE BEING STRUCK BY LIGHTNING. BETTER THAN BULLETS.
I WAIT HERE FOR YOU, YES?
THANK YOU. I'LL BE FINE, IGOR.
THEN I WILL GO MEET OTHER AGENTS, OKAY?

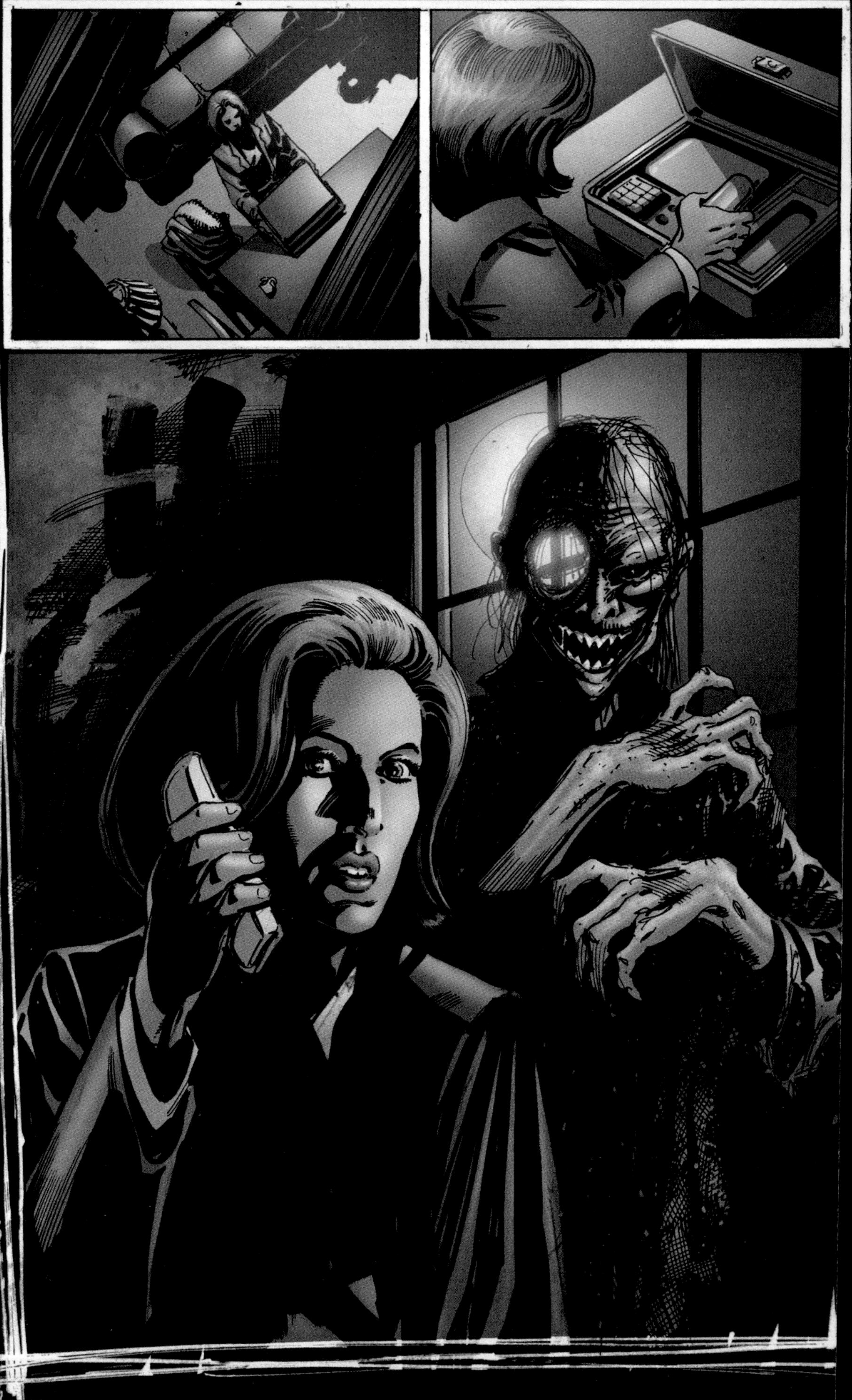

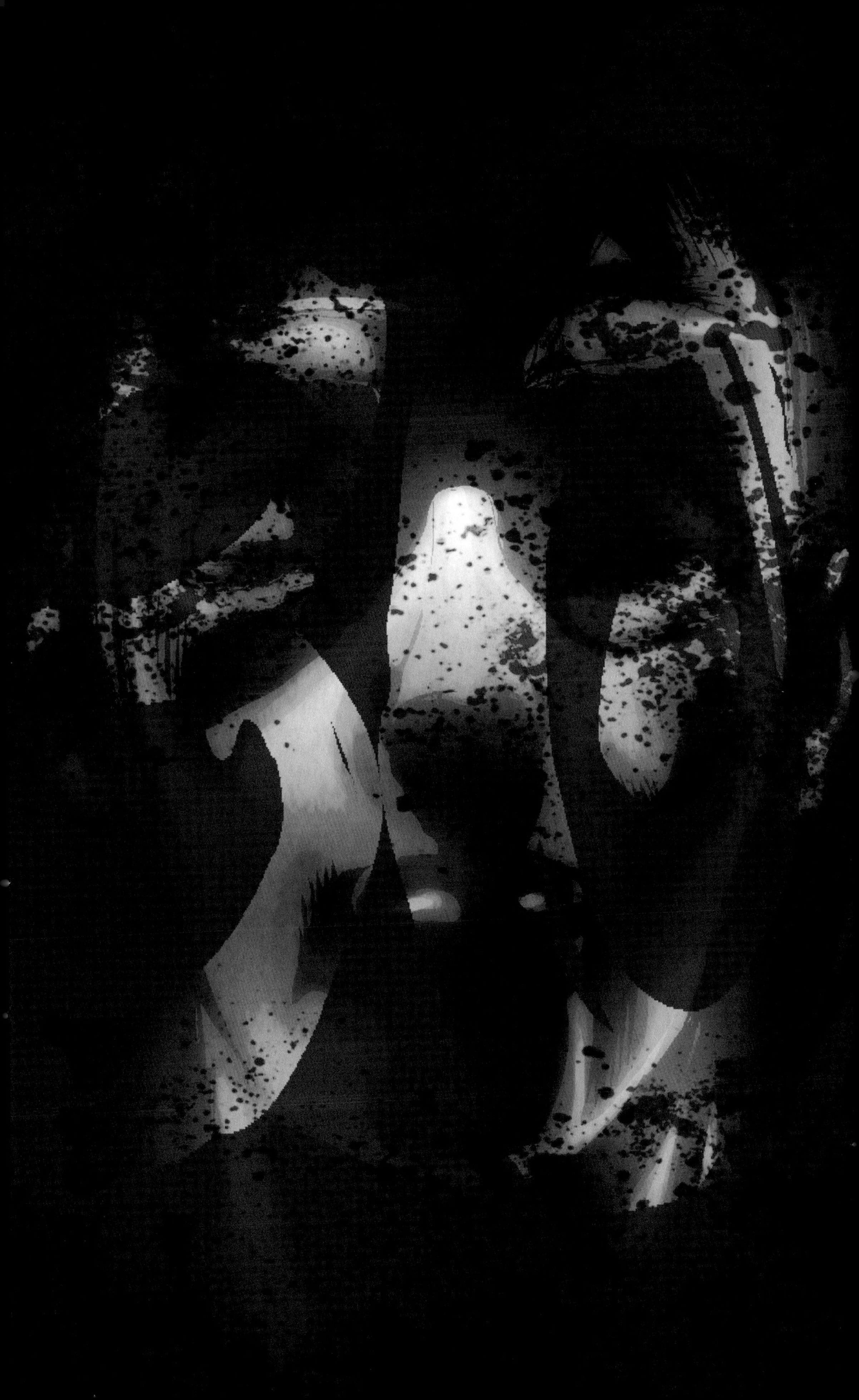

art by: Andrea Sorrentino

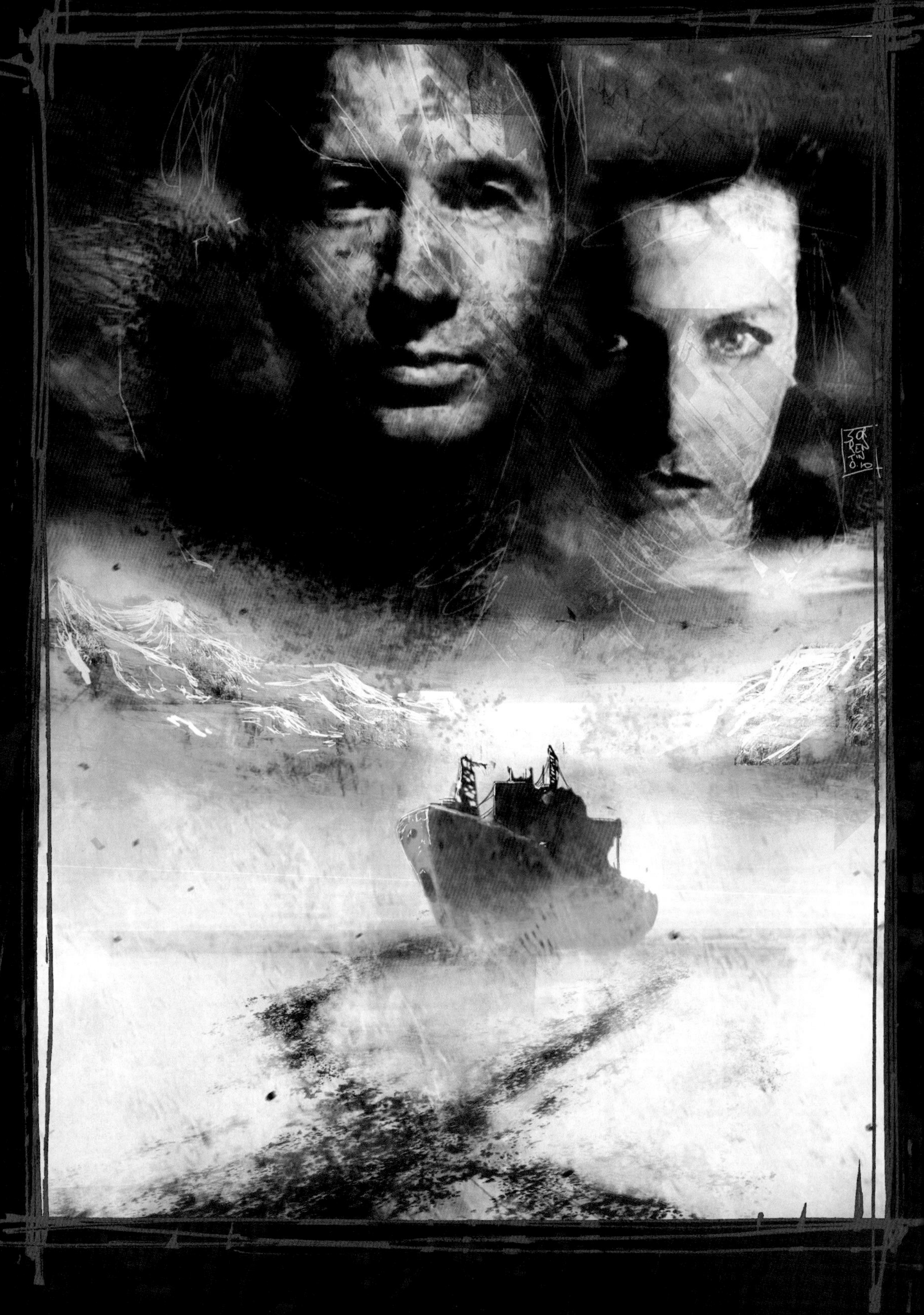

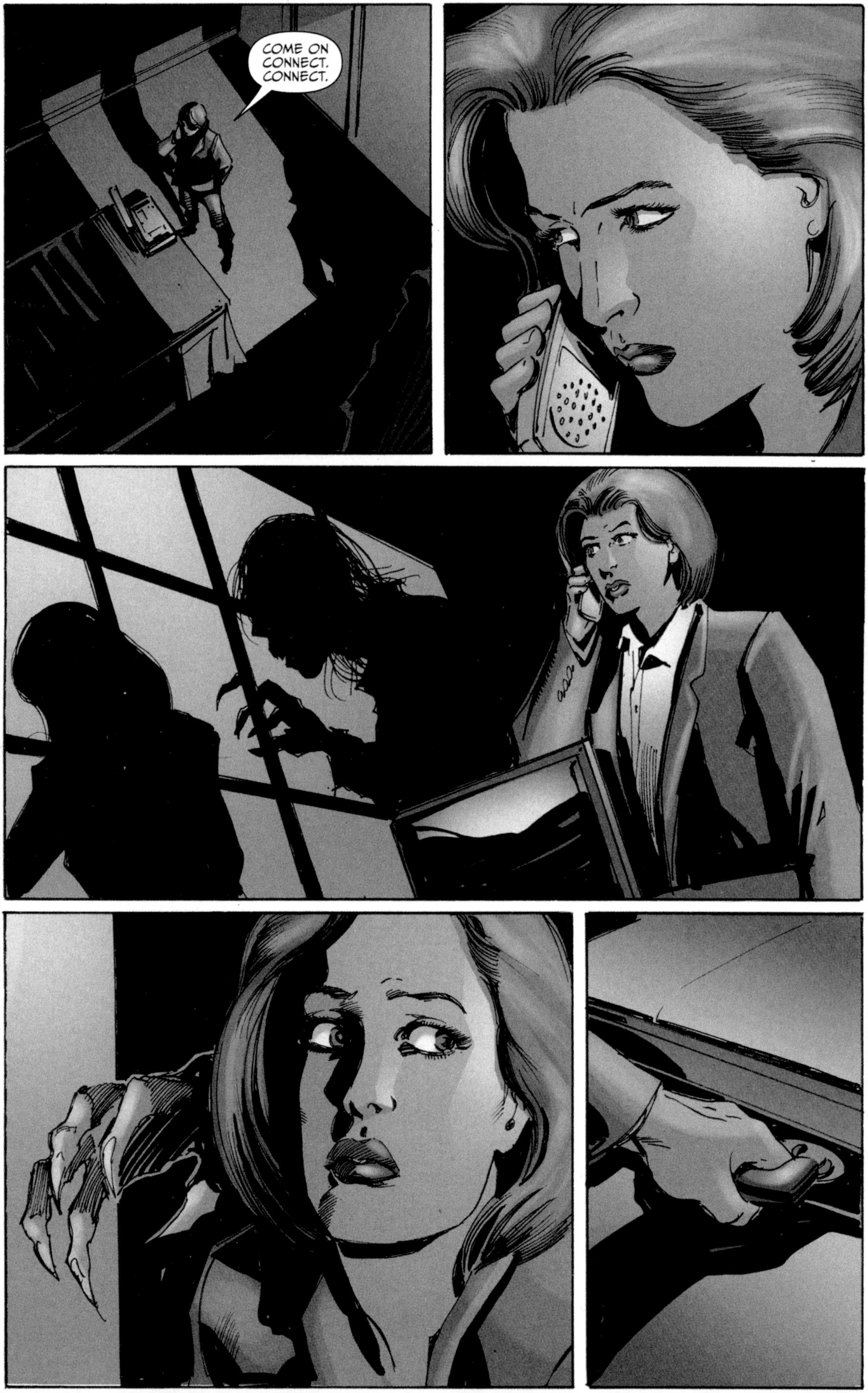
COME ON
CONNECT.
CONNECT.

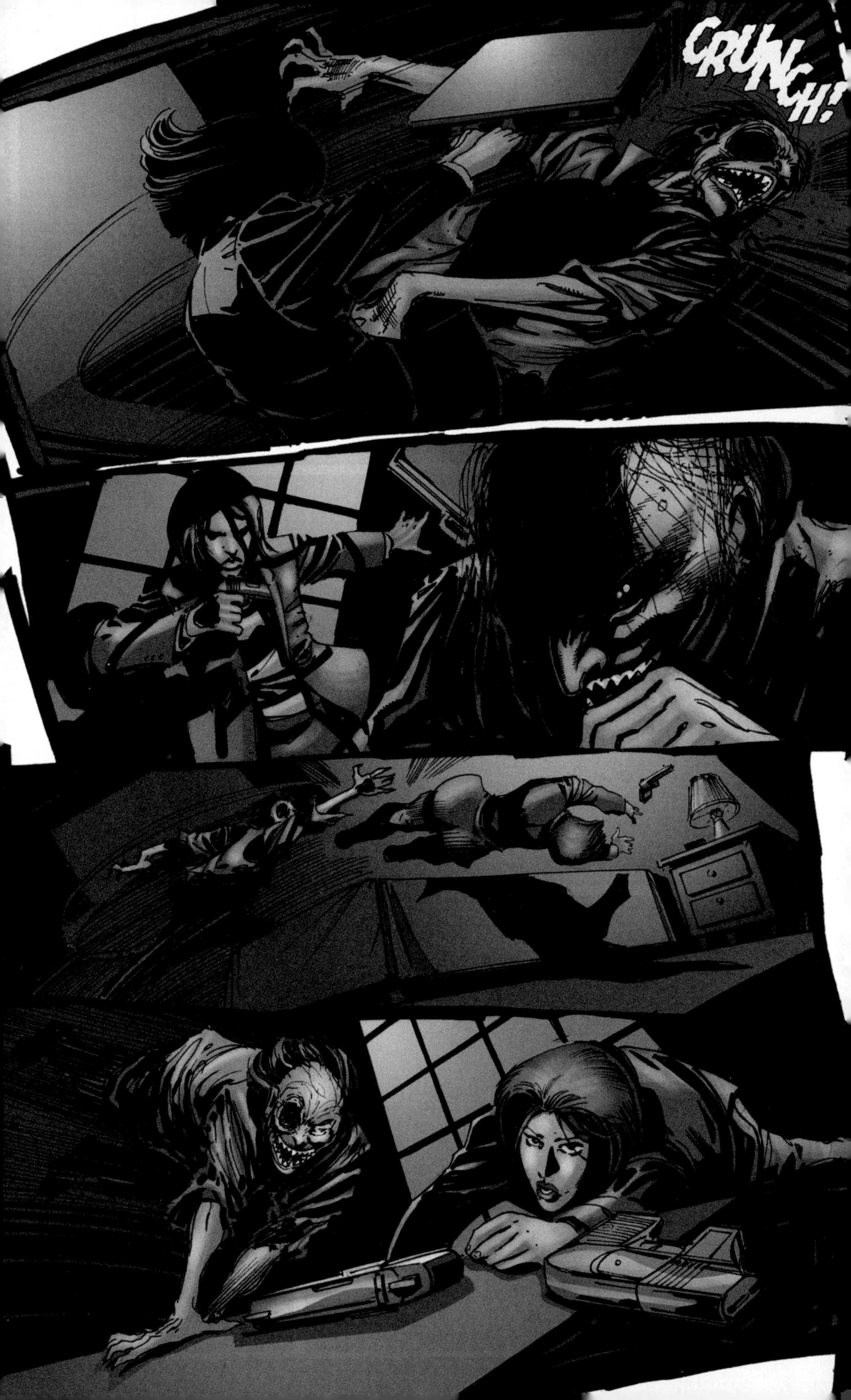
CRUNCH!

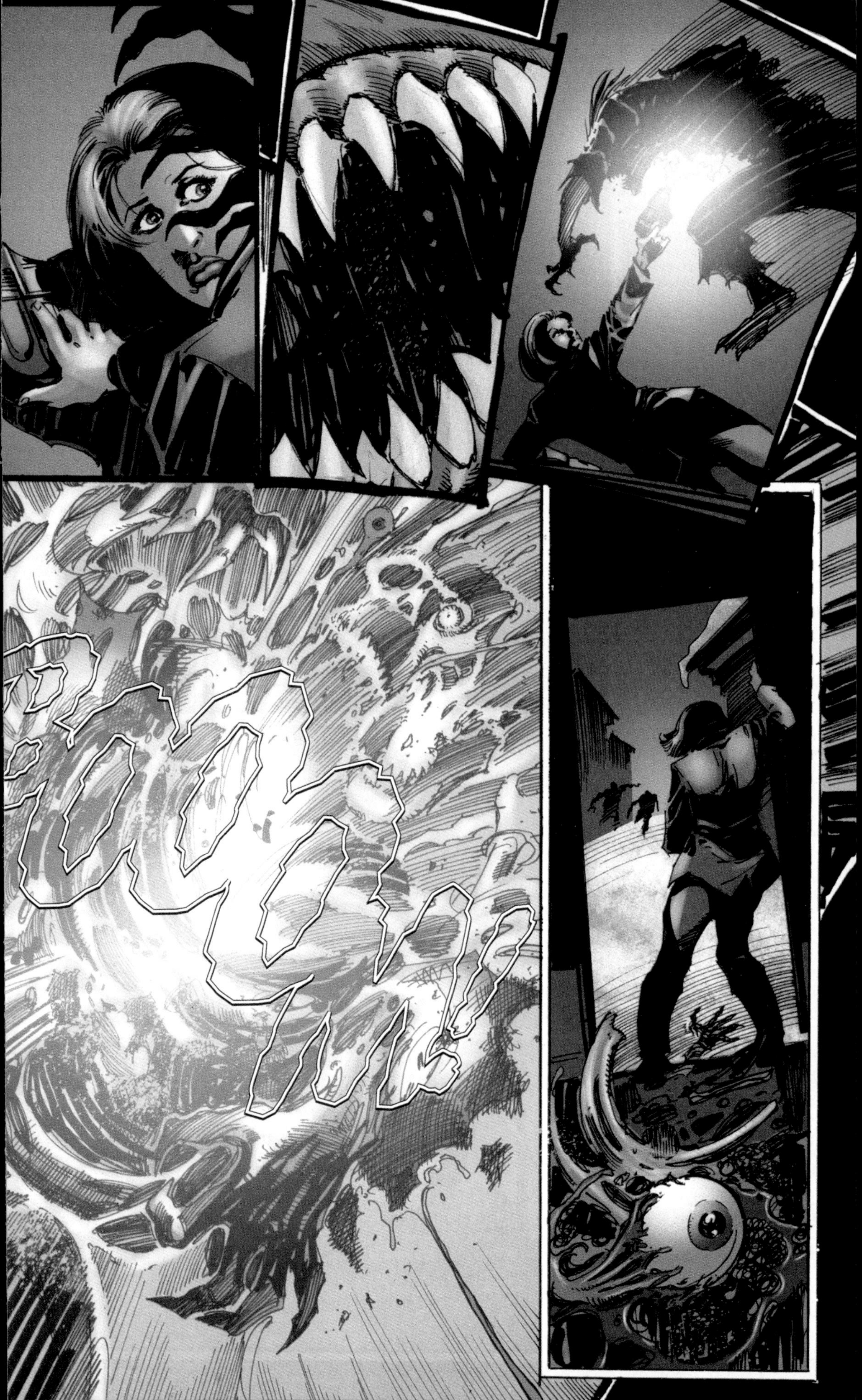

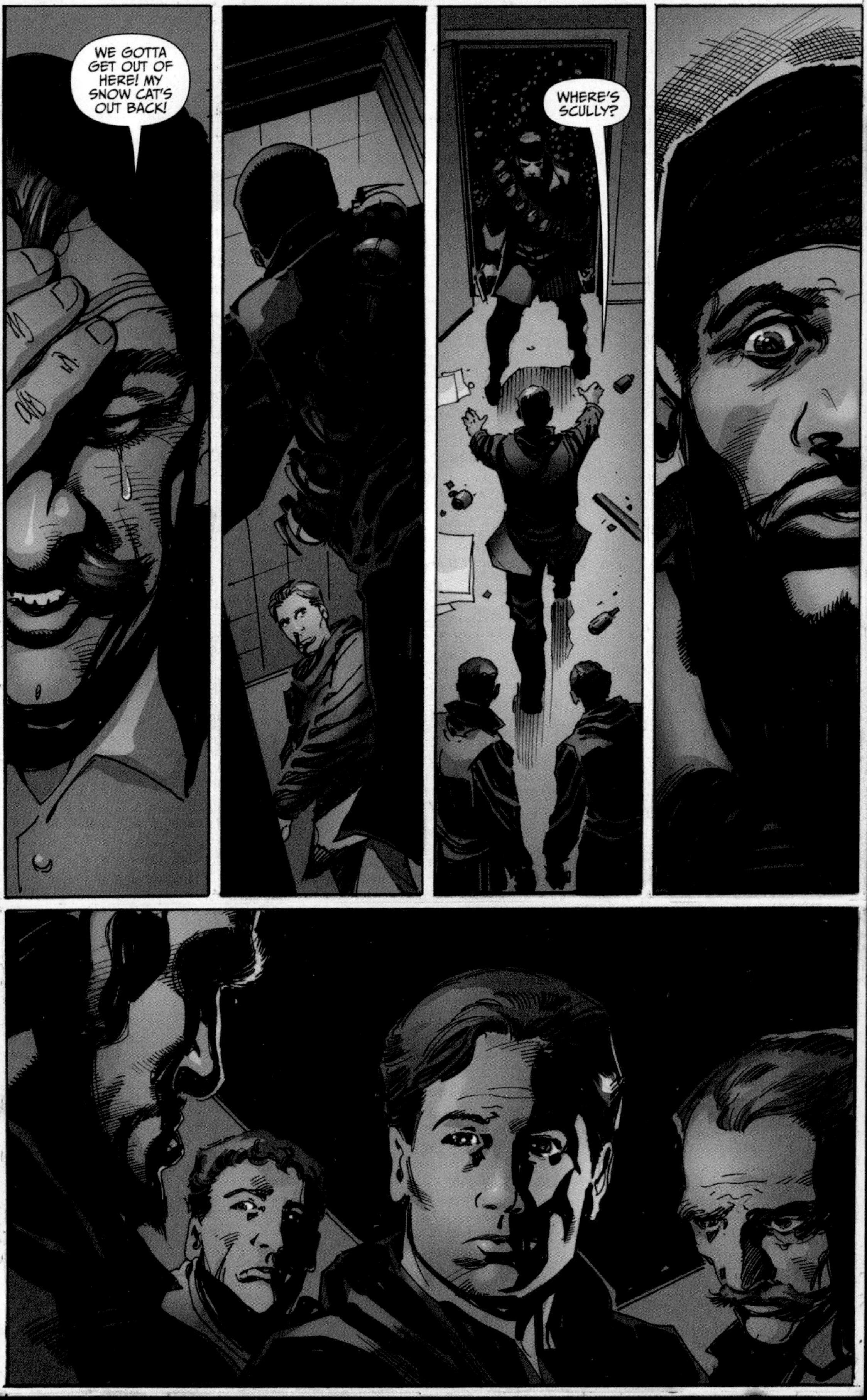
WE GOTTA GET OUT OF HERE! MY SNOW CAT'S OUT BACK!
WHERE'S SCULLY?

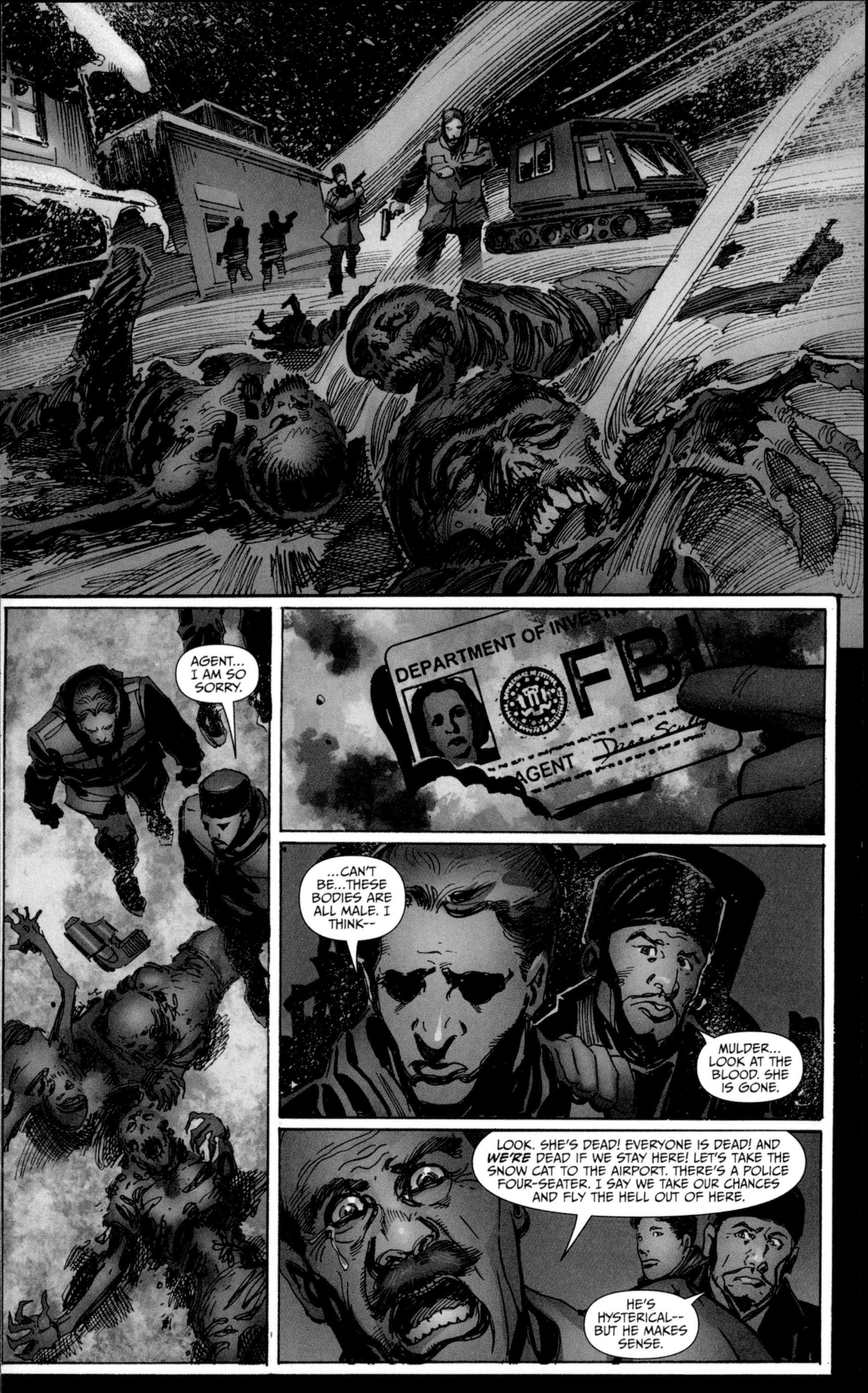
AGENT... I AM SO SORRY.
DEPARTMENT OF INVEST
FBI
AGENT
...CAN'T BE...THESE BODIES ARE ALL MALE. I THINK--
MULDER... LOOK AT THE BLOOD. SHE IS GONE.
LOOK. SHE'S DEAD! EVERYONE IS DEAD! AND WE'RE DEAD IF WE STAY HERE! LET'S TAKE THE SNOW CAT TO THE AIRPORT. THERE'S A POLICE FOUR-SEATER. I SAY WE TAKE OUR CHANCES AND FLY THE HELL OUT OF HERE.
HE'S HYSTERICAL-- BUT HE MAKES SENSE.

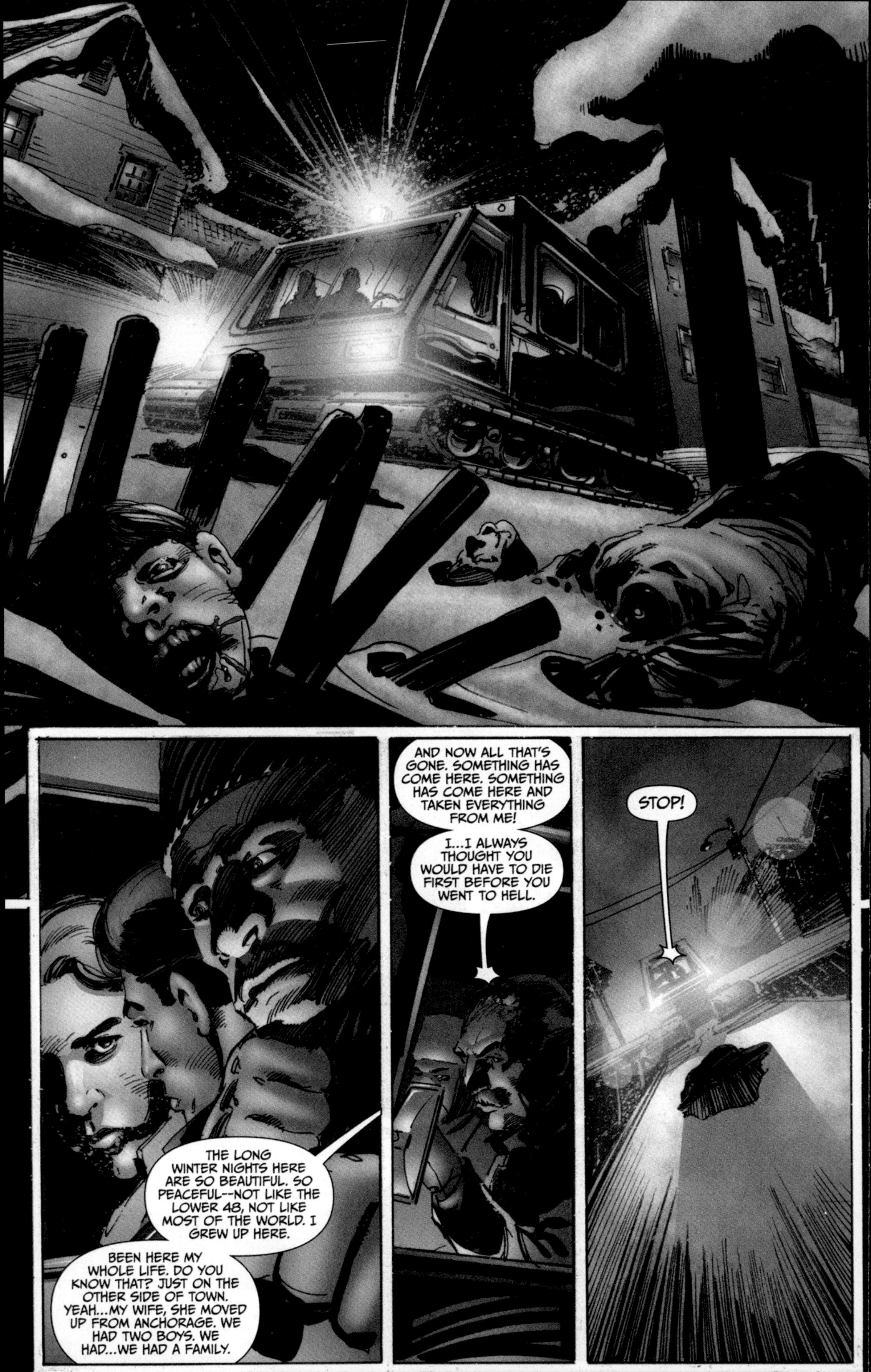

THE LONG WINTER NIGHTS HERE ARE SO BEAUTIFUL. SO PEACEFUL--NOT LIKE THE LOWER 48, NOT LIKE MOST OF THE WORLD. I GREW UP HERE.
BEEN HERE MY WHOLE LIFE. DO YOU KNOW THAT? JUST ON THE OTHER SIDE OF TOWN. YEAH...MY WIFE, SHE MOVED UP FROM ANCHORAGE. WE HAD TWO BOYS. WE HAD...WE HAD A FAMILY.
AND NOW ALL THAT'S GONE. SOMETHING HAS COME HERE. SOMETHING HAS COME HERE AND TAKEN EVERYTHING FROM ME!
I...I ALWAYS THOUGHT YOU WOULD HAVE TO DIE FIRST BEFORE YOU WENT TO HELL.
STOP!

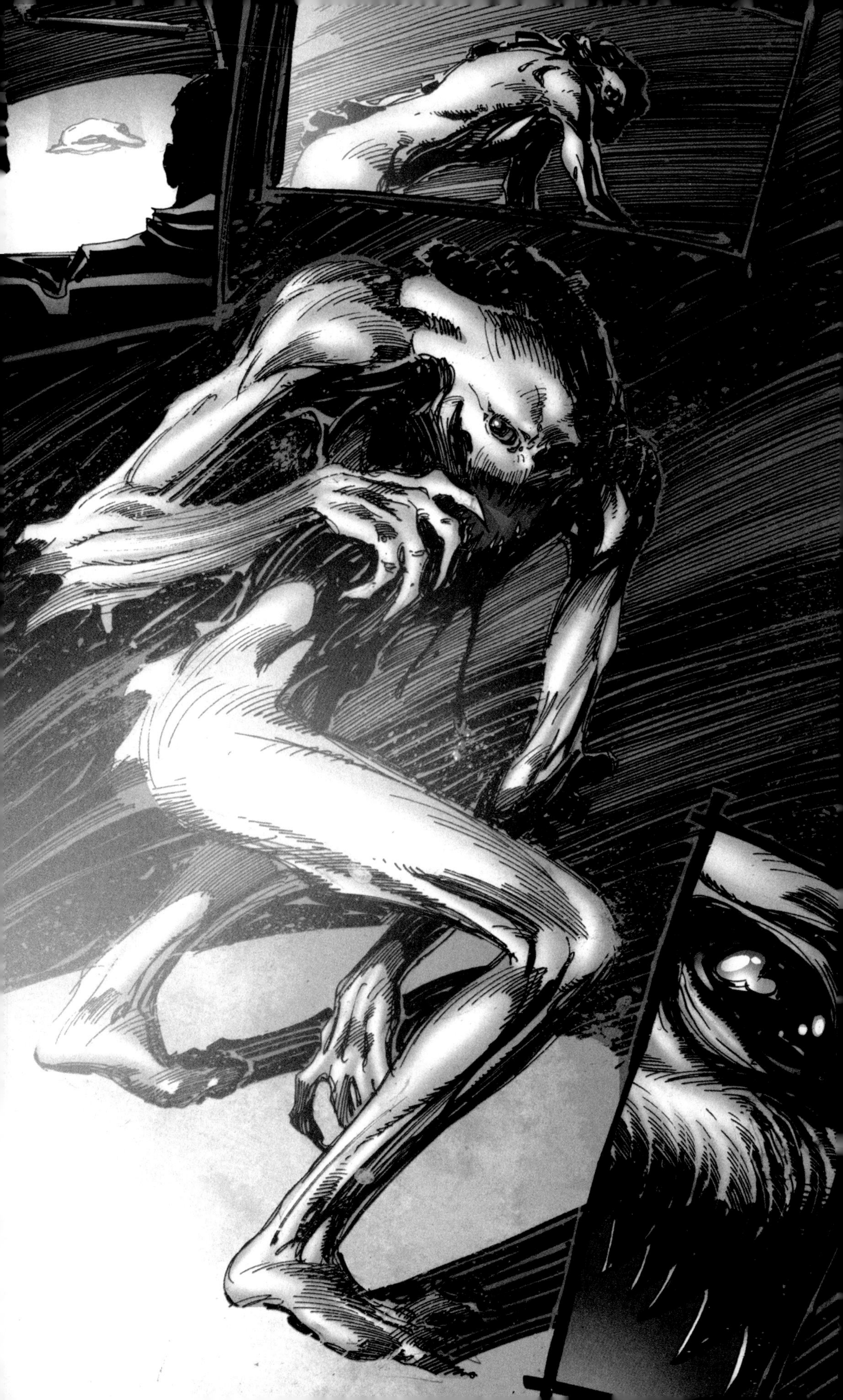

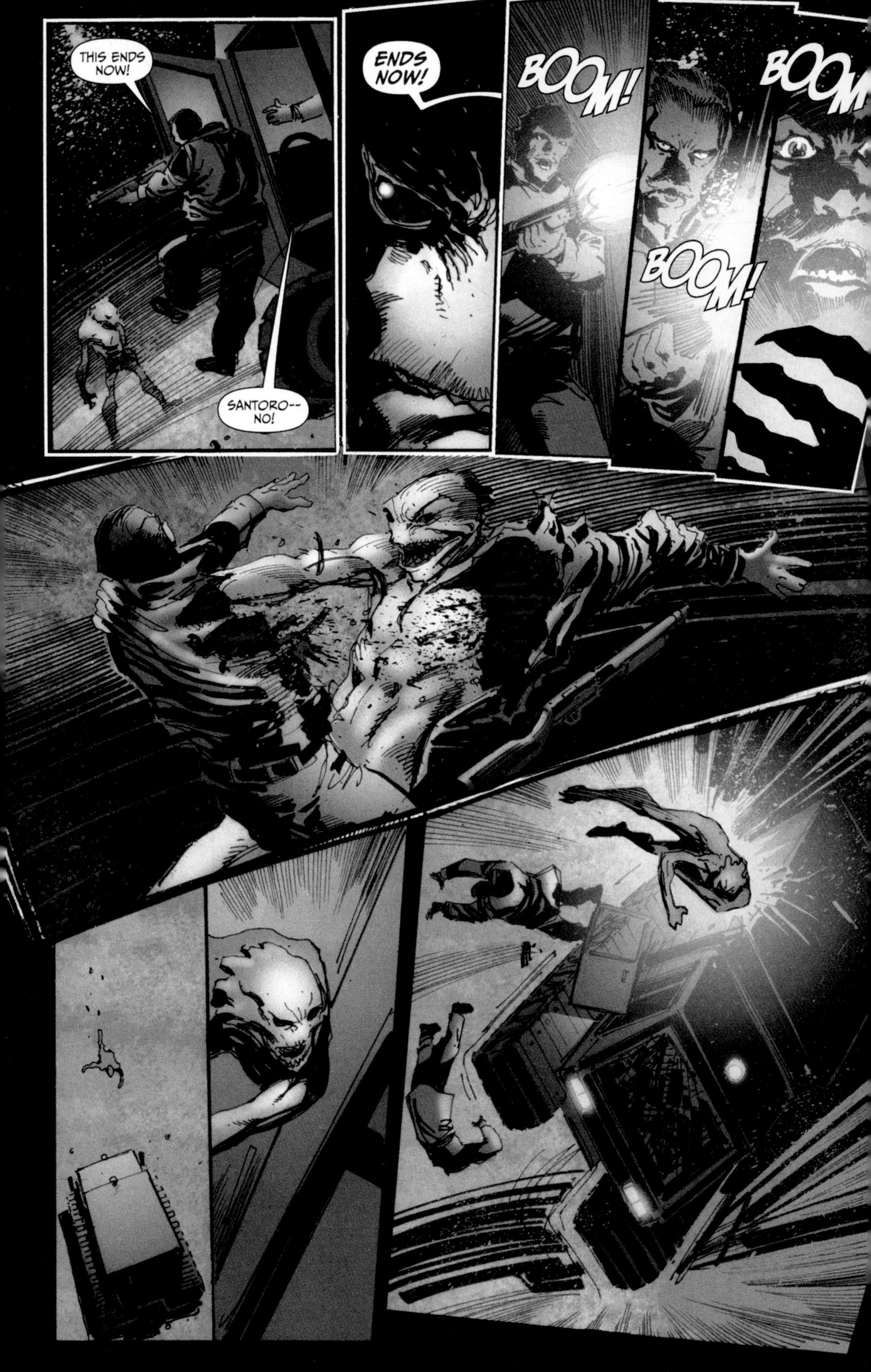
THIS ENDS NOW!
SANTORO-- NO!
ENDS NOW!
BOOM!
BOOM!
BOOM!

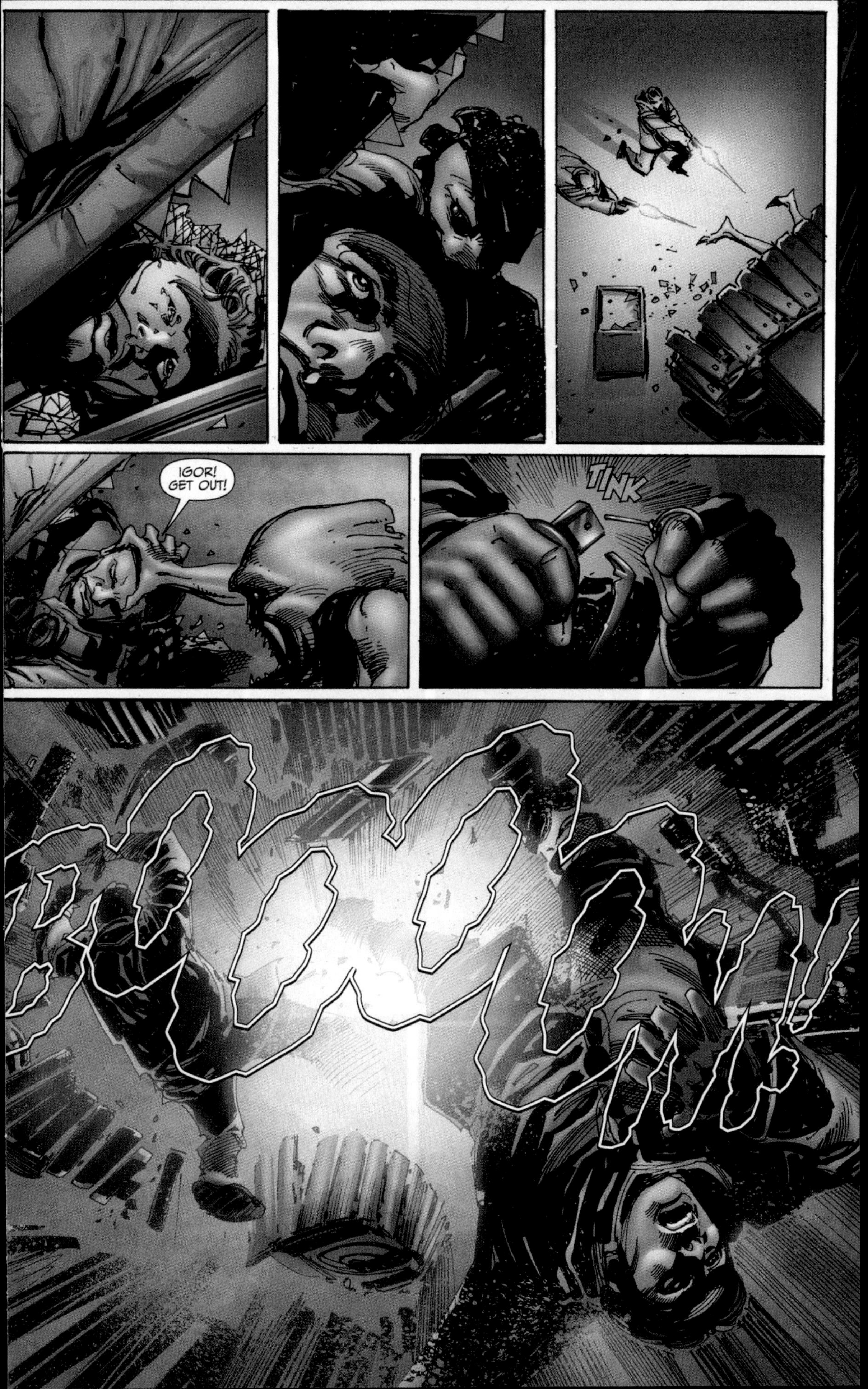
IGOR! GET OUT!
TINK

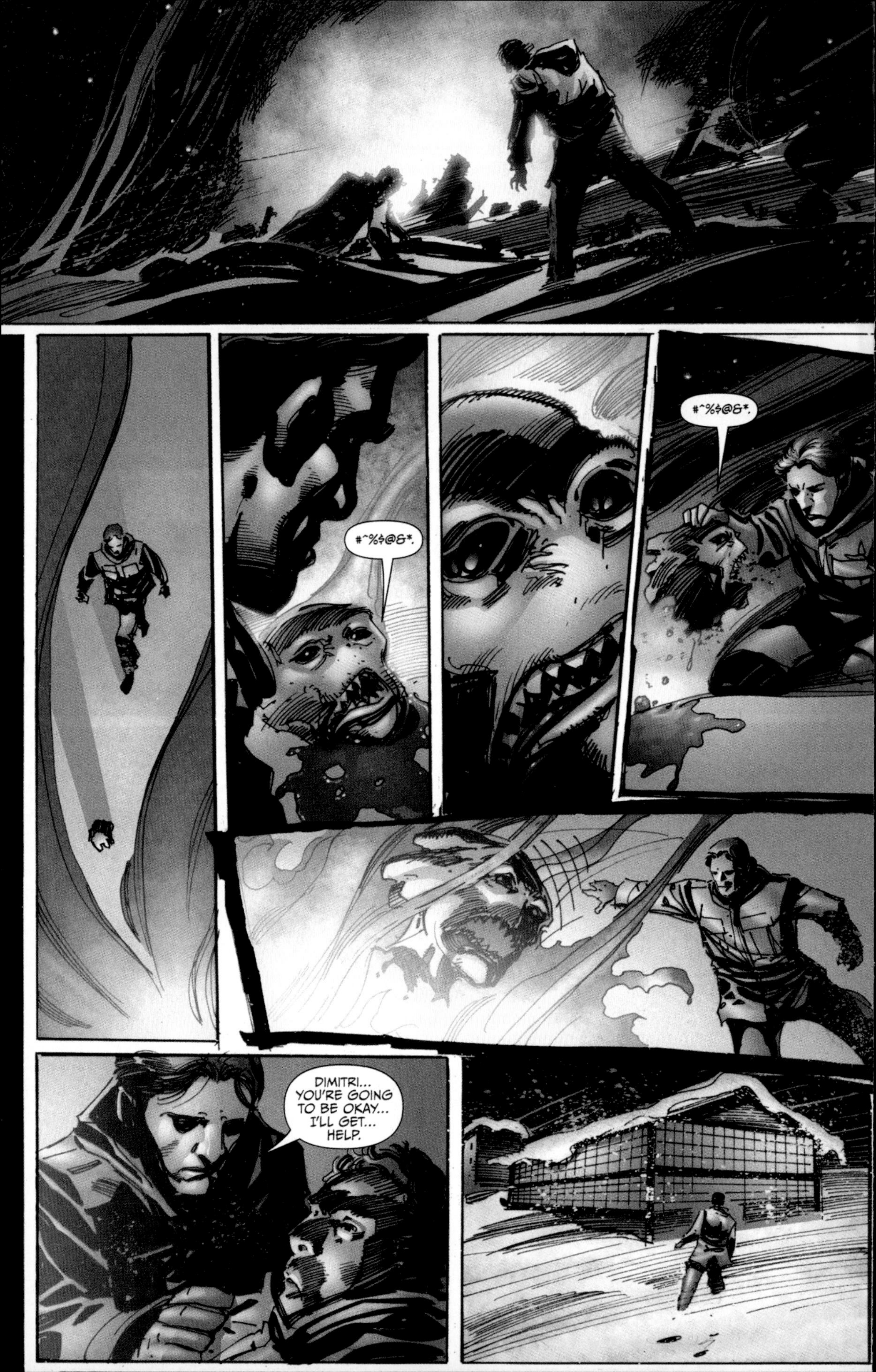
#^%$@&*.
#^%$@&*.
DIMITRI... YOU'RE GOING TO BE OKAY... I'LL GET... HELP.

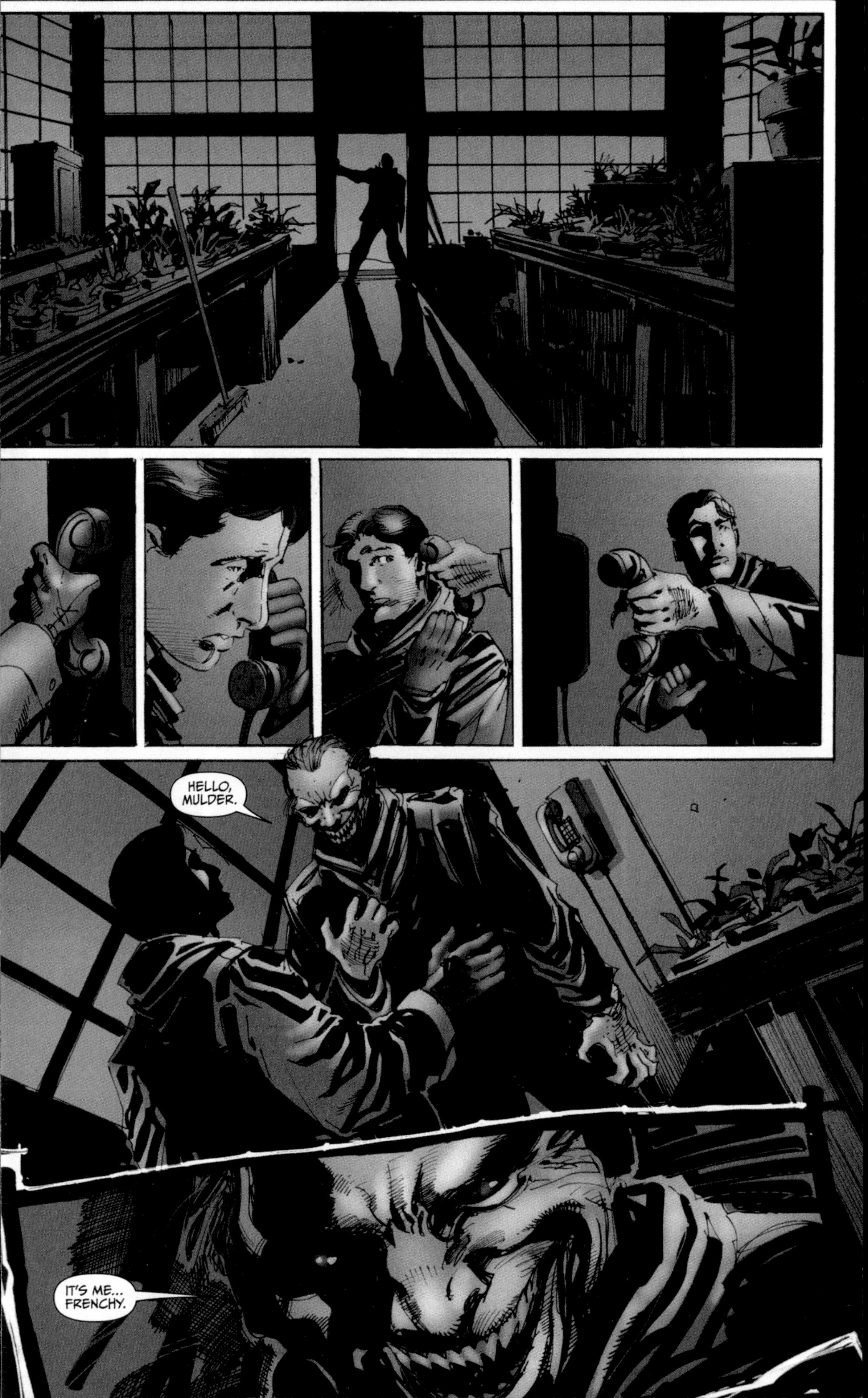
HELLO, MULDER.
IT'S ME... FRENCHY.

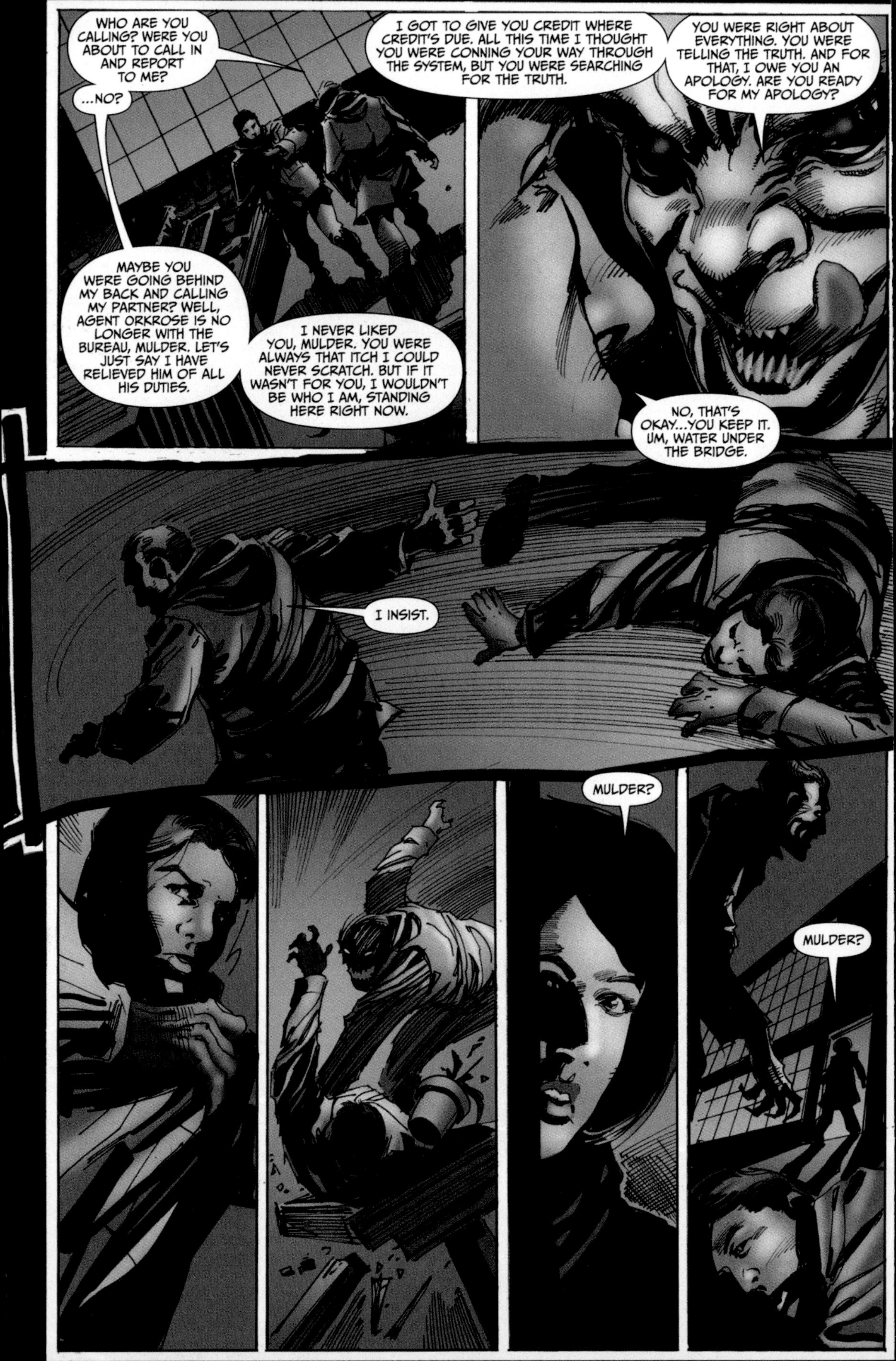
WHO ARE YOU CALLING? WERE YOU ABOUT TO CALL IN AND REPORT TO ME?
...NO?
MAYBE YOU WERE GOING BEHIND MY BACK AND CALLING MY PARTNER? WELL, AGENT ORKROSE IS NO LONGER WITH THE BUREAU, MULDER. LET'S JUST SAY I HAVE RELIEVED HIM OF ALL HIS DUTIES.
I NEVER LIKED YOU, MULDER. YOU WERE ALWAYS THAT ITCH I COULD NEVER SCRATCH. BUT IF IT WASN'T FOR YOU, I WOULDN'T BE WHO I AM, STANDING HERE RIGHT NOW.
I GOT TO GIVE YOU CREDIT WHERE CREDIT'S DUE. ALL THIS TIME I THOUGHT YOU WERE CONNING YOUR WAY THROUGH THE SYSTEM, BUT YOU WERE SEARCHING FOR THE TRUTH.
YOU WERE RIGHT ABOUT EVERYTHING. YOU WERE TELLING THE TRUTH. AND FOR THAT, I OWE YOU AN APOLOGY. ARE YOU READY FOR MY APOLOGY?
NO, THAT'S OKAY...YOU KEEP IT. UM, WATER UNDER THE BRIDGE.
I INSIST.
MULDER?
MULDER?

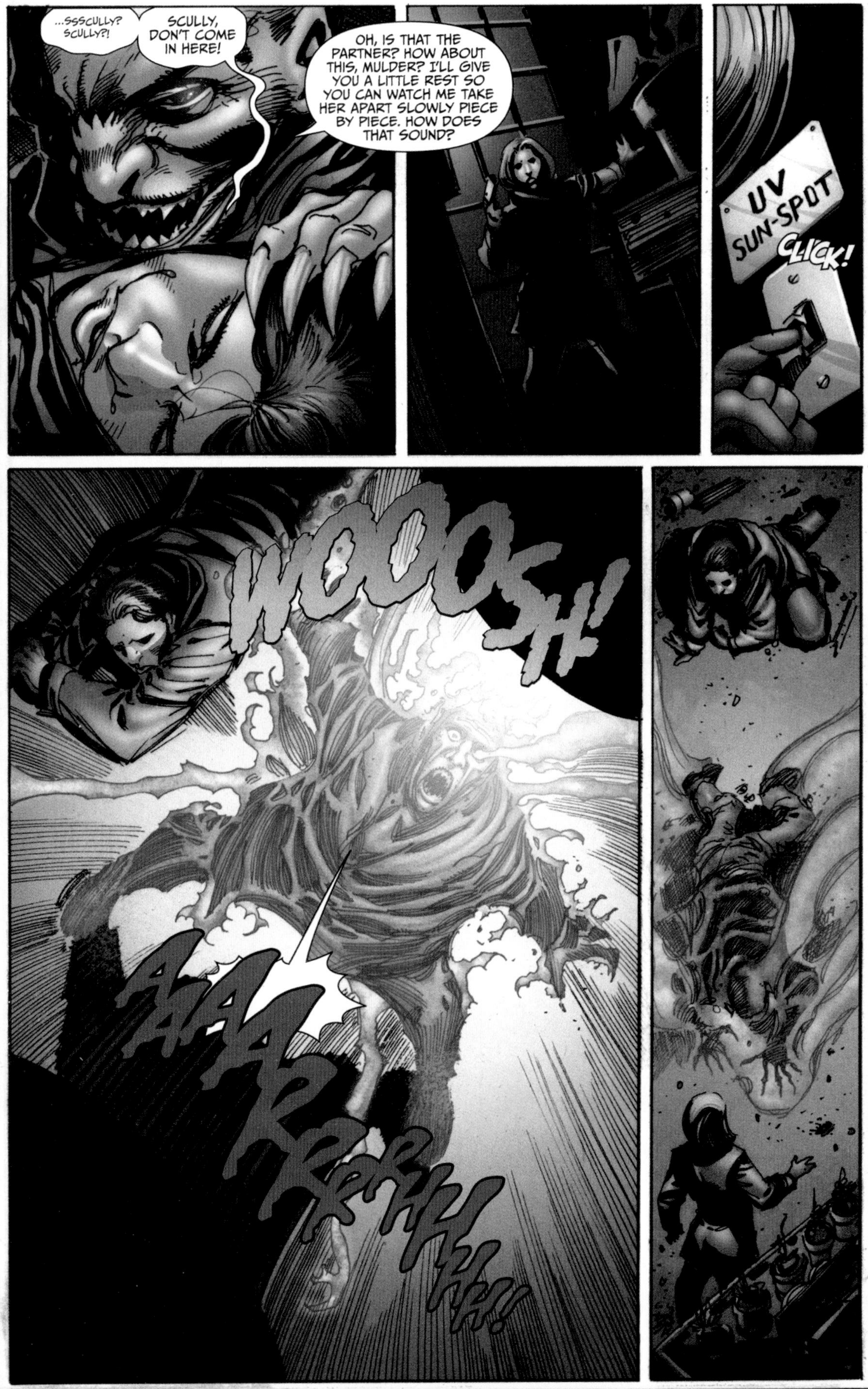
...SSSCULLY? SCULLY?!
SCULLY, DON'T COME IN HERE!
OH, IS THAT THE PARTNER? HOW ABOUT THIS, MULDER? I'LL GIVE YOU A LITTLE REST SO YOU CAN WATCH ME TAKE HER APART SLOWLY PIECE BY PIECE. HOW DOES THAT SOUND?
UV SUN-SPOT
CLICK!
WOOOSH!
AAAARRRHHHHH!

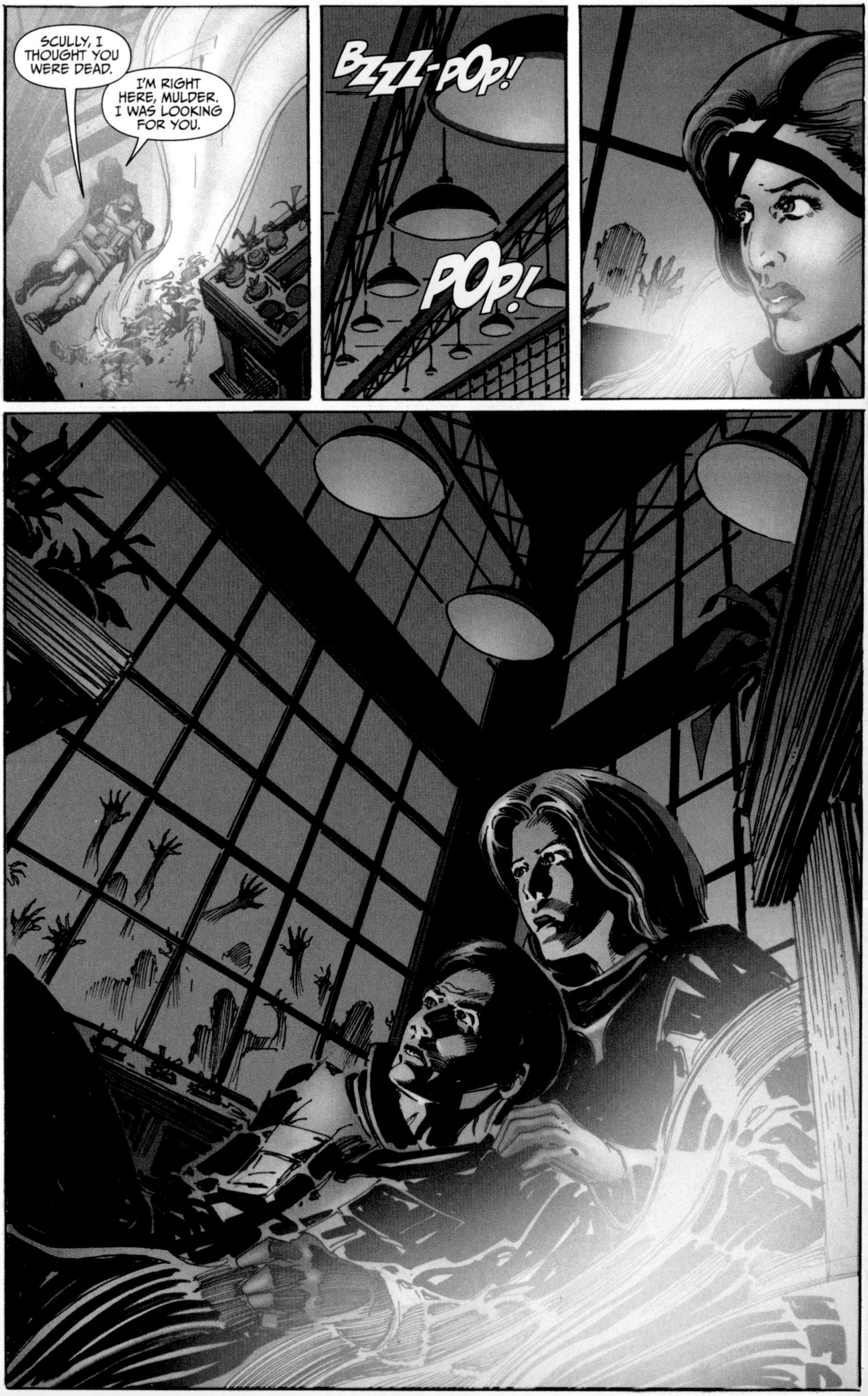
SCULLY, I THOUGHT YOU WERE DEAD.
I'M RIGHT HERE, MULDER. I WAS LOOKING FOR YOU.
BZZZ-POP!
POP!

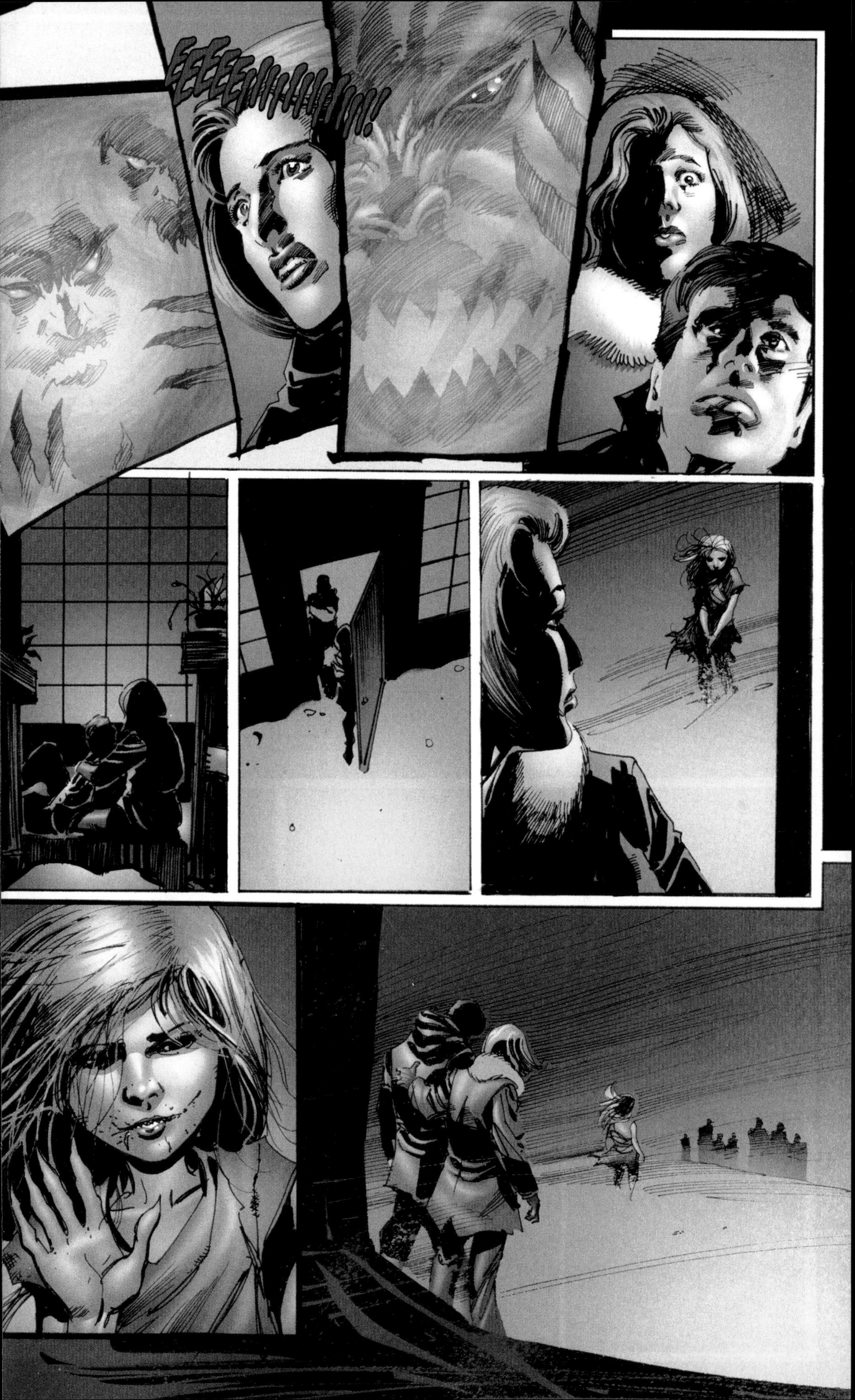
EEEEIIIIIIIIIIIII!

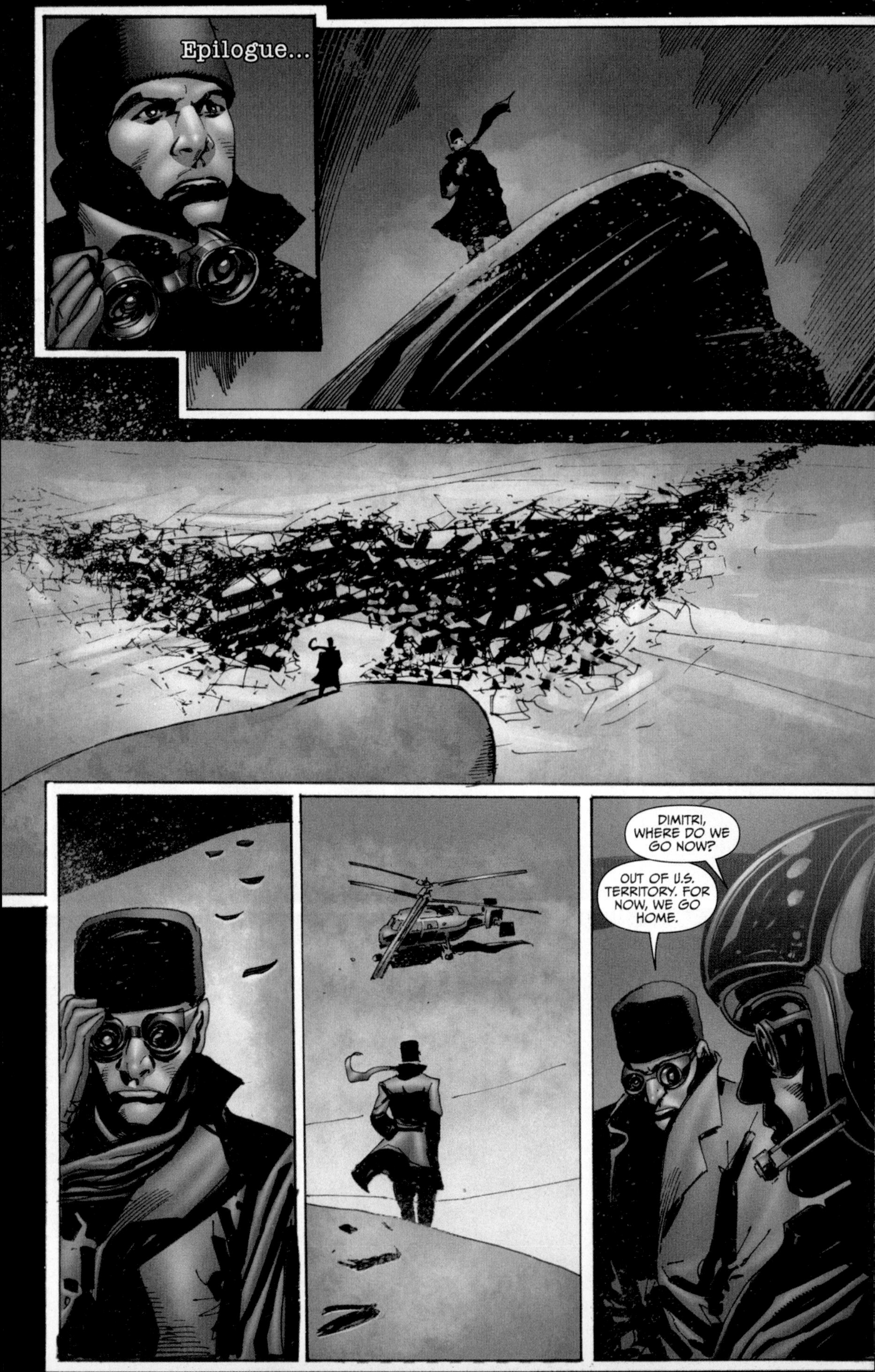
Epilogue...
DIMITRI, WHERE DO WE GO NOW?
OUT OF U.S. TERRITORY. FOR NOW, WE GO HOME.

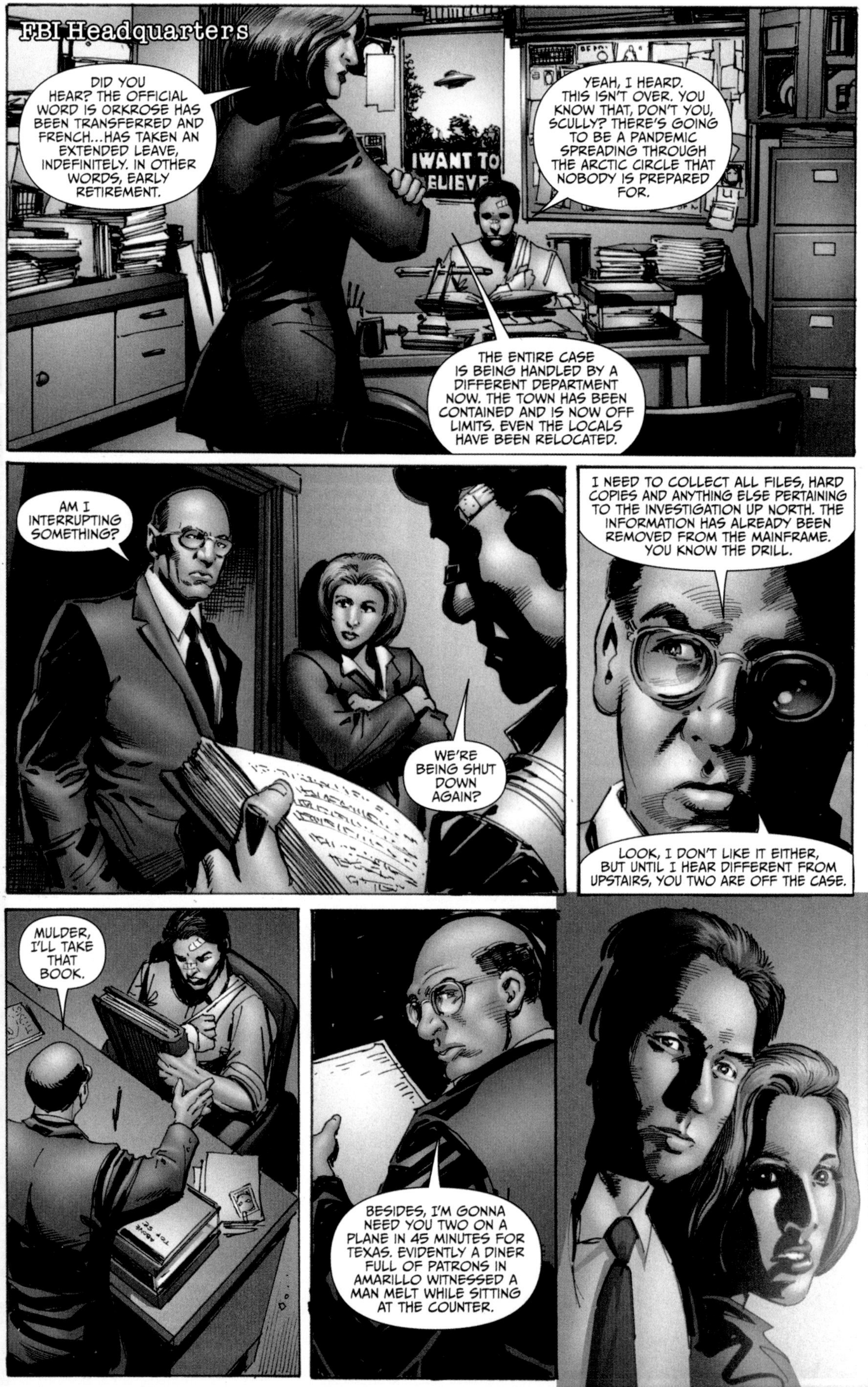
FBI Headquarters
DID YOU HEAR? THE OFFICIAL WORD IS ORKROSE HAS BEEN TRANSFERRED AND FRENCH...HAS TAKEN AN EXTENDED LEAVE, INDEFINITELY. IN OTHER WORDS, EARLY RETIREMENT.
YEAH, I HEARD. THIS ISN'T OVER. YOU KNOW THAT, DON'T YOU, SCULLY? THERE'S GOING TO BE A PANDEMIC SPREADING THROUGH THE ARCTIC CIRCLE THAT NOBODY IS PREPARED FOR.
THE ENTIRE CASE IS BEING HANDLED BY A DIFFERENT DEPARTMENT NOW. THE TOWN HAS BEEN CONTAINED AND IS NOW OFF LIMITS. EVEN THE LOCALS HAVE BEEN RELOCATED.
AM I INTERRUPTING SOMETHING?
WE'RE BEING SHUT DOWN AGAIN?
I NEED TO COLLECT ALL FILES, HARD COPIES AND ANYTHING ELSE PERTAINING TO THE INVESTIGATION UP NORTH. THE INFORMATION HAS ALREADY BEEN REMOVED FROM THE MAINFRAME. YOU KNOW THE DRILL.
LOOK, I DON'T LIKE IT EITHER, BUT UNTIL I HEAR DIFFERENT FROM UPSTAIRS, YOU TWO ARE OFF THE CASE.
MULDER, I'LL TAKE THAT BOOK.
BESIDES, I'M GONNA NEED YOU TWO ON A PLANE IN 45 MINUTES FOR TEXAS. EVIDENTLY A DINER FULL OF PATRONS IN AMARILLO WITNESSED A MAN MELT WHILE SITTING AT THE COUNTER.

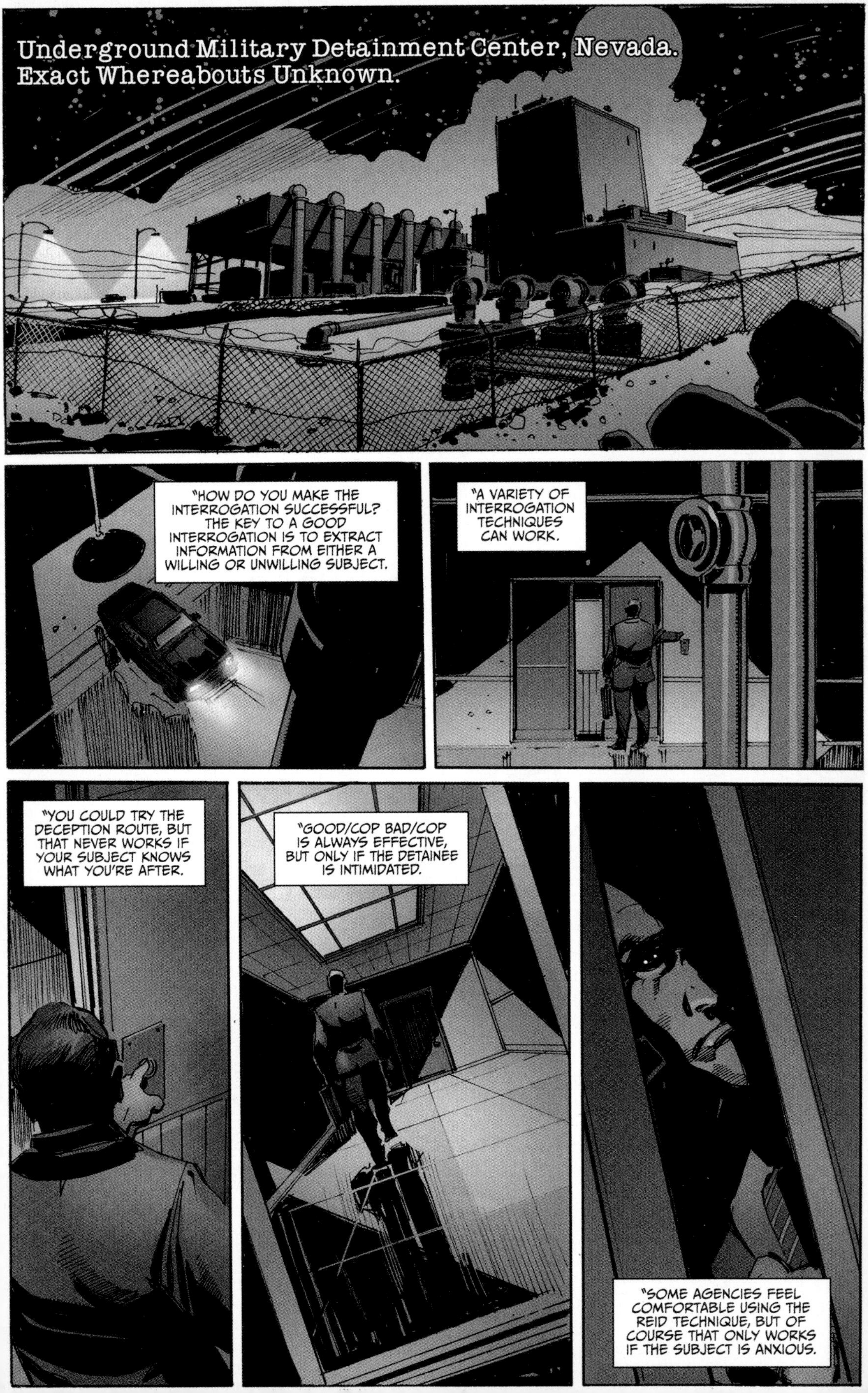

Underground Military Detainment Center, Nevada. Exact Whereabouts Unknown.
"HOW DO YOU MAKE THE INTERROGATION SUCCESSFUL? THE KEY TO A GOOD INTERROGATION IS TO EXTRACT INFORMATION FROM EITHER A WILLING OR UNWILLING SUBJECT.
"A VARIETY OF INTERROGATION TECHNIQUES CAN WORK.
"YOU COULD TRY THE DECEPTION ROUTE, BUT THAT NEVER WORKS IF YOUR SUBJECT KNOWS WHAT YOU'RE AFTER.
"GOOD/COP BAD/COP IS ALWAYS EFFECTIVE, BUT ONLY IF THE DETAINEE IS INTIMIDATED.
"SOME AGENCIES FEEL COMFORTABLE USING THE REID TECHNIQUE, BUT OF COURSE THAT ONLY WORKS IF THE SUBJECT IS ANXIOUS.

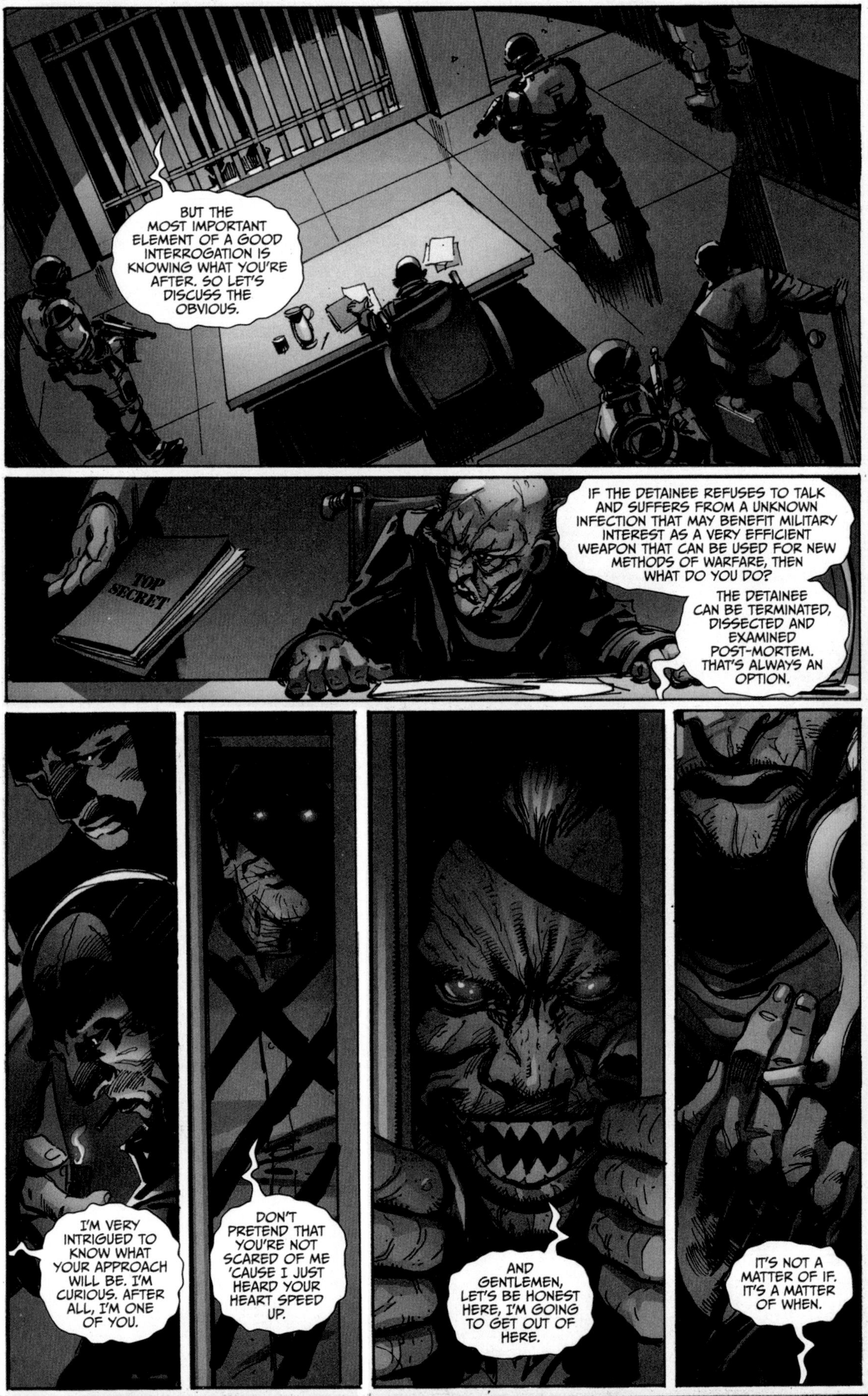
BUT THE MOST IMPORTANT ELEMENT OF A GOOD INTERROGATION IS KNOWING WHAT YOU'RE AFTER. SO LET'S DISCUSS THE OBVIOUS.
TOP SECRET
IF THE DETAINEE REFUSES TO TALK AND SUFFERS FROM A UNKNOWN INFECTION THAT MAY BENEFIT MILITARY INTEREST AS A VERY EFFICIENT WEAPON THAT CAN BE USED FOR NEW METHODS OF WARFARE, THEN WHAT DO YOU DO?
THE DETAINEE CAN BE TERMINATED, DISSECTED AND EXAMINED POST-MORTEM. THAT'S ALWAYS AN OPTION.
I'M VERY INTRIGUED TO KNOW WHAT YOUR APPROACH WILL BE. I'M CURIOUS. AFTER ALL, I'M ONE OF YOU.
DON'T PRETEND THAT YOU'RE NOT SCARED OF ME 'CAUSE I JUST HEARD YOUR HEART SPEED UP.
AND GENTLEMEN, LET'S BE HONEST HERE, I'M GOING TO GET OUT OF HERE.
IT'S NOT A MATTER OF IF. IT'S A MATTER OF WHEN.

Pacific Ocean

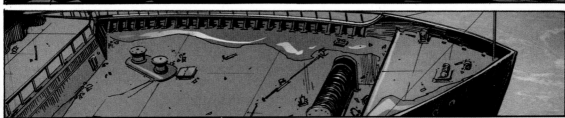

Barrow

Point Hope

Kotzebue

Fai

155

The end.

art by: Sam Kieth

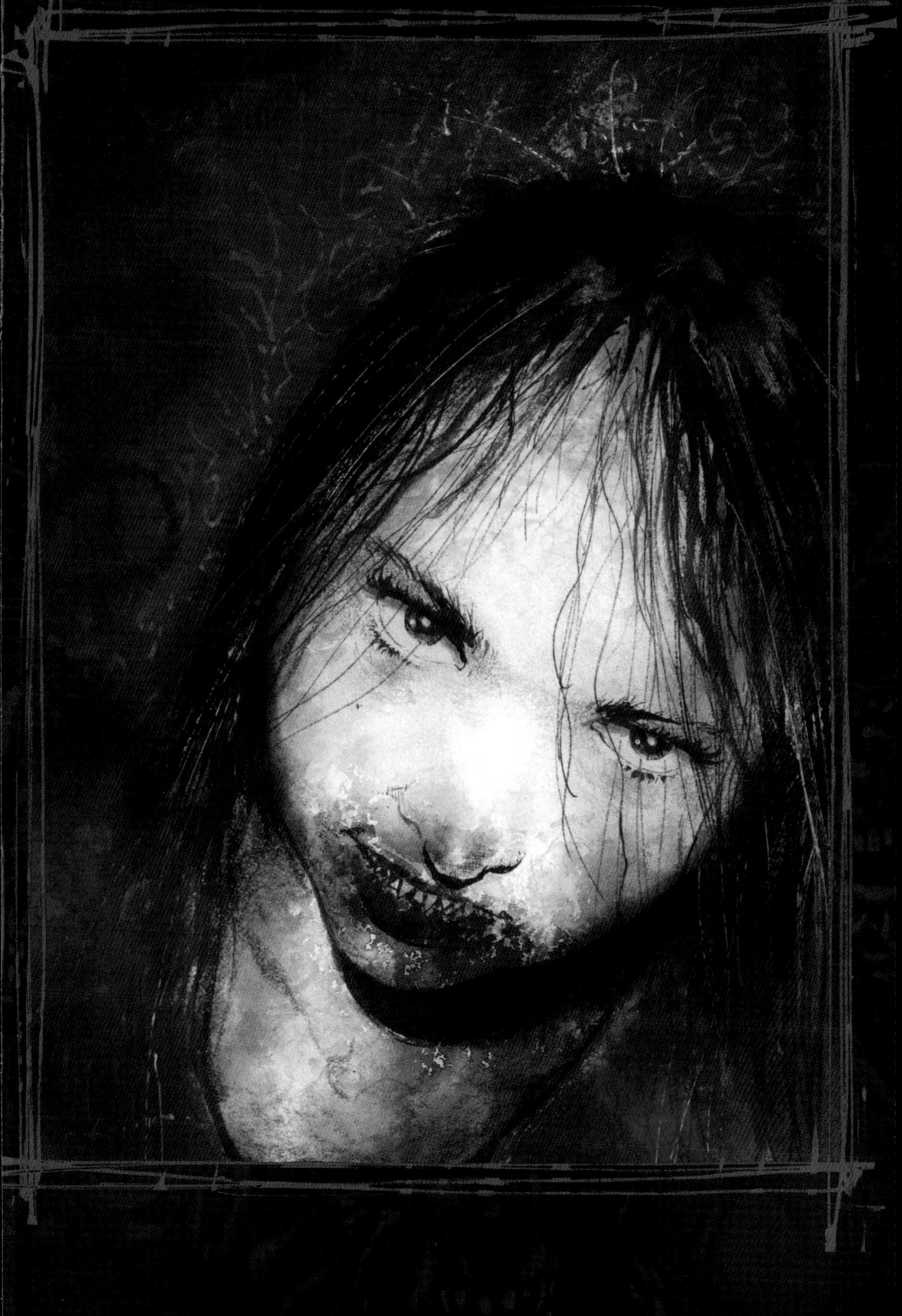

art by: Tom Mandrake

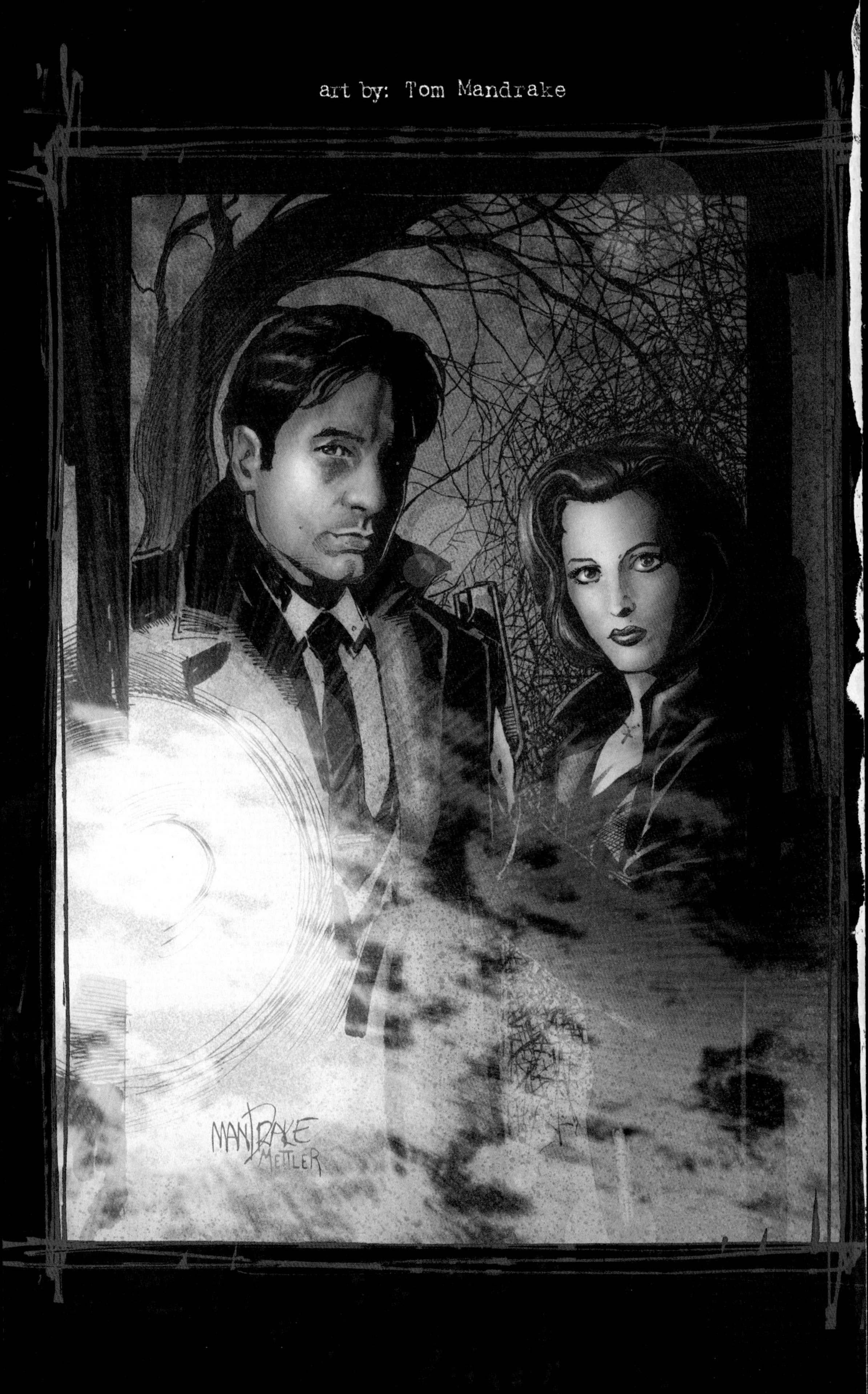
MANDRAKE
METTLER